First published in 2004 by
COLLINS
An imprint of,
HarperCollins*Publishers*
77–85 Fulham Palace Road
Hammersmith, London W6 8JB

The Collins website address is **www.collins.co.uk**

Collins is a registered trademark of HarperCollins Publishers

Copyright © HarperCollins*Publishers* Ltd 2004
Edited and designed by D & N Publishing, Marlborough, Wiltshire

British Library Cataloguing in Publication Data:
A catalogue record is available from the British Library

Printed and bound in Italy by LEGO, Vicenza

ISBN 0 00 716639 7

The Collins Atlas of Military History

HarperCollins*Publishers*

Editorial Direction: Philip Parker
Editorial and Picture Research: Céire Clark and Terry Moore
Cover Design: David Wardle

Cartographic and Design Direction: Martin Brown

D&N Publishing
Editorial and Design Direction: David Goodfellow
Design: Shane O'Dwyer
Proof-reading: Michael Jones

Further proof-reading: Margaret Gilbey
Index: Chris Howes

Picture credits
Front cover and page 3 Christopher F. Foss; **8–9** 1990, Photo Scala, Florence –
courtesy of the Ministero Beni e Att. Culturali; **30–31** and **44–45** Ancient Art & Architecture
Collection Ltd, London; **58–59** akg-images; **72–73** akg-images/Erich Lessing;
88–89 Getty Images/Hulton Archive; **106–107** Getty Images/Hulton Archive;
126–127 Yevgeny Khaldei/CORBIS; **158–159** Hulton- Deutsch Collection/CORBIS

The Collins Atlas of Military History takes an entirely new look at the history of warfare through the ages. It takes as its starting points the visual representation of major battles, campaigns and wars through maps. Covering the entire span of military history, from the earliest recorded battles in the ancient Near East to the recent conflicts in Afghanistan and Iraq, the present volume's scope is vast, but its fundamental premise is very simple. By actually seeing the routes of the Roman legionaries laid down just as they would be in a modern atlas or tracing lines portraying the Soviet offensive on Berlin in 1945, it is relatively simple to understand in graphic form what would otherwise take ten thousand words to describe.

The story of how warfare developed from the chariots of the ancient world to the smart weaponry of the 21st century is a complex one. It is not the intention of this book to cover each and every war and battle in detail. Instead, campaigns and conflicts which exemplify major developments in tactics and the waging of war have been chosen. The text focuses on great military leaders such as Alexander the Great of Macedonia, Frederick the Great of Prussia, Napoleon and Zhukov, on the tactics they evolved and the changes in technology which have shaped the face of warfare through the ages.

A wide historical perspective is vital to understanding the roots of conflicts in the modern world. Without an appreciation of the supremacy of defensive warfare in the First World War, for example, the terrible cost in lives suffered by both sides on the Western Front is difficult to understand. In just 192 pages, the reader can see the battles of the Roman legions visually represented, follow the campaigns of Napoleon, understand the course of the Thirty Years' War in Europe, trace the routes of the Crusades and follow the course of the American Civil War. Although the maps are at the core of this book and its approach, they are supported by a comprehensive and analytical text which act as a companion to their coverage and together with them create a package of unrivalled breadth and accessibility. **The Collins Atlas of Military History** offers an easy, informed and pleasurable way into the subject. Particularly suitable for students, but intended to appeal to all lovers of military history, this book truly brings past wars into focus.

CONTENTS

egyptians and hittites

- **c. 2500 BC**
  first indications of warfare with large numbers of troops

- **c. 1500 BC**
  first use of the bow and the horse in warfare

- **early 15th century BC**
  first 'known' battle – Megiddo

- **1282 BC**
  battle of Kadesh between Ramses II and Hittites

- **c. 1200 BC**
  introduction of chariot

The first military campaigns for which enough evidence survives took place in the Middle East, involving Egypt, Assyria, the Hittites and the Persians as the main protagonists. From Sumerian culture of southern Mesopotamia, around 2500 BC, we have indications of warfare involving large numbers of troops. The Sumerians fielded a clunky forerunner to the war chariot: pulled by what appears to be the Middle East version of today's donkey, these functioned as mobile platforms for archers.

Two major developments occurred around 1500 BC: the first military use of the bow and use of the horse in combat. The combination of both produced armies with excellent mobility on open ground – and relatively long-range killing capabilities. These two inventions turned Middle Eastern armies towards a mobile, missile-based force (in contrast to the massed, armoured infantry that Greece was later to develop). From 1200 BC the chariot became the key weapon system, one that would remain in service for 1,000 years.

1 **kingdoms and empires, c. 1500–1100 BC**

- Hittite empire established by Suppiluliuma I, 1344–1322 BC
- Mitanni territory at its greatest extent, c. 1480–1340 BC
- Mitanni after c. 1340 BC (under Hittite and Assyrian control)
- Assyrian territory gained by Ashur-uballit I, 1353–1318 BC
- Babylonia under Burnaburiash II, 1347–1321 BC
- Elam under Tepti-ahar, c. 1353–1318 BC
- Egypt under Amenophis IV and Tutankhamun, 1352–1335 BC

The most prolific users of chariots were the Egyptians who, in the 2nd millennium BC, under such pharaohs as Tuthmosis III and Ramses II, achieved their pinnacle of military power, dominating modern Palestine. The worth that the Egyptians held in the chariot is illustrated by the large numbers of representations of pharaohs driving chariots through piles of enemies. The first 'known' battle – Megiddo – occurred in the early 15th century BC, when Tuthmosis III shattered a Canaanite coalition. His victory allowed Egypt to extend its borders to their greatest extent in history, as far north as Syria and as far east as the Euphrates. However, Egyptian campaigns into the north aroused the fear of another nation, centred on what is now Anatolia in Turkey: the Hittites.

The Hittite army possessed chariots similar to the Egyptians', but some were heavier, with a crew of three. Advancing into modern Syria, a Hittite army under King Suppiluliumas, marched to confront the Egyptian Pharaoh Akhenaten. Akhenaten died, and his daughter Ankhsenamun (widow of Tutenkhamun) bought off Suppiluliumas by her offer to marry one of his sons. However, two Egyptian ministers had the Hittite prince assassinated at the border, and the war was on again.

Egyptian–Hittite rivalry culminated in the Battle of Kadesh in 1282 BC. Ramses II was intent on stopping Hittite forays into western Syria and sought to destroy the army of the Hittite king, Muwatallis. With Ramses at their head, the Egyptians smashed the Hittite chariots, forcing Muwatallis to take refuge inside Kadesh. Both commanders claimed victory. The result was a non-aggression treaty, but the Hittites remained in control of Syria.

1 The second half of the 2nd millennium saw the growth of a number of competing powers in the Near East. The map (below left) indicates the territorial position in *c.* 1330 BC. To the west, New Kingdom Egypt fought for control of Syria–Palestine first with Mitanni and then with the Hittites, while to the east the Kassite kings of Babylon were increasingly threatened by the emergent powers of Assyria to the north and Elam to the east. Mitanni archives record the existence of professional troops and militia, the striking force of the Mitanni army being a corps of 200 chariots.

2 The strip of fertile land between the Mediterranean and the Syrian desert was a target for Egyptian imperialism, beginning with the campaigns of the early pharaohs of the 18th Dynasty (map right). By the reign of Tuthmosis, Egypt's power reached north from the Third Cataract in Nubia to the Euphrates. His grandson, Tuthmosis III, fought 17 campaigns in Palestine and Syria, setting up a monument next to his grandfather's on the Euphrates in the region of Carchemish. Boundaries were established by treaties first with the land of Mitanni, later with the Hittites. After much of this empire had crumbled away in the next 130 years, Seti I and Ramses II temporarily recovered some of the region.

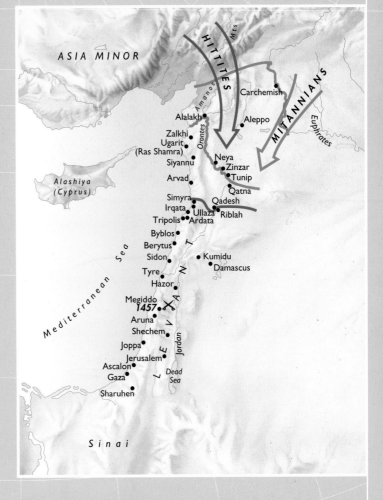

2 **Egyptian campaigns in Syria and Palestine**

— northern limit of campaigns of Tuthmosis I (1507–1494 BC) and Tuthmosis III (1490–1436 BC)

— boundary between Egyptian and Mitannian zones of influence at the end of the reign of Amenophis II (1438–1412 BC)

— boundary between Egyptian and Hittite zones of influence at the end of the reign of Akhenaten, 1347 BC

assyrians and persians

853 BC
Battle of Qarqar; Shalmaneser III defeats an alliance of western states, including Ahab of Israel

early 7th century BC
Assyrians under Ashurbanipal (668–627 BC) control almost the entire Middle East

612 BC
fall of Nineveh to the Babylonians and Medes

550 BC
Cyrus the Great seizes the throne of Media

500 BC
Ionian city-states revolt against their Persian overlords

In about 1200 BC new waves of invaders descended on the eastern Mediterranean. The Sea People, as the Egyptians called them, dramatically reshaped the political landscape of the Middle East: Egypt barely survived the onslaught; the Hittite kingdom collapsed; the city states of Syria were overrun; and the Egyptians lost all their lands east of and including the Sinai. The only power to be unaffected was the kingdom of Assyria in Mesopotamia.

Over the next 500 years Assyrian armies, led by such kings as Shalmaneser III, Sennacharib and Ashurbanipal, conquered and ruled a great empire. Their campaigns prefigured those of the Mongols in terms of their ruthless treatment of those they defeated. By the 7th century BC, the Assyrians controlled almost the entire Middle East, from Egypt to the Taurus mountains, from Sidon and Tyre to the capital of the Medes, Susa, just north of the Persian Gulf.

Assyria reached its zenith in the beginning of the 7th century BC, before it imploded, caught between the powers it had previously trampled, and new powers from the east: Babylon and the Medes. The fall of Nineveh, in 612 BC, signalled the death knell for this remarkable society. Assyria's disintegration left the field open for four smaller powers to fight over the remains: Babylon, which had some success under Nebuchadnezzar; Egypt, which was in decline; and two mini-powers, Lydia to the west and Media in the east.

1 Cyrus the Great carved out an empire that continued to expand under his successors (map right). The Persians adapted from an infantry-based army to an all-arms force in which heavy cavalry was combined with professional bow- and spear-armed foot soldiers. Having conquered the Near East, the Persians turned to the Greek city states of the eastern Aegean.

1 persia, 550 – 330 BC

| approximate extent of Achaemenid heartland |
| added by Cyrus the Great by 550 BC |
| added by Cyrus the Great by 530 BC |
| added by Cambyses by 525 BC |
| added by Darius I by c. 500 BC |
| approximate maximum extent of Achaemenid empire, c. 500 BC |

campaigns and battles
- ⊠→ Cyrus the Great
- ⊠→ Cambyses
- ⊠ Darius

— satrapy
● satrapal capitals

The power of the Median kings was usurped from within by a Persian faction, led by Cyrus the Great, who seized the throne in 550 BC, conquered Babylon and Lydia, and within a few years had overwhelmed Egypt. By the early 6th century BC Persia was the superpower of the Middle East, the Persian kingdom one of the largest in the known world. The élite force in its army was not the chariot wing but 'The Immortals', the King's personal guard of 10,000 infantry, so-named because the division was always kept up to strength. The Immortals, however, were not heavy infantry, such as predominated in Greece, but more moderately-armoured spear and bow men.

By the time King Darius turned his attention to Europe, the Persian cavalry was the best of its time, but the light infantry consisted of levies from usually reluctant allies. In the 5th century BC the Ionian city states revolted against their Persian overlords, supported by several cities on mainland Greece. The result was a confrontation between the Greek citizen armies of hoplite farmers, and Persia, with its light cavalry and infantry. Within 175 years, the Greeks ruled the western world and the Persian empire had ceased to exist.

Black Sea

URARTU

Malazgirt

Meliddu

Marqasi

Adana

Sam'al

Carchemish
✕ 605 BC

Tarsus

Sissu

Aleppo

Kullania

MEDES

Nineveh

Nimrud · Arbail

Assur · Kirkuk

Harhar?

Hamath
✕ 605 BC

Arwad

Byblos ▽ Zabah
Sidon ▲

Tyre ▽ Damascus

Der

Babylon

PERSIANS
(by 640)

Samaria ▽

Nippur

Susa

▽ Jerusalem

CHALDAEANS

Petra

Tigris

Euphrates

671, 667 BC
Assyrian campaigns
against Egypt

2 The Near East that emerged from the upheavals of the late Bronze Age was characterized by new forms of political organization (map above). Along the Mediterranean coast city-states developed, sometimes united by powerful rulers into temporary kingdoms. Meanwhile, Assyria recovered to become the main power of the region until its overthrow by the Babylonians and Medes. The later Assyrian empire dominated the region with an army that included cavalry as well as chariots, and improved siege techniques that enabled them to overrun the walled cities of Judea. A state policy of terror served to intimidate their enemies into surrender: cities that resisted were razed to the ground, their populations exterminated.

Aral Sea

MASSAGETAE

Maracanda · Cyreschata ·

Oxus

SATRAPY OF BACTRIA

campaign against the
Shakas 520 BC

Zadracarta ○
HYRCANIA

· Rhagae

Bactra ○

PARTHIA

campaign against Massagetae c. 539– c. 530 BC

Ghazni ·

Taxila ·

ARIA

○ Herat

Kandahar ○

× Pasargadae
✕ 550 BC

○ Persepolis

PERSIS

ARACHOSIA

INDIANS

Indus

2 the near east,
1000–600 BC (above)

Israelite kingdom at its greatest extent,
c. 1000–922 BC

Urartu at its greatest extent,
c. 745 BC

Neo-Assyrian empire,
745 BC

Neo-Assyrian empire at its greatest extent,
c. 705–610 BC

Neo-Babylonian empire under Nebuchadnezzar II,
604–562 BC

■ Neo-Hittite city-states

▲ Phoenician city-states

▽ Aramaean city-states

march of Cyrus the Younger against Artaxerxes and return route of the 'Ten Thousand' Greek mercenaries

ARABS neighbouring populations

Arabian Sea

13

500 BC
Ionian Greek city-state colonies revolt against Persian empire of Darius I

494 BC
Battle of Lade: Persian Darius I's navy defeats the Greeks

492 BC
Persians under Mardonius conquer Thrace and Macedon

490 BC
Battle of Marathon

480 BC
Persian victory at Thermopylae. Greeks win crushing naval battle at Salamis

479 BC
Greek victory at Plataea

The Greek military system relied principally on the hoplite, an armoured infantryman so named for his shield, the hoplon. The Persian military in contrast was better suited to the open spaces of Southwest Asia, where speed and manoeuvrability won battles. Given its training and experience, Persian cavalry was far superior to that of the Greeks, but Persian infantry was ill-equipped to stand toe-to-toe with hoplites.

The Persian empire continued to expand under Darius I, conquering the Greek city-state colonies in Anatolia (modern-day western Turkey). Around 500 BC these cities rose in revolt, appealing to their mother cities in Greece to give them aid. Athens and Eretria sent a small naval contingent. Darius' navy defeated the Greek squadrons at the Battle of Lade (494 BC) and his army put several Ionian cities to the torch. Darius despatched an expeditionary force to punish Athens and Eretria.

The Persian forces captured Eretria, then shipped their army to a beach on the Marathon plain, 19 miles from Athens, near a convenient road that lead to the city. Forewarned, the Athenian army arrived just after the Persians had disembarked and occupied a narrow valley, Vrana, that flanked the Persian route of advance to the city. Although victorious, the Athenians only managed to capture seven ships; a rearguard action by the Persian cavalry covered their escape. Internal conflict delayed the Persian riposte until 480 BC, when Xerxes, the new King of Kings, led a fresh expedition to avenge Marathon.

Most of the Greek cities in the north surrendered without a fight. In the south, a Hellenic league, with Sparta as its leader, sent a land and naval force to buy time to prepare fortifications on the isthmus. At Thermopylae, 300 Spartans held off the entire Persian army for several days, while an inconclusive naval battle took place off Artemisium. The Spartan delaying force, under their king, Leonidas, was wiped out to the last man; the galley fleet withdrew when its land flank was uncovered.

The Persians marched into a poorly defended Athens, which they sacked. But their fleet was lured into closed waters near the island of Salamis and destroyed by the Athenian and Corinthian navies. With its logistic support destroyed, the majority of the Persian army withdrew to Asia while some 20,000–25,000 men remained behind near Plataea. In 479 BC a Hellenic army representing most of Southern Greece defeated the Persians. The Persian rout was then completed by their defeat at Mycale the same year. With the Persians expelled from Europe the Spartans returned home, while an appeal from the Ionian Greeks to Athens created the Delian League.

MAC

ILLYRIA

THESSAL

The

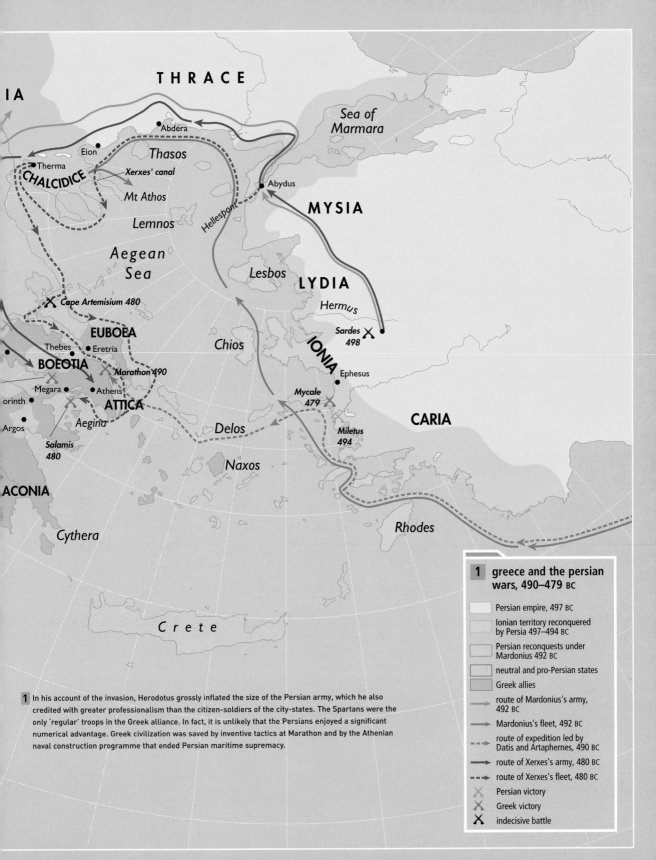

THRACE

Sea of
Marmara

Abdera

Eion

Therma

Thasos

Xerxes' canal

CHALCIDICE

Mt Athos

Abydus

MYSIA

Lemnos

Hellespont

Aegean
Sea

Lesbos

LYDIA

✕ *Cape Artemisium 480*

Hermus

EUBOEA

Chios

Sardes
498 ✕

Thebes

Eretria

Ephesus

BOEOTIA

✕ *Marathon 490*

IONIA

Megara

Athens

*Mycale
479*

Corinth

ATTICA

Argos

Aegina

Delos

*Miletus
494*

CARIA

*Salamis
480*

Naxos

LACONIA

Cythera

Rhodes

Crete

1 greece and the persian
wars, 490–479 BC

	Persian empire, 497 BC
	Ionian territory reconquered by Persia 497–494 BC
	Persian reconquests under Mardonius 492 BC
	neutral and pro-Persian states
	Greek allies
→	route of Mardonius's army, 492 BC
→	Mardonius's fleet, 492 BC
⇢	route of expedition led by Datis and Artaphernes, 490 BC
→	route of Xerxes's army, 480 BC
⇢	route of Xerxes's fleet, 480 BC
✕	Persian victory
✕	Greek victory
✕	indecisive battle

1 In his account of the invasion, Herodotus grossly inflated the size of the Persian army, which he also credited with greater professionalism than the citizen-soldiers of the city-states. The Spartans were the only 'regular' troops in the Greek alliance. In fact, it is unlikely that the Persians enjoyed a significant numerical advantage. Greek civilization was saved by inventive tactics at Marathon and by the Athenian naval construction programme that ended Persian maritime supremacy.

431 BC
Peloponnesian War starts

429 BC
Athenian naval victory at Naupactus

425 BC
Athens captures Sphacteria. Spartan peace overtures rebuffed

422 BC
Spartan victory at Amphipolis. Brasidas and Cleon both killed

421 BC
negotiation of Peace of Nicias (new Athenian leader)

418 BC
Battle of Mantinea: Sparta defeats Argive-led army

407 BC
Spartan fleet wins naval battle off Notium

406 BC
Athenians win victory at Arginusae, and again decline offer of peace

405 BC
Athenian fleet destroyed while beached at Hellespont

404 BC
Athens surrenders

The war between the Peloponnesian League, led by Sparta, and the Delian League, led by Athens, pitted a land power against a sea power. The asymmetric nature of the conflict helped prolong hostilities for 25 years. Athens collected tribute from allies who were bound to her by treaty, and their fleet of 300 triremes allowed them to win the majority of its naval battles, even when outnumbered. Although the Peloponnesian League's naval forces were outnumbered, it could muster some 30,000–35,000 hoplites, more than twice as many as Athens. At the League's core was the Spartan army, the only professional fighting force in Greece.

The first phase of the war, the Archidamian War (431–421 BC), saw the Spartan army invade Attica each year, while the Corinthian navy attempted to break out of the Gulf of Corinth. The Athenian admiral, Phormio, operating from Naupactus, defeated a succession of Corinthian sorties and prevented Corinth from maintaining its economic links to colonies in Italy. Athens established a base at Pylos on the western coast of the Peloponnese. Sparta landed a small army on an adjacent island (Sphacteria), but Athenian naval forces isolated them. After a series of failed negotiations, Athenian naval forces were able in 425 BC to land superior Athenian land forces on to the island, destroying the majority of the Spartan force and capturing the survivors.

Negotiations followed, culminating in the Peace of Nicias in 421 BC, but it was no more than an armistice. Many of Sparta's allies became disaffected and formed a new league with Argos. At the Battle of Mantinea (418 BC), Sparta won the one and only large hoplite battle of the Peloponnesian War when it defeated an Argive-led army which included an Athenian contingent. This victory, plus the Athenian invasion of Sicily, prompted a renewal of hostilities.

In 415 BC, Athens launched a pre-emptive attack on Syracuse, a potential Spartan ally. The fact that the Athenians could launch the original expedition and subsequently reinforce it without hindrance from the Peloponnesian League testifies to their control over the western sea routes to Sicily. But the

1 The whole Greek world became involved in the prolonged war between Athens and Sparta from 431 BC (map right). Sparta was stronger on land, but Athens kept firm control of the sea. After ten years an uneasy peace was made (421 BC), but when Athens lost almost its entire fleet in Sicily, the Spartans pressed home their advantage. Even so, it was only with considerable naval and financial support from the Persians that they were able to overcome the Athenian navy.

Rome

LATIUM

Cumae
Neapolis

Tyrrhenian Sea

MAGNA GRAECIA

Lipara

Messana

Segesta

Himera
Rhegium

Sicily

Selinus
Catana

Gela
Syracuse 41

Camarina

1 the peloponnesian war, 431–404 BC

Athens and members of the Delian League

ally of Athens

Sparta and allies

neutral states

allies of Athens in Magna Graecia

allies of Sparta in Magna Graecia

Athenian campaigns

Spartan campaigns

Athenian victory

Spartan victory

loss of 160 Athenian and 56 allied triremes in the confined waters of Syracuse harbour equalized the naval forces available to both sides for the first time in 50 years.

Sparta was now able to establish a series of fleets in western Asia Minor that contested Athens' sea lines of communication across the Aegean and the Hellespont. Although Athens had lost naval superiority and had suffered a series of political upheavals at home, its superior tactical prowess still enabled its navy to win a series of naval battles over an eight-year period. Yet these were not enough; Athenian allies rebelled and ceased paying tribute, further weakening the Athenian navy. In 405 BC the Athenian fleet, maintaining its eastern sea lanes in the Hellespont, was destroyed while beached and Athens, faced with imminent starvation, surrendered a year later.

 At their third attempt, the Syracusan army extended a defensive wall past the Athenian siege lines, preventing the total blockade of the city (map right). Spartan general Gylippus then trapped the Athenian fleet within the great harbour and the besiegers found themselves cut off. The surrender and enslavement of the expeditionary force was a catastrophe for Athens and her fleet never recovered its qualitative advantage.

2 **siege of syracuse, 416 BC**

- Syracusans
- Athenians

0 — 1 km
0 — 1 mile

alexander the great and the successor wars

338 BC
Battle of Chaeronea: Macedon (under Philip II) overpowers Theban-led coalition

336 BC
Philip assassinated. Son, Alexander III, secures Greece and the Balkan Peninsula

334 BC
Alexander invades Persia

333 BC
Battle of Issus

331 BC
Battle of Arbela (or Gaugamela): Alexander defeats Darius

321 BC
Alexander dies

280 BC
Three main successor states emerge: Macedon, Egypt and the Seleucid kingdom

217 BC
Battle of Raphia between Antiochus and Egypt

200 BC
Rome declares war on Philip V of Macedon

197 and 168 BC
Macedonians defeated

1 The meteoric career of Alexander brought the Macedonian army to the limits of the known world. In ten years of unceasing warfare, he led his men to victory over the Persian army, the cities of Phoenicia, mountain tribes and Scythian horsemen. That his empire would not outlive him was evident before his death: false news of his demise triggered several revolts prior to his fatal sickness at Baghdad.

Wars between the Greek city states continued after the Peloponnesian War until the northern state of Macedon overwhelmed a Theban-led coalition at the Battle of Chaeronea in 338 BC.

The victorious Macedonian king, Philip II, was assassinated in 336 BC. Two years later, his son Alexander III led the Macedonian army into Asia, on a one-way journey that won him the reputation of the greatest field commander of the Ancient world. He shattered a Persian army led by local satraps in western Asia Minor, personally leading a headlong cavalry charge that nearly cost him his life. Alexander's communications with Macedon were vulnerable to the Persian fleet, which was also capable of supporting revolts within Greece, so he led the army against the coastal cities of the eastern Mediterranean. King Darius III of Persia arrived in 333 BC, but he was defeated at Issus, and his army disintegrated. The Persian empire began to fracture. Its provinces included a wide variety of races, subject peoples with no particular allegiance to the ruling Achaemenid dynasty. Egypt's cities surrendered to Alexander. Alexander's general Ptolemy was to found the last dynasty of pharaohs, which ended with Cleopatra VII. In 331 BC Alexander marched into the heartland of Asia for a final confrontation with Darius, who had raised and equipped another army. Darius fled the field at Arbela, and was pursued for some months by Alexander until assassinated by Bessus, the satrap of Bactria.

Alexander devoted the next ten years to conquering the farthest reaches of the Persian empire. In 321 BC, aged only 33, and having conquered most of the civilized world, he died of fever (or possibly poison).

1 the empire of alexander

–·–·– empire of Alexander, 323 BC

———— states federated to the empire

———— independent states

⟶ route of Alexander the Great

⟶ route of Nearchus's naval expedition, 325 BC

⟶ return route of Alexander's veterans and elephants under Craterus, 325 BC

✕ Alexander's major battles

● new cities founded, 336–100 BC

● cities partly replanned or rebuilt, 336–100 BC

Alexander's sudden death precipitated a series of wars that only ended with the arrival of Roman power in the region. Alexander's generals (the Diadochoi, or Successors) fought to inherit, if not his throne, at least an empire of their own. By the assassination of Seleucus, the last of Alexander's officers, in 280 BC, three main successor states emerged: Macedon, Egypt and the Seleucid kingdom that stretched from the eastern shores of the Mediterranean to Baghdad.

Over a century after Alexander's death, the Egypt of the Ptolemys and the Seleucids in the Middle East/Syria were at war over the ports and cities that were part of Coele-Syria, the modern-day Mediterranean Middle East. In 218 BC, fresh from suppressing a series of eastern rebellions, the Seleucid kingdom's young ruler, Antiochus III, invaded Coele-Syria and marched against Egypt. The ensuing Battle of Raphia (217 BC) left Palestine in Egyptian hands while Antiochus devoted his considerable energy to further campaigns in Bactria, Arabia and as far east as the Punjab.

2 Antigonus 'one eye' was killed at the Battle of Ipsus in 301 BC, ending the most serious attempt by one of Alexander's generals to control the entire empire (map below). By the time the last of the original 'successors' was killed in 280, Alexander's empire had fractured into many states. The most powerful were based on Egypt, the old Persian heartland and Macedonia itself. Macedonian intrigues with the Carthaginians during the Second Punic War were not forgotten in Rome which declared war on Philip V in 200 BC. The Macedonians were defeated in 197 and again in 168. Between the Macedonian wars, Rome intervened in the eastern Aegean where smaller states allied with her against Antiochus III, ruler of the Seleucid empire. Antiochus was defeated at Magnesia in 190, the success of cavalry under his own command failing to stop the legions demolishing his phalanx.

2 the hellenistic world, 188 BC

- independent Greek states
- Antigonid kingdom (and dependencies 241 BC)
- Ptolemaic kingdom and dependencies
- kingdom of Pergamum
- Hellenized non-Greek kingdoms

Inset map 2 labels

ROMAN REPUBLIC
ILLYRIANS
THRACIANS
Pella
MACEDON
Pydna 168
Cynoscephalae 197
Pergamum
BITHYNIA
PAPHLAGONIA
GALATIA
PONTUS
Apamea
CAPPADOCIA
ARMENIA
PERGAMUM
Magnesia 190
Antioch
COMMAGENE
Nemrut Dag
MEDIA ATROPATENE
Black Sea
Caspian Sea
SELEUCID KINGDOM (AND VASSAL STATES)
PARTHIA
GRAECO-BACTRIAN KINGDOM
GEDROSIA
Panias 200
EGYPT
Alexandria
LIBYANS
ARABIA
Persian Gulf

Main map labels

Caspian Sea
Cyrus
Araxes
Oxus
MASSAGET
SCYTHIA
DAHAE
Tashkent
Alexandria Eschate
(Bukhara)
Maracanda (Samarkand)
Cyropolis
Zadracarta
Hecatompylos
Bojnurd
Meshed
Susia
Nautaca (Karshi)
Derbent
Sogdian Rock besieged 328
SOGDIANA
Alexandria (Merv)
Rhagae (Teheran)
Amol
HYRCANIA
Thara
Ai Khanoum (?Alexandria Oxiana)
Bactra (Balkh)
BACTRIA
Drapsaca
Caspian Gates
Ecbatana
Laodicea
PARAETACENE
PARTHIA
ARIA
Artacoana
Alexandria Areion (Herat)
Nicaea
Alexandria ad Caucasum
Begram
Nysa
Charsadda (Shaikhan Dheri)
Aornos
Taxila
KINGDOM OF ABHISARA
Indus
COSSAEI
UXII
Gabae
salt desert
DRANGIANA
Alexandria (Shaikahn Dheri)
Alexandria (Ghazni)
KINGDOM OF OMPHIS
326
Bucephala
Nicaea
Artemita
BABYLONIA
Susa
Seleucia
Tigris
SUSIANA
Alexandria Prophthasia
Alexandria Arachoton (Kandahar)
Hindu Kush
KINGDOM OF PORUS
Chenab
Pasargadae
CARMANIA
ARACHOSIA
Sangela
Persian Gates
Persepolis
PERSIS
Nad-i-Ali
SEISTAN
Multan
Hydraotes (Ravi)
Hyphasis (Beas)
probable ancient coastline
Alexandria (Gulashkird)
Quetta
Alexandria Opiana
Sutlej
Harmozia
Pura
GEDROSIA
Indus
INDIA
Persian Gulf
Las Bela
Alexandria
City of the Brahmans
Indian Desert
Pasni
ORITAE
Kokala
Gwadar
Pattala
probable ancient course of Indus
Arabian Sea

19

the **punic** wars

264 to 146 BC

264–242 BC
First Punic war

259 BC
Victory of Roman fleet off Cape Ecnomus. Later lands in Africa

241 BC
Romans destroy the Carthaginian fleet off the Aegates. Carthage sues for peace. Cession of Carthage's possessions in Sicily to Rome

219 BC
Rome fights Carthaginian general Hannibal for control of Spain

218–201 BC
Second Punic War

217 BC
Battle of Lake Trasimene

216 BC
Battle of Cannae

202 BC
Roman General Scipio Africanus (237–183 BC) defeats Hannibal

146 BC
Romans take and destroy Carthage, ending the 3rd Punic War

1 The acquisition of overseas provinces by Rome was seldom by design (map right). Although Roman commanders needed little encouragement to undertake military campaigns, they preferred to make treaties with defeated enemies rather than turn their territories into provinces. However, the wars against the Hellenistic kingdoms of the eastern Mediterranean in the 2nd and 1st centuries BC left the Romans with possessions that could yield substantial tribute.

By the 4th century BC, Rome had extended its power to southern Italy. Rome, Carthage and the Macedonian successor state of Epirus were vying for control of Sicily. Epirus fought Rome from 281–272 BC when its king, Pyrrhus, died; he defeated Rome's armies, but at such heavy cost the expression 'Pyrrhic victory' was coined. Against the Carthaginians Rome fought a series of Punic Wars. The first lasted from 265–242 BC. Rome conquered Sicily, but an invasion of North Africa met with disaster. After a period of uneasy peace, the two powers clashed over control of Spain in 219 BC, while Hannibal led his army towards the Alps.

Hannibal beat the Roman armies at Trebbia and Lake Trasimene (217 BC), leading Rome to adopt a defensive policy championed by Fabius, but a populist consul, Varro, claimed the nobility were prolonging the war for their own profit and that he could end it immediately. This 'political general' led 80,000 Roman infantry against 50,000 Carthaginians, of which half were Gallic auxiliaries. Unlike Alexander the Great, who left his infantry to advance according to a pre-planned timetable while he charged at the head of his cavalry, Hannibal remained in the centre where he could coordinate the battle. The Carthaginian centre held, albeit at heavy cost.

Rome had the political will to survive 15 years of campaigning in Italy. New legions were raised, the city resorting to the recruitment of freed slaves. Rome's fortifications were formidable; it was impossible for Hannibal to storm the city. The Fabian strategy was tried again, and this time the Romans persisted with it; keeping their army close to Hannibal's, but never risking battle. The Romans habitually fortified their camp, nullifying the Carthaginians' cavalry superiority. Isolated detachments of Carthaginians were attacked, the Romans retiring behind their fortifications if pressed. Rome could replace its losses in such skirmishes, but Hannibal could not. The few Italian cities that had deserted Rome came to regret it, the fate of Capua anticipating that of Carthage. The Roman navy prevented reinforcements reaching Hannibal by sea. Hannibal's brother marched an army overland from Spain, but Hannibal only learned of the attempted reinforcement when Hasdrubal's severed head was tossed into his camp.

Rome's superior manpower enabled a second front to be opened; sustained by Roman naval superiority, new armies were deployed to Spain where they drove out the Carthaginians. This 'indirect approach' stampeded the Carthaginian senate into negotiations. An armistice was arranged and Hannibal's army sailed home. Its arrival stiffened the Carthaginians' resolve, and a final battle took place near the small town of Zama (202 BC). Publius Cornelius Scipio won the nickname 'Africanus' for this, his most famous and important victory.

In 146 BC, the Romans ended 150 years of hostilities with Carthage by storming the city. The survivors were sold as slaves and the city demolished. The Carthaginian language was eventually lost and only the writings of later historians shed any light on Carthage's military institutions and its most famous general, Hannibal.

1 the roman world, 264–44 BC

limits of Carthaginian control, c. 264 BC	territory under Roman control by 133 BC
limits of Carthaginian control, 218 BC	territory taken under Roman control, 133–44 BC
controlled by Carthage by 149 BC	*146* date of establishment of a formal province
Italy, 197 BC	dependencies of Rome by 44 BC
	independent states

naval warfare in the mediterranean

490 to 31 BC

c. 700 BC
Phoenicians have the first dedicated warships

5th century BC
trireme (three banks of oars) replaces bireme (two banks)

4th–3rd centuries BC
warships grow larger: Roman and Carthaginian fleets use quadremes and quinquiremes

31 BC
Naval Battle of Actium. Quinquereme is standard battleship on the Mediterranean

By around 700 BC the Phoenicians had developed the first dedicated warships. Experience soon stimulated the design of oar-propelled warships. Independent of the wind, these narrow-beamed ships had the manoeuvrability and acceleration to force an action with lumbering sail-driven merchant ships. By the 5th century BC the Phoenician bireme had been largely superseded by the triple-banked trireme.

In 480 BC, ten years after Marathon, the Persians launched a second invasion of Greece. The Persian soldiers, battle-hardened conquerors of an already vast empire, were accompanied by a large fleet of perhaps 400 warships. It came as a disagreeable surprise to encounter a Greek fleet of similar size off Artemisium. Themistocles, the far-sighted leader of Athens, had persuaded the citizens to spend the profits from their new-found silver mines on a massive programme of naval construction. The Athenian navy held off the Persian fleet.

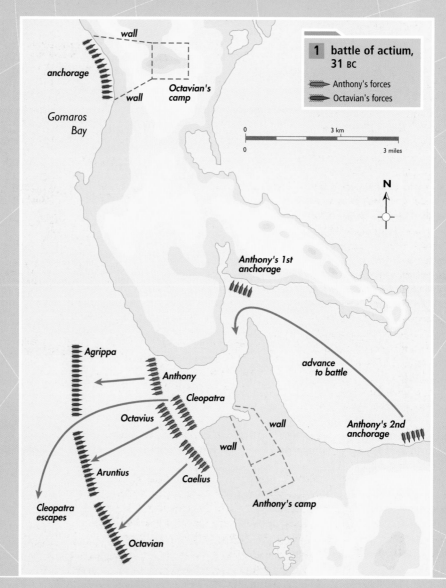

1 battle of actium, 31 BC

➤ Anthony's forces
➤ Octavian's forces

1 The final battle of the civil war following Caesar's murder was fought off the Greek coast at Actium. Cleopatra's squadron broke through the enemy centre, but she hoisted sail and escaped to Egypt with the treasury. Mark Anthony's flagship was a gigantic warship with multiple banks of oars, but most ships on both sides were quinquiremes, the standard Roman warship since the Second Punic War.

2 A Roman invasion fleet of 330 vessels sailed for Africa but was intercepted off Sicily by 350 Carthaginian ships. The Romans won the battle, capturing 64 enemy ships and sinking 30 for the loss of 24 of their own. Both the Carthaginian admiral and one of the two Roman consuls were later tortured to death by the Carthaginian authorities.

By offering battle in the Bay of Eleusis, the Athenians lured the Persian fleet to defeat. The Greek crews lacked the experience of their opponents, their triremes were heavier and less manoeuvrable, but they were able to concentrate on the leading Persian squadrons as they entered the bay. Caught in a bottleneck, the Persians had no room to exploit their superior seamanship. A flanking attack by their Egyptian squadron was similarly defeated by Corinthian triremes on the western side of Salamis, and the Persian warships withdrew in confusion.

All major sea battles in the ancient Mediterranean took place close to the shore. Oar-powered warships demand large crews and because triremes could only carry a few days' provisions the fleets put ashore each night for food and water. This made it difficult to impose a blockade. Fleets were vulnerable when beached for the night, a weakness highlighted during the Peloponnesian war when the Athenian navy was annihilated at Aegospotami in 405 BC. Lysander, the Spartan commander, massacred the Athenian oarsmen. Athens had demonstrated extraordinary powers of economic recovery in nearly 30 years of conflict, but while the city might be able to rebuild ships, trained seamen were irreplaceable. Athens surrendered.

Warships grew larger during the fourth and third centuries BC. Roman and Carthaginian fleets used quadriremes and quinquiremes. The Roman fleet relied on boarding rather than ramming and they achieved naval superiority during the first Punic War, and maintained it during the Second Punic War (218–201 BC).

By 31 BC, when the Battle of Actium decided the Roman Civil War in favour of Octavian (later Augustus), the quinquireme was the standard battleship of the ancient Mediterranean. Larger vessels had been tried, but proved too cumbersome. Lighter warships, some relying as much on their sails as their oars, proved of greater value, and would play a greater role as Roman naval power waned in the absence of organized opposition. During the following centuries of the Pax Romana, warships all but vanished from the Mediterranean.

Carthaginian centre
174 ships,
2nd position

Roman wedge
164 ships,
2nd position

right division
(87 ships)

centre divisions

87 ships   87 ships

left division
(87 ships)

2nd position,
right division

2nd position,
3rd division

2nd position,
4th division

2nd position,
left division

1st division
(82 ships)

2nd division
(82 ships)

3rd division
(82 ships),
towing 82
transports

4th division
(82 ships)

2 **battle of ecnomus, 256 BC**

Romans
Carthaginians

58 to 52 BC

386 BC
Gallic invasion almost reaches Rome

295 BC
Battle of Sentinum, prompted by Gallic invasion

58 BC
Julius Caesar's first Gallic campaign

57 BC
Caesar pacifies Belgica

55 BC
Caesar goes to the Low Countries to repel a group of invading Germans, and in turn invades German territory

53 BC
Caesar puts down another Belgian revolt and enters Germany again. Winter – all central Gaul raises a revolt. Caesar crosses Alps and suppresses the Gauls

52 BC
siege of Alesia: Caesar forces surrender of Vercingetorix

51 BC
last Gallic resistance put down

Throughout the Early Republic, Rome had been subjected to frequent invasions from the north. The Gauls had come within a stone's throw of Rome in 386 BC and two major battles, Sentinum (295 BC) and Telamon (225 BC), had been fought against them. The Gauls were made up of conglomerations of aggressive tribes, most of which had settled in what is now France and Germany. Some moved as far south as the Po Valley. Warfare was for them a way of life, bravery in battle a sure road to elevation in the tribal hierarchy. As a result, the Gauls could be most impressive and difficult foes, especially with their savage initial charge, which could sweep all before it. The Romans called it *furor*, and they feared its effect mightily. It required all the legion's discipline, as well as their superiority in armament, to keep the Roman soldiers in place when confronted by the Gallic *furor*.

The Gauls that Caesar met in the 1st century BC were the same tribes the Romans had encountered in Italy in the 3rd century BC. Their armies employed *furor*, although their weapons and armour had improved. Despite Caesar's efforts to gather votes at home by putting a spin on how fearsome they were, through his famous book *de Bello Gallico*, it is obvious that Caesar had little trouble smashing three large Gallic armies: the Helvetii at Bibracte (58 BC); the Nervii, at the Sabis (57 BC) ; and the Germanic tribes under Ariovistus, somewhere west of the Rhine.

Caesar's Gallic campaigns involved several naval ventures. In order to neutralize the Armorican tribes, Caesar built a fleet of Liburnian biremes from scratch and engaged in a full-scale battle

1 Divided among themselves, the Gallic tribes were defeated one after another by the Romans (map right). Caesar exploited their inability to maintain a large army for any length of time. Avoiding battle in the early stages of a campaign, Caesar went over to the offensive as the Gauls began to disperse. He probably outnumbered the tribal armies by the time they met on the battlefield, something he was determined to conceal in his published account of the wars.

2 Vercingetorix, chief of the Arveni tribe in central Gaul, waged a 'scorched earth' policy against Gallic tribes that allied themselves to Rome (map left). Caesar besieged him at Gergovia, but had to break off the siege to deal with another revolt. In 52 BC he besieged him at Alesia (Alise-Sainte-Reine) where he defeated another Gallic army that attempted to raise the siege. Vercingetorix led many attempts to break out, but was ultimately obliged to surrender.

Mt. Rea

N

Alesia

Ose

Gallic relief army

Oserain

Brenne

0   1 km

0   1 mile

1 the siege of alesia

Gauls — Roman forts
Roman camps — Roman siegeworks

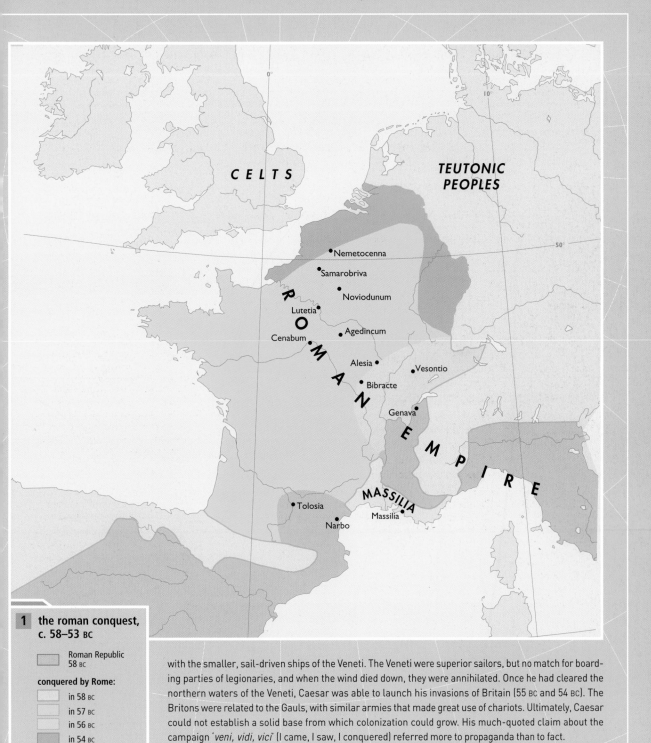

CELTS

TEUTONIC
PEOPLES

Nemetocenna

Samarobriva

Noviodunum

Lutetia

Agedincum

Cenabum

R·O·M·A·N

Alesia

Vesontio

Bibracte

Genava

E·M·P·I·R·E

MASSILIA

Tolosia

Massilia

Narbo

1 the roman conquest,
c. 58–53 BC

Roman Republic
58 BC

conquered by Rome:

in 58 BC

in 57 BC

in 56 BC

in 54 BC

frontiers, 53 BC

with the smaller, sail-driven ships of the Veneti. The Veneti were superior sailors, but no match for boarding parties of legionaries, and when the wind died down, they were annihilated. Once he had cleared the
northern waters of the Veneti, Caesar was able to launch his invasions of Britain (55 BC and 54 BC). The
Britons were related to the Gauls, with similar armies that made great use of chariots. Ultimately, Caesar
could not establish a solid base from which colonization could grow. His much-quoted claim about the
campaign 'veni, vidi, vici' (I came, I saw, I conquered) referred more to propaganda than to fact.

The climax of the Gallic wars, the epic siege of Alesia, saw Vercingetorix holing up in the hilltop village of Alesia,
but the Gauls had not developed skills in siege-craft. They also did not have the 250,000 men in the relief force that
Caesar claims in his account. The logistics of assembling and feeding such a huge army were far beyond the
ability of the Gallic chiefs. The military genius on display at Alesia was, rather, in the Roman preparations for the
assault of the relief force. Vercingetorix was forced to surrender and Gallic resistance was effectively ended.

rome, germany and parthia

109 BC
Revolt of Numidia king Jugurtha (finally defeated 104 BC)

102 BC
Romans (under Marius) crush the Teutons at Aquae Sextiae

101 BC
Romans defeat the Cimbri at Vercellae

53 BC
Battle of Carrhae – Parthian victory over the invading Marcus Crassus, who is killed

AD 9
Battle of the Teutoburger Wald – Rome's most famous defeat in Germany

By the end of the 2nd century BC, Gallic migrations in northern Europe had pushed some of the 'Germanic' tribes towards the expanding Roman frontier. The foremost of these were the Teutons and Cimbri, who, in the 15 or so years before 100 BC, pushed west and south towards the Roman frontier. In 113 BC, they came into contact with Rome, winning four victories against small, poorly led Roman armies. When it counted, however, the Romans crushed first the Teutons, at Aquae Sextiae, and then the Cimbri, at Vercellae. Nevertheless, the halt to German aggression was temporary, as Caesar and the emperors were to find out.

The Germans tended to rely more in battle on physical bulk and brute force than the Romans. They had a few swords and virtually no armour. What they did add to the tactical mix was a method of attack Romans called 'the wedge'. A section of Germans would charge in a solid block with the idea of concentrating effort and energy at one point. Against mediocre troops, or other tribes, this could be a most effective tactic. Against veteran legions, it proved useless. Nowhere was this better demonstrated than at the Battle of Vercellae (date). King Beorix, his Cimbri, and the German wedge could do little against the implacability of Marius' legions.

The Numidians, in Africa, and the Parthians, in the regions east of Syria, were similar in their approach to warfare. Both armies consisted almost entirely of light cavalry, and the Romans had great difficulty countering them. Numidians excelled at a hit-and-run style of warfare. Their cavalry would charge up to an enemy line of infantry, discharging their javelins as they got near, then wheeling and galloping away. If the infantry, stung by too many spears, moved out to challenge them, they swooped in, isolated the rash few and hacked them to pieces. The Romans, lacking cavalry suitable to handling this tactic, usually went on the defensive. The more and the better the contingent of Roman cavalry, the more able it was to take the offensive.

Against the last King of Numidia, Jugurtha, who had revolted in 109 BC against Roman attempts to turn him into a puppet, the Roman legions came close to being picked apart but their discipline, just enough cavalry to make a difference, and Marius' leadership, provided Rome with two victories – and Jugurtha in chains.

Against the Parthians, they had less success. The Parthians perfected the 'Parthian shot', the ability of their cavalry to fire accurately while galloping away. They were so adept at hit-and-run that a large consular army under Publius Crassus (triumviral associate of Julius Caesar) was picked to death and destroyed at Carrhae (53 BC). Crassus' fate put Rome off any advance east of Syria for generations.

1 The Parthians overran much of the territory of the Seleucid empire (map right). Their advance westwards brought them into contact with the expanding power of Rome and in 53 BC their mounted archers surrounded and destroyed the legions of the Roman general Crassus. Parthian armies consisted mainly of these horse archers, whose ability to shoot behind them gave rise to the expression 'Parthian shot'. A core of heavily armoured lancers (cataphracts) stood ready to charge, once the arrow storm had depleted the enemy ranks and disordered their formation.

1 persia under the parthians, 247 BC–AD 224

territory gained by Parthians 247–176 BC

Parthian territory 53 BC–AD 224

vassal or allied kingdoms

Roman naval expedition

Tiberius' fleet
AD 14

BURGUNDIONES

CHAUCI

AD 15

tribes loyal to Rome
11 BC–AD 15

approximate route of Roman expedition

LANGOBARDI

Elbe

Weser

Aller

CHERUSCI

line of temporary forts

SUGAMRI

Caecina's expedition
AD 15

Noviomagus

Vetera
main Roman
garrison town

Lippe

Aliso
Drusus' depot 11 BC;
Tiberius' winter quarters;
besieged by Germans AD 16

Ruhr

(Arnsburg)

river navigable in summer

Rhine

CHATTI

Colonia
Agrippensis
(Cologne)

Drusus AD 15

Mosel

(Friedburg)
Drusus' fort AD 15
supply route

HERMUNDURI

Mogontiacum (Mainz)

Main

2 Unlike the Gallic tribes, the semi-nomadic Germans had no fixed bases for the Romans to attack (map left). Animal herds were their main source of food so there were no grain stores for the Romans to seize. However, by exploiting the rivers and the coast, the Romans were able to launch a series of summer campaigns, their armies sometimes overwintering at a temporary base established at Aliso. Tribes were bribed or bullied into alliance with Rome, but their long-term loyalty could only be ensured by an immediate military presence.

2 roman campaigns in germany

☐ Roman empire,
AD 15

▨ under Roman occupation,
AD 75

■ Roman fort

3 Rome's most famous defeat in Germany occurred in AD 9 when Varus' three legions were wiped out during their retreat to the fort at Aliso (map right). Roman vengeance followed: Germanicus led a punitive expedition in AD 14 and Drusus launched a two-pronged assault the following year. The Roman frontier seemed set to reach the Elbe, but Tiberius halted the war, afraid that victorious generals might emulate Caesar and return to Rome to seize power.

3 battle of the teutoburger wald, AD 9

▨ areas raided by Romans

N.B. the whole area was forested

Teutotoburger wald

(Minden)
approximate site of
Varus' camp

Varus' retreat AD 9

approximate site of
Teutoburg battlefield*

raids by Germnicus
AD 14

Lippe

Aliso
Roman fort

Varus' intended route
to Aliso

Weser

Leine

Ruhr

Diemel

Fulda

Lenne

area laid waste by
Drusus AD 14

Drusus AD 15

*Varus's army annihilated losing 3 legions (XVII, XVIII & XIX), plus 6 cohorts of German allies and 3 squadrons of cavalry. (12-18,000 soldiers and followers; column 9-12 miles long)

Rhine

Westerwald

60 BC
first triumvirate divides Roman empire between Julius Caesar, Marcus Crassus and Gnaeus Pompey

53 BC
Crassus killed in Parthia

49 BC
Caesar declares war on Pompey, instigating five years of civil war, from which he emerges victorious

44 BC
Caesar murdered on Ides of March

31 BC
Battle of Actium: Caesar's nephew Octavian's victory makes him sole ruler of Rome

27 BC
Octavian granted title 'Augustus' by the Senate; Roman republic becomes an Empire

AD 357
Battle of Argentoratum: Emperor Julian defeats the German invaders

AD 378
Roman army defeated by Goths, led by Fridigern, at Adrianople

After Caesar crossed the Rubicon to initiate his bid for supreme power, senatorial limitations on the armies became irrelevant. The numbers of Romans under arms rose to staggering proportions in the ensuing civil wars. For the next 150 or so years, most of the major battles involved legions fighting other legions, with some 'time outs' to fight Germans in the north and to subdue rebellions in the east.

In 49 BC Caesar's army faced one loyal to Pompey (Cnaeus Pompeius) in Spain. Caesar outmanoeuvred his opponents, cutting them off from their water supply and forcing a surrender. Caesar then shipped his army to the Balkans to attack Pompey at Dyrrhachium (Dubrovnik). The rival armies fought a pitched battle at Pharsalus in August 48 BC. Pompey's legions made little progress against Caesar's veterans and he fled to Egypt where he was murdered.

Caesar was in turn assassinated in 44 BC. His nephew Gaius Julius Caesar Octavianus (Octavian), who with Mark Antony had defeated the assassins, became sole ruler of Rome. In 27 BC, victorious at Actium (the last major naval battle of the ancient world), he was granted the title Augustus by the Senate and the republic's transformation into an empire was all but complete.

By the reign of Septimius Severus (AD 193–211), the factors that led to the decline of the Roman military system were in place.

By the early 3rd century, social and economic power had devolved to the provinces. Citizenship was extended to most peoples within the empire and the importance of Rome itself diminished. This affected the legions, most of which were not only stationed on the frontiers but were now allowed to settle where they served, raise families and take jobs. Integration with local communities had a corrosive effect on the legions' military quality. The fearsome discipline of the legion disappeared, and with it, the legions' advantage over 'barbarian' forces. By the beginning of the 4th century, the legion had effectively disappeared.

Two major battles towards the end of the 4th century illuminate the changes that time and policy had brought. At Argentoratum (or Strasbourg) in 357, Emperor Julian routed an army of German tribes under King Chnodomer, but at Adrianople in 378, an over-eager Roman army under Emperor Valens, seeking to rid Thrace of the Goths for ever, attacked the Gothic camp only to be driven back by Gothic cavalry, enveloped, and then smashed.

But by the end of the 4th century, Rome's 'legions' were now no more than a local militia; cavalry dominated the battlefield and both arms were largely recruited from 'barbarian' allies.

1 From 27 BC the emperor himself was responsible for the administration of the imperial provinces (those in which legions were stationed). The others were governed by pro-consuls appointed by the Senate (map above). At the start of the imperial period some parts of the empire were ruled by friendly client kings; as they died their lands became Roman provinces. Emperors could gain great glory by extending the empire. Although campaigns in the 1st century AD in Germany had only limited success, the eastern Balkans, north Africa, Arabia and Britain were all added to Rome in the following century. Trajan added Dacia, Armenia, Assyria and Mesopotamia, pushing the frontiers to their greatest extent. Hadrian, his successor, abandoned Trajan's conquests, save Arabia and Dacia, to consolidate more defensible frontiers.

2 battle of adrianople

Goths
- tribesmen
- cavalry

Romans
- infantry
- cavalry

waggon laager

Emperor Valens

2 Determined to get sole credit for ridding Thrace of the Ostrogoths, Emperor Valens led the Roman army of the east into battle before the army of the western empire could arrive (map left). The Gothic cavalry was away foraging when Valens assaulted their wagon laager, but it returned with decisive effect. The Romans were attacked from the flanks and rear and Valens himself was killed.

1 the roman empire, 31 BC–AD 250

- under administration of the Senate
- imperial provinces
- public provinces
- provinces added after AD 14, with date
- later subdivisions of provinces, with dates

SARMATAE

ARMANIA

NDURI

OMANNI
QUADI

Danube · Vindobona · Aquincum
Lauriacum
NORICUM
TIA · Virunum
107 · PANNONIA SUPERIOR
leia
na · Siscia · Sirmium
Ravenna
nonia
Ariminum · Salonae
Narona · Doclea
Arretium
e · Corfinium
Dyrrhachium
Neapolis · Tarentum
Brundisium

IAZYGES · Porolissum
Potaissa · POROLISSENSIS 124–68
PANNONIA INFERIOR · 107 · DACIA SUPERIOR 118–68
Sarmizegetusa · 106
DACIA · DACIA INFERIOR 118–68
Oescus · Danube · MOESIA INFERIOR
MOESIA SUPERIOR · 85
Naissus · Serdica
ILLYRICUM · Trimontium
Stobi · THRACIA · 46
MACEDONIA · Thessalonica · Alexandria
Beroea · Troas

COSTOBOCI · ROXOLANI
Tomi

BOSPORAN KINGDOM · Panticapaeum
Chersonesus · client kingdom from 63 BC
Black Sea
Sinope
Heraclea Pontica · Amisus · Trapezus
Amasia · Nicopolis
BITHYNIA AND PONTUS · 107
Perinthus · Byzantium
Prusa · Ancyra · Caesarea
Dorylaeum · GALATIA · CAPPADOCIA · 17 · Melitene · 72
Pergamum · Antiochia · Iconium · Tarsus · COMMAGENE
Sardis · P · Side · CILICIA
Smyrna · PAMPHYLIA · Antioch · 200
Athens · Attaleia · LYCIA 43 · Apamea · Palmyra · 200

ALANI · COLCHIS · ALBANIA
Phasis
PARTHIAN PERSIAN EMPIRE Sasanid from 224
ARMENIA 114–17 temporary acquisition · Artaxata
Randeia · Tigranocerta
ASSYRIA 116–17 temporary acquisition · Amida · Tigris · Nisibis
MESOPOTAMIA 115–117 temporary acquisition · Dura Europos · Euphrates · Babylon

EPIRUS 140 · Nicopolis
E · M
X
Actium 31 BC · Patrae · Corinth · ACHAEA · Sparta
Demetrias
ASIA
Halicarnassus · Rhodus

Panormus
SICILIA · Catana · Syracuse
thage
Thapsus

CRETE · Gortyn

Mediterranean Sea

CYPRUS · Salamis · Tripolis · Berytus · PHOENICIA · 200
JUDAEA (PALESTINA) client kingdom 41–4 · Jerusalem · Gaza · 106 · Petra · PETRAEA
ARABIA · NABATAEI

Pelusium
Alexandria · Memphis
Cyrene · Apollonia
F · Sabrata · Leptis Magna
Berenice
HAZANIA · CYRENAICA · AEGYPTUS · Oxyrhynchus · Hermopolis · Nile · Ptolemais
Red Sea

29

the **fall** of the **roman empire**

AD 410
Alaric and Visigoths sack Rome

AD 418
Visigoths found kingdom of Toulouse in Gaul

AD 429
Vandal kingdom founded in North Africa

AD 451
Battle of Catalaunian Fields (Chalons) in Gaul: Romans and Germanic tribes together defeat Attila and his Huns

AD 476
the last emperor in the west, Romulus Augustulus, deposed by Odoacer, the commander-in-chief of the Roman army.

from AD 481
Clovis, the Frankish leader rules over Gallo-Germans and Franks in northern Gaul

AD 507
Battle of Vouillé: Frankish King Clovis defeats Visigoths

In the course of the 5th century, a flood of Germanic and other tribes brought down the western Roman empire. In 407, Britain was abandoned; Gaul and North Africa were lost before the middle of the century. By 489, the heart of the empire, Italy, had been taken over by the Ostrogoths. In many ways, the defeat of the western empire was surprising; the Eastern, or Byzantine, empire survived for another 1,000 years. In numbers, organization, tactics and strategy, the 'barbarians' were far inferior to the Romans. So why did the Germanic tribes emerge victorious?

With threats all along the imperial frontiers, the invasions had first of all to be resisted locally. Thus the relative weight of forces did not favour the Romans as much as the overall, absolute balance suggested. But, more importantly, the empire proved easy to fragment. Institutionally and ideologically, the empire turned out to be too weak for its citizens to feel forced or obliged to provide the taxes and manpower necessary to defeat the invasions. All too often, regions faced the invaders in isolation and many cities that could have withstood a siege failed to summon the necessary resistance. The invaders, on the other hand, utilized their military potential more efficiently.

After an enormous plundering spree, which left few parts of the empire unaffected, the tribes settled within it. Fascinated and impressed by the empire, the 'barbarians' tried hard to become Romans. As they acquired Roman titles and functions from the waning imperial powers, they also fought wars competing for claims of succession to the empire, in whole or in part. Also important was the idea that victory in war was a sign of Divine approval. For many chieftains and their followers, conversion to Christianity was clinched by the perception that the Christian God was a 'God of hosts' who provided the ultimate aid in their just pursuit of worldly power.

1 Clovis founded the Frankish empire (map left). From modern-day Belgium and northern France, he launched raids against the Visigoths in Aquitaine, the Gallo–Roman remnant of the Roman Empire under Syagrius, the Burgundians and the Alamans. His plundering and occasional battles created a 'Frankish' empire, based not on conquest but on the acceptance of overlordship and the payment of tribute. The looseness of the Empire is illustrated by the penetration of Germanic words into the local languages. Rule was an ephemeral, constantly contested, superimposition over existing societies.

1 the frankish kingdom, 511

Frankish territory at the beginning of Clovis's rule, 481

controlled by Syagrius before the Frankish conquest

conquered by Clovis by 497

conquered by Clovis, 507

boundaries between the kingdoms of Clovis's sons from 511

frontiers, 511

dates are those of Frankish conquest

North Sea

Hadrian's Wall
Eburacum
ANGLES
Glevum
ANGLES
Londinium
SAXONS JUTES

JUTES
ANGLES
FRISIANS
SAXONS
FRANKS
SLAVS 500
Baltic Sea
BALTIC PEOPLES
S L A V S
AVARS 558
HUNS c. 370

451
500
625
AVARS 568–803
OSTROGOTHS 150–370
ALANS overrun by Huns c. 370, reappear 406

TOXANDRIA
FRANKS
BURGUNDIANS
Colonia Agrippina
VANDALS
ALEMANNI (Worms)
BAIOVARII
RUGII
SUEVES
OSTROGOTHS
Crimea

Rotomagus
FRANKS Lutetia
Catalaunian Fields 451 ✕
ALEMANNI Aventicum
LOMBARDS
SLAVS 590
HUNS (from 425) VISIGOTHS
Attila's headquarters 434–53
Pliska
Odessus
Marcianopolis 447
Black Sea

VANDALS
SUEVES
AQUITANIA
Vouillé 507
KINGDOM OF THE VISIGOTHS
Tolosa (Toulouse)
Lugdunum
BURGUNDIANS 443–534
Mediolanum
Augusta Taurinorum
Genua
Pisae
VISIGOTHS 418–507
Massilia
568 LOMBARDS
Augusta Treverorum
BURGUNDIANS 407–43
Verona
OSTROGOTHS (from 454)
SLOVENES
CROATS
Salonae
SERBS (after 626)
Margus
Viminacium
Ratiaria
Naissus
Serdica
BULGARS 680 ✕ 447
443
Adrianople 378
Constantinople

Corsica
VISIGOTHS 410
Rome
OSTROGOTHS 489–552
Faleri
Neapolis ✕ Mons Lactarius 552
Tarentum
Byrundisium
THRACE
Philippopolis
MACEDONIA
SLAVS 600
✕ Gallipoli 443
Thermopylae where Attila was held in 447

Tarraco
Sardinia
Caralis
Palma
Valentia
Pompaelo
Panormus
Syracuse
Alaric dies 410
GREECE
Thermopylae
Athens
Piraeus
Corinth
VISIGOTHS 395
Sparta

Mediterranean Sea

Carthago Nov
Caesarea
Carthage
VANDALS, ALANS SUEVES 439–534
KINGDOM OF THE VANDALS
Ad Decimum 533

B E R B E R S

WESTERN ROMAN EMPIRE
EASTERN ROMAN EMPIRE

---

2 the germanic settlements, 395–476

movements of peoples

→ Huns and campaigns of Attila
→ Vandals, Alans, Sueves
→ Visigoths
→ Ostrogoths
→ Franks
→ other Germanic peoples
→ Slavs
→ Scots and Britons

— frontiers, 395
☐ official Roman withdrawal, 410
☐ kingdoms established by Germanic federates and the Vandals in the western Roman empire by 443
☐ regions settled by other federates in the western Roman empire, 450
☐ given up by the Romans to the Huns by 446
☐ other western Roman territories occupied by Germanic peoples by 476
☐ western Roman empire, 476
☐ eastern Roman empire, 476

---

2 In the frontier regions of the Roman empire, there was much interchange with, as well as raids by, neighbouring peoples (map above). On occasion entire peoples were settled as 'federates' associated with the army for defence purposes. Other 'barbarians' served in the ranks and in the top military posts of the imperial armies. The Huns created a major disruption and pushed groups such as the Goths and Vandals from the frontier regions of the empire. By the early 6th century, especially in the west, a number of successor states of mixed population had emerged on its former territory.

Wars were not about the conquest of territory with a view to its long-term exploitation; they provided immediate profit in the form of plunder. If there was a longer-term perspective, it usually went no further than the annual extraction of tribute from defeated enemies.

The Frankish king Clovis (born 466; ruled 481–511) provides an excellent example of these developments. His very name meant 'glory by combat' and his spectacular success in war was interpreted as a sign of divine favour (he converted to Christianity) which also brought him recognition from the Romans. The Byzantine emperor Anastasius made him consul after his victory over the Visigoths at the Battle of Vouillé in 507. Nonetheless, his campaigns did not usually consist of battles, which he fought rarely, but rather of yearly plunder raids deep into enemy territory.

the **arab** invasions

632
Death of Mohammed

caliph Abu Bakr completes
Mohammed's conquest of
Arabia and enters southern
Palestine

caliph Omar advances to
Damascus

636
Omar's victory over the
Byzantines at Yarmuk river.
Moves east into Mesopotamia
and northwest into Asia Minor

638
capture of Jerusalem

643
Battle of Alexandria: Alexandria
occupied

651
final defeat of Persians at Merv

673–78
Constantinople besieged

699
Byzantines abandon North
Africa

711
Battle of Rio Barbate: conquest
of Spain

712
Arab conquest of Sind

732
Battle of Poitiers on 25th
October: Frankish victory over
Arabs

751
Arab victory against Chinese at
Talas River

The speed of the 7th-century Arab conquest still astonishes. The Prophet Mohammed established himself in the Arabian peninsula in a period of little more than a decade. After his death in 632, Abu Bakr completed the conquest of the peninsula in two years. His successors moved into Egypt, Syria, Mesopotamia and beyond. By 669, Arab forces had briefly laid siege to Constantinople. Before the century was out, they had penetrated deep into Persia, knocked at the gates of the Byzantine Empire in Asia Minor and stood poised at the Straits of Gibraltar to move into Visigothic Spain.

Their main opponents, the Byzantines and Persians, had been greatly weakened by their interminable wars and the Visigoths, Persians and Byzantines were not closely integrated with the populations they ruled. For many it made no difference who their rulers were. Once defeated, one regime was easily replaced by another. Moreover, the Arabs were usually quite lenient in their treatment of conquered peoples. They required no conversion to Islam, only tribute, often at a rate lower than the tax burden imposed by the old regime.

Arab armies had a number of strengths. The traditional motive of lust for loot was reinforced by religious enthusiasm. With armies largely on horseback, they also possessed the twin advantages of initiative and mobility. Their knowledge of the desert enabled them to attack the old empires from a new direction. Rather than returning home every year, the Arabs, like the Vikings a little later, established armed camps along the way of their major expeditions from which they systematically launched further attacks. Famous examples with a long and distinguished future were Fustat in Egypt (which later grew into Cairo) and Basra in Iraq. Shorter-lived establishments were Qairawan, founded south of Carthage in 670, Cyzikos, just south of Constantinople (674–677) and Fraxinet, near Marseilles (c. 894–972).

The Arabs achieved another major feat in taking to the seas. In the 9th century, naval raids multiplied and led to long-term presences on Sardinia, Sicily and Crete, as well as the Italian mainland and southern France.

Arab expansion appears to have faltered through a combination of geographic and socio-political factors. In Spain, Asia Minor and Armenia, the Pyrenees, Taurus and Caucasus mountains marked the limit respectively; in the east, the vast expanses of inner central Asia put a temporary halt to expansion. In addition, north of the Pyrenees and beyond the Taurus mountains, the core areas of the Frankish and Byzantine realms were more loyal to their overlords than the frontier regions had been. Resistance stiffened and establishing a permanent presence became more difficult.

The Arabs also fell prey to their own internal bickering. There was no strong central power. By the ninth and 10th centuries, the Abbasid caliphate had begun to fracture, and local dynasties seized power. In time, their divisions handed opportunities to enterprising individuals from Western Christendom and the Byzantine empire to try and turn the tide back.

1 the arab conquest

- growth under Mohammed
- growth under Abu Bakr (632–4)
- growth under Omar (634–44)
- growth under Othman (644–56) and Ali (656–61)
- expansion of Umayyad Caliphate (661–750)
- expansion under the early Abbasids (750–850)
- ○ military camps/ new cities
- **638** date of Muslim conquest
- → routes of advance
- – – – principal trade routes

The Arab Conquest of Spain (map 2)

Toulouse 719
Carcassonne 721
Narbonne 720–759
AQUITAINE
Gegia
Pamplona
Roncesvalles
Pyrenees
Gerona
ASTURIAS
Santiago
Astorga
Amaya
714
Zaragoza
Lérida
Barcelona
Pilgrim Road
Tarragona
S P A I N
(AL-ANDALUS)
714
Guijelo
Guadalajara
Coimbra
713
Coria
714
Toledo
712
Valencia
Balearic Islands
Mérida 713
Albacete
Orihuela
715 Murcia
Córdoba
Ecija
Granada
Almería
Huelva
Niebla
Ocsonoba
Málaga
Guadalete 711
Djabal Tárik (Gibraltar)
Strait of Gibraltar 711
Mediterranean Sea

2 By 708 Arab armies had reached Tangier and, reinforced by Berbers, they crossed over to Spain in 711 under the leadership of Tariq ibn Ziyad, a Berber chief. After the death in battle of the Visigothic king, Roderick, resistance collapsed. Tariq took Cordoba and Toledo, whilst Merida fell in 713. By 716 almost the whole peninsula, except for the Pyrenees and the northern region of Asturias, was under Muslim control. Raids were even conducted into the Frankish kingdom until the Arabs were repelled by Charles Martel at Poitiers in 732.

2 the arab conquest of spain

— medieval roads
— northern limit of Muslim conquest, 732

campaigns of conquest
→ Tarik 711,713,714
→ Músa 712, 713, 714
→ Abd al-Aziz 714,715
→ al-Hurr 716, 718
→ al-Samah 719
→ Ambasa 721

Talas River 751
TRANSOXANIA
FERGHANA
Aral Sea
Oxus
KHAZAR EMPIRE
Bukhara 710
Samarkand 710
PUNJAB
Caspian Sea
Derbent
Merv 651
Balkh 651
Hindu Kush Mts
Kabul 664
Caucasus Mts
Tiflis
AZERBAIJAN
Ardabil
Nishapur 651
Herat
Multan 712
Black Sea
Erzurum
ARMENIA
Tabriz
Rai
GURGAN
KHURASAN
PERSIA
SEISTAN
Constantinople
besieged 673–8
717–18
EMPIRE
Tarsus
Mosul 641
Jalula
Nihavand 642
Isfahan
Indus
SIND
Cyprus 649
Antioch
Edessa
MESOPOTAMIA
Sus
FARS
KIRMAN
MAKRAN
To India
SYRIA
Damascus 635
Kerbela 680
Baghdad
Kufa
Ctesiphon
Wasit 702
Persepolis (Istakhr) 648
Yarmuk 636
Al Qadisiyya 637
Basra 656
Alexandria 643
Ramla
Fihl
Jerusalem 638
Persian Gulf
OMAN
Suhar
Muscat
Heliopolis
Ajnadain 634
BAHRAIN
Fustat (Cairo) 640
YAMAMA
640 670
EGYPT
Nile
Tabuk
Hiji
HEJAZ
ARABIA
Medina
Badr 624
Mecca
flight from Mecca, 622
HADHRAMAUT
Red Sea
NUBIANS
Dongola
Najran
YEMEN
KINGDOM OF AKSUM
Aden

1 The spread of Islam outside the Arabian Peninsula began almost immediately after the Prophet's death in 632. By 711, Arab armies were simultaneously attacking Sind in northeast India and preparing for the conquest of the Iberian peninsula. In general, the conquests in the east exceeded those in the west both in size and importance. By 750, when the Abbasids ousted the Umayyad dynasty, the empire to which they succeeded was the largest civilization west of China.

2 The themes were administrative districts in which peasants were granted farms in exchange for service in the local army. Their establishment from the mid-7th century onwards stabilized recruitment problems. In effect the themes militarised the state by creating a capacity for a mobilization of manpower from all over the Empire as well as a defence in depth.

The Byzantine empire grew out of the partition of the Roman empire by the Emperor Diocletian in 293. This division was made mainly for military reasons. Separate sectors, with their own armies and command structure, were intended to make the defence of the frontiers more effective. During the 5th century, the Eastern empire was not as hard hit by invasions as the West, and it managed to survive until its capital, Constantinople, finally fell to the Ottoman Turks in 1453.

The Byzantines inherited a well-educated military, with a core of long-serving, well-paid conscripts. The élite regularly reformed the military, partly in response to having to deal with different and changing enemies, and partly to adapt to the changing resources of the empire. Paying the army proved as much of a headache as fending off invaders. The chronic problem of raising sufficient tax money for wages led to a subdivision of the empire into 'themes' in the mid-7th century. Each theme could raise a field army from soldiers who were given local land grants in return for military service. The land grant provided the soldier not only with a steady source of income, but also gave him a stake in the defence of the empire, or at least of that region. Although it helped reduce financial pressures, the themes gave rise to the problem of local armies which were effectively independent from the state. This encouraged

1 The Byzantines needed a significant tax and manpower base to support their armies. The Empire possessed this in Asia Minor, protected by mountains in the east and sea on the other sides. Nonetheless, enemies penetrated into Asia Minor and other parts of the Empire. Constantinople itself was besieged many times. Byzantine emperors tried to push the borders outward to keep the threats further away, gain access to more manpower and boost their revenue through loot and tribute. Much fighting thus took place beyond the Taurus Mountains and deep into the Balkans, as well as across the Mediterranean in Italy and North Africa.

2 the development of the themes

organization of *themes* in late 9th century

first five *themes* with date of foundation the army in 840

Armeniac, 667	● 1,000 soldiers (a drungus)
Anatolic, 669	● 1,000 soldiers added in 809
Opsician, 680	● 1,000 soldiers added in 840
Carabisiani, 680	■ 1,000 oarsmen
Thracian, 680	▲ 80 soldiers (an archontate)

Bosporus
Chersonesus
ABASGIA
IBERIA
Tiflis
ALBANIA
LAZICA
Black Sea
Ani
Araxes
MOESIA
Singidunum
Danube
Nicopolis
Silistra 971
Odessus
DACIA
Serdica
Philippopolis
Scupi
Ragusa
Dyrrhachium
THRACE
Adrianople
Constantinople
Nicomedia
BITHYNIA
PAPHLAGONIA
Sinope
Halys
PONTUS
Trebizond
Neocaesarea
Sebastea
Manzikert
1071
L. Van
PERSIA
Tigris
Mosul
Iadera
Salonae
DUCHY OF POLETO
DUCHY OF BENEVENTO
Barium
Brundisium
Tarentum
NEW EPIRUS
ANCIENT EPIRUS
MACEDONIA
Salonica
Larissa
THESSALY
Cotiaeum
PHRYGIA
Smyrna
LYDIA
Ephesus
Miletus
PAMPHYLIA
ISAURIA
GALATIA
PISIDIA
Iconium
Caesarea
CAPPADOCIA
CILICIA
Tarsus
Antioch
Samosata
Edessa
Euphrates
Palmyra
Aegean Sea
Athens
Patras
Rhodes
Cyprus
Tripolis
to Byzantium 965
Damascus
Bostra
Messana
Syracuse
Ionian Sea
to Byzantium 961
Crete
M e d i t e r r a n e a n   S e a
Caesarea
PALESTINE
Jerusalem
Gaza
Petra
ARABIA
Apollonia
Ptolemais
Damietta
Pelusium
Alexandria
Mareotis
Memphis
Arsenoe
EGYPT
Nile
Tabuk
LITANIA

military uprisings, which came with particular frequency from the Opsician Theme around Constantinople. The military success and longevity of the empire is nevertheless remarkable. It often found itself fighting two- and even three-front wars.

The empire contracted and expanded at regular intervals. The most notable period of expansion was under Justinian (527–565), whose generals Belisarius and Narses repeatedly defeated the Persians, destroyed the Vandals in North Africa and forced the Ostrogoths in Italy into submission. Justinian even managed to take back territory from the Visigoths in Spain. The Byzantines succeeded in maintaining a presence in Italy into the 11th century, but they permanently lost the western Mediterranean with the growth of Muslim naval power in the 7th century.

The Byzantine fleet enjoyed a long period of success. Byzantine possessions continued to dot the Italian and Balkan coasts, even when much of the interior was lost. The same was true for Asia Minor after the Seljuk Turks arrived in the 11th century and permanently breached the eastern defence. In 1071 the Byzantine emperor, Romanus IV, suffered a catastrophic defeat at the hands of the Seljuq Sultan, Alp Arslan. This defeat ultimately spelled the end of the empire. Its territory began to contract to such an extent that it could no longer support adequate defences. In the late 13th century, with the rise of the Ottoman Turks, the writing was on the wall. In the 1340s, on the invitation of a pretender in one of the interminable struggles for the Byzantine throne, they crossed into the Balkans. Soon only Constantinople's walls delimited the borders of the once-powerful empire.

the **carolingians**

486 to 814

732
Charles Martel defeats Arabs at Tours

768–814
reign of Charlemagne

774
Charlemagne conquers Lombard kingdom

788
Charlemagne annexes Bavaria

834
Viking attacks begin

899–955
Magyars launch 33 attacks against Germany, Italy, France and Spain

955
Otto (the Great) defeats Magyars on the Lechfield

The Carolingian empire was founded on and brought down by war. The early rulers – Charles 'the war hammer' Martel (714–741), Pepin the Short (741–768) and the greatest of all, Charlemagne (768–814) – were outstanding warlords. Virtually every year of their reigns, the Carolingians led their armies in major military campaigns, gradually turning the direction of the campaigns outward – Saxons, Avars, Lombards, Moors and Bretons all suffered the depredations of the Franks, year after year. As these peoples realized that it was better to be inside than outside the Frankish realm, they began to submit and thus, particularly under Charlemagne, the empire expanded greatly. In 800 Charlemagne had himself crowned as 'Emperor of the Romans' by Pope Leo III in Rome.

However, after these submissions, the Franks found campaigning further east unrewarding. In Italy, geography hindered expansion, while in Spain, a strong Moorish presence made it difficult. The distances armies needed to cover to reach their enemies increased. For armies that needed to be mobilized anew for each campaign from all over the empire, more and more time was taken up by profitless travel. Cavalry became more important in Frankish armies, not so much because of their value in combat (this came later), but because mobility within the large empire was useful.

2 the campaigns of charlemagne

- Frankish realm 714
- added to Frankish empire by 814
- Frankish dependencies (with date of formation)
- ⚜ Frankish royal residences
- → campaigns, with dates
- FRIULI 776 province, with date of acquisition

ICELAND
to Greenland 982
Atlantic Ocean
of invasion
Faroe Is. c.870
Shetland Is.
Orkney Is.
NORWEGIANS
SCANDINAVIA
SWEDES
GÖTAR
DANES
North Sea
Baltic Sea
Staraya Ladoga
Novgorod
KIEVAN RUSSIA
Kiev
Iona
Derry 856
Inishmurray
IRELAND
Wexford
Dublin 838
Limerick
Cork
Waterford
Chester 893
WALES
Northampton
Winchester
WESSEX 860
Derby
Lincoln
Stamford
Thetford
London
BRITAIN
York 866
Lindisfarne 793
Jarrow 794
Hamburg 845
FRISIA
Porestad 834
Nijmegen 881
SAXONY (906–38)
THURINGIA (908–33)
Cologne
Louvain 884
Quentovic 820
Rouen 841
Clermont 864
Paris 845, 885–6
Le Mans 865
St-Lô 889
St Malo 872
799, 842, 891 Nantes
799 Noirmoutier
SWABIA (909–54)
BAVARIA (907–54)
937 Bavarian army destroyed by Magyars, 907
926
954 Lechfeld 955
954 Pressburg 907
Hungarian Plain
MAGYARS
boundary of Christian west on eve
FRANCE (GAUL)
Poitiers 864
Bordeaux 844
Gijón 844, 1013
Santiago de Compostela 968
859
Toulouse
Narbonne 844
Nimes 844
Valance
Arles 844
Fraxinetum 890–973
859
Pavia
Luna 844
Pisa 844
926
937
Rome 936
Agropoli 890
Corsica
Sardinia 1015
Bari 841–71
Taranto 840–80
Otranto
Santa Severina c. 840–86
BYZANTINE EMPIRE
Constantinople 907, 944
Black Sea
CALIPHATE OF CÓRDOBA
Karmona (Córdoba)
Seville 844
859
859
Balearic Is.
Mediterranean Sea
SARACENS (ARABS)
Tunis
Sicily (occupied 827)
Malta 824

Lower-left map:
MARK
NTHIA 788
820, 821
791
PANNONIA 795–6
796
AVAR KINGDOM (destroyed 796)
Drava
820, 821
CROATIA 795
Sava
rol disputed by ntines and Venetians 798
DALMATIA 803
Adriatic Sea
BARDY

With fewer opportunities for plunder and with weaker military leadership, the Carolingian empire faltered under Charlemagne's son, Louis the Pious. Instead of channelling their energies outwards, the warrior nobility started fighting amongst itself. The collapse of central power was hastened by the quarrelsome division of the empire, according to Frankish custom, among Louis' three sons in 840 and by a wave of Viking, Magyar and Muslim raids. Viking attacks began in 834 and only let up in the late 10th century. Between 899 and 955 the Magyars launched 33 major expeditions from the east against Germany, Italy, France and even Spain. At the same time, Muslims repeatedly attacked Italy and the south of France.

Just as with the late Roman empire, the response to these attacks from all directions was primarily a local one. Many cities and monasteries – prime targets for the plunderers – were refortified. Local strongmen received an opportunity to distinguish themselves. In the east, a strong Saxon dynasty organized the defence of the Holy Roman Empire (greatly benefiting from the old Carolingian organization of the border into numerous military districts, or marches). In 955, Otto, later nicknamed the Great, defeated the Magyars on the Lechfeld and slaughtered so many that major attacks ceased for almost a century. In the west, numerous territorial principalities emerged, some, such as Flanders and Normandy, under dynasties with Viking connections.

warfare in the high middle ages

900 to 1500

10th–11th centuries
the Peace of God movement in France

1066
Battle of Hastings

1346
Battle of Crécy

1337–1453
Hundred Years' War between England and France

1415
Siege of Harfleur: Battle of Agincourt

1455–85
Wars of the Roses

Feudalism was a by-product of the extreme political fragmentation that Europe suffered with the collapse of Carolingian public order. Power became vested in a multitude of local strongmen who jealously guarded their recently acquired right to use force and administer justice. The symbols of these rights and the embodiment of their independence were the castle and the war-horse. A striking feature of medieval warfare was the extent to which it was subject to rules and rituals. This was nowhere more apparent than in siege warfare and pitched battles.

The Church suffered considerably from the collapse of public order. The depredations of the 10th and early 11th centuries gave rise to a movement called the 'Peace of God' in the south of France. Central to the movement was the call on knights to protect the unarmed, that is clerics and common people. This gave rise to a code of conduct which became known as 'Chivalry'. This was an ethos fostered partly in war and, in peacetime, through tournaments. These emerged in France in the middle of the 11th century and experienced their greatest popularity in the 12th century.

The set of laws governing siege warfare started from the premise, provided by the Bible in Deuteronomy XX, 14, that in towns or castles that had resisted, 'all males' should, on surrender, be 'put to the sword' and 'the loot divided among the army'. This harsh principle, meant to induce immediate surrender, was tempered by the equally uncompromising principle that immediate surrender constituted treason to one's own party, which was also punishable by death. As a result, an intricate body of customs emerged by the late Middle Ages that allowed resistance and

1 Castles proliferated in the 11th century (map right). The Charente is a good example of an early start. The number of castles multiplied by a factor of three to five, in some cases even many times that in a century. In Maine, there were none before 1000, 11 by 1050 and 62 by 1100. It used to be thought that this was in response to the Viking invasions. In fact, the surge began after these attacks stopped. The root cause was a failure by central, or even regional, authorities to control the process. This is suggested by such counter-examples as Normandy which was ruled by powerful dukes. There, castle numbers increased at a much slower pace, from 12 in 1035 to just 20 in 1100. All were controlled by the duke, who prevented nobles from building castles without his permission.

1 the spread of castles

- castles before 1000
- castles 1000–1050
- castles 1050–1100
- castles 1100–1200
- diocese boundary
- forest and woodland
- coastal marsh

2 the 100 years' war

— · — · —	Edward III, 1339–40
- - - →	Edward III, 1346
· · · · · →	Edward III, 1359–60
- - →	Lancaster, 1345
- - - →	Lancaster, 1346
· · · · · →	Lancaster, 1356
━━►	The Black Prince, 1355
━ ━►	The Black Prince, 1356
	The 'Great Companies', 1360–5
- - →	Robert Knolles, 1370
- - - →	John of Gaunt, 1373
· · · · · →	Buckingham, 1380

2 England's attempt to conquer France began in 1337, and came close to success with the great victories of Crécy (1346) and Poitiers (1356) (map right). France recovered after 1360 (Peace of Brétigny), but Henry V's invasion in 1415 again gave England control of northern France. In the first half of the war the campaigning consisted largely of giant raids or *Chevauchées*, which laid waste everything in their path, aimed at damaging the French king's economy and calling into question his ability to protect his subjects, whilst simultaneously satisfying the desire for plunder on the part of the English nobility.

surrender under certain circumstances. In the typical siege of Harfleur in 1415, the English king Henry V, for example, allowed the besieged formally to ask the king of France to relieve them. The town would surrender if a French relieving army failed to turn up within a set period of time to do battle with Henry. Thus Henry and the king of France could both show magnanimity.

Pitched battles were rare in the Middle Ages. When they did occur, they were highly ritualized. Generally, the protagonists agreed a time and place in advance (hence pitched battle). The preparation for the fight was accompanied by religious ceremony. After battle, a victor was expected to demonstrate his victory by staying in possession of the field for three days and nights, rather than pursue his enemy. The key actor in battle by the 11th century was the knight. This medieval heavy cavalry fought, not as individuals, but in units, based on feudal and kinship bonds. Because virtually every knight was caught in the web of kinship and feudalism, an extensive network of ready-made military units and command structures existed.

Chivalry made Europe, not more peaceful, but more ordered as war was fought according to widely accepted rules. These codes of conduct would influence the conduct of war for generations to come.

3 The English army formed a densely-packed shield-wall that resisted Norman archers, infantry and even a series of cavalry charges (map right). But when part of the duke's army fell back, the English broke ranks in pursuit. William rallied his knights and overwhelmed the disordered English. In hard fighting, punctuated by a number of Norman feigned flights, Harold was killed and the English fled. The battle between the two claimants for the English throne is depicted in the accounts of the time as a divine judgement.

1) William's infantry advances, but Saxons stand firm. Infantry begins mock retreat.

2) Saxons lured in from high ground. William commits his cavalry and archers. Saxons defeated.

HAROLD 8,000 — final position of the Standard

light armed infantry — housekarls or bodyguard — light armed infantry

housekarls housekarls

WILLIAM — Normans (4,000)

Bretons (2,400)

Franco-Flemish (1,600)

3 hastings, 1066

━━	Harold's position
- - -►	Saxon movement from high ground
━━	Norman cavalry and infantry, deployed at 9 a.m.
● ● ●	Norman archers
► ► ►	Norman infantry advance and retreat
→	Norman cavalry and archer attacks

the **crusades**

1095 to 1291

| 1096–99 |
| First Crusade |

| 1146–48 |
| Second Crusade |

| 1189–91 |
| Third Crusade |

| 1202–1204 |
| Fourth Crusade |

| 1228–29 |
| Fifth Crusade |

| 1395 |
| Crusade of Nicopolis |

| 1444 |
| Crusade of Varna |

Towards the end of the 11th century the Chivalric idea culminated in its supreme expression, the Christian enterprise of the Crusade. The Church offered remission of sins for those who would fight to liberate and defend the Holy Land. The Crusades were the most ambitious military operations undertaken by the Christian West in the Middle Ages. Beginning in 1095, with the preaching of a crusade by Pope Urban II, and ending in 1291, with the loss of the last outpost in Palestine, Christian warriors attempted to restore Jerusalem and the surrounding Holy Land to Christianity.

First and foremost, the Crusades were the expression of an idea. All the material motives usually ascribed to crusaders – lust for power, land and loot – were secondary to this religious purpose, the liberation of Jerusalem. Since the material motives could have been satisfied much closer to home, without an arduous journey across inhospitable lands and seas, it required considerable conviction for the tens of thousands of crusaders to undertake the dangerous and expensive expedition. Nonetheless, land and loot were important subsidiary considerations. Both provided an attractive and expected bonus to the spiritual salvation offered by the Church.

The crusaders have often been criticized for their lack of unity. The army of the First Crusade (1096–99) started out with perhaps 4,500 knights and 30,000 foot soldiers. It not only suffered serious casualties in an astonishingly high number of 12 battles and four sieges before reaching Jerusalem, but also lost significant numbers to the ambitions of such leaders as Baldwin, Bohemond of Taranto and Raymond of Toulouse who sought to create principalities around Edessa and Antioch. The army that took Jerusalem may have counted only 1,200 knights and 12,000 infantry. The new principalities, however, served an important purpose by providing strategic depth to the defence of the new kingdom of Jerusalem.

Later crusaders sought to avoid the difficult land journey to and from Palestine and, instead, travelled by sea. When the centre of Muslim power shifted to Egypt in the 13th century, the direction of the later Crusades (the Fifth, 1228–1229, and Sixth, 1248–1254) changed accordingly. The best sources of plunder automatically led to strategically important areas and

2 the battle of arsouf

| Crusaders | Muslims |

1 Hospitallers
2 Burgundians
3 Champagnois
4 Poitevins
5 Angevins

0 — 1 km
0 — 1 mile

N

skirmishers

KING RICHARD

Arsoef

Reconquista: gradual conquest of southern of Iberian peninsula completed by 149...

Lisbon

ALMORAV...

GRANADA (1238–1492)

Granada

AL MO H A...

(1140–1269)

Las N... Tolosa

PORTUGAL

2 Marching from Acre to Jaffa in September 1191, a crusading army under Richard 'Coeur de Lion' met the army of Saladin (map left). Richard advanced with infantry and crossbowmen protecting the cavalry from Muslim archers. The right flank was protected by the sea, the left by cavalry, so that they and the cavalry in the centre could sally forth to beat off attacks or, God willing, smash the main body of the enemy. On 7 September, Saladin's forces closed in but were shattered by three successive charges.

1 Beginning with the First Crusade, preached by Pope Urban II at the Council of Clermont (1095), the crusading movement inspired Christian Europe's struggle against the enemies of the faith – both internal and external – for four centuries (map above). Even after the fall of the last stronghold in Palestine in 1291, Crusades were fought to defend the Balkans against the Ottoman Turks, to complete the Reconquista in Spain and against pagans around the Baltic.

SCOTLAND

NORWAY

SWEDEN

North Sea

eastward expansion 12th–13th centuries

1220

TEUTONIC ORDER (from 1237)

against Novgorod, 1240

by Sword Brothers, early 13th century

against Estonians, 1220

Baltic Sea

DENMARK

RUSSIAN PRINCIPALITIES

VOLGA-BULGARIA (to 1237)

ENGLAND

against Slavs, 1147

expansion by Teutonic order, 13th century

GERMANY

POLAND

against Hussites, 1420–31

GOLDEN HORDE (from 1241)

Paris

HOLY

Prague

BOHEMIA

Regensburg

FRANCE

ROMAN

Buda

HUNGARY

Szeged

Milan

Venice

Zara

Spalato

SERBIA (1185–1459)

Nicopolis

Varna

BULGARIA (1186–1396)

Black Sea

GEORGIA (from 1136)

bigenisan Crusade nst Cathars, 08–29

Aigues-mortes

Marseille

EMPIRE

PAPAL STATES

Rome

OTTOMAN (expanding during 14th and 15th centuries)

Constantinople

SELJUK

COUNTY OF EDESSA (1098–1146)

EMPIRE (in decline from 1092)

1217–21

KINGDOM OF SICILY (from 1130)

Durazzo

BYZANTINE EMPIRE (to 1204; from 1261)

LATIN EMPIRE (1204–61)

RUM (ICONIUM) (to 1307)

Smyrna

LESSER ARMENIA (1081–1375)

Edessa

PRIN. OF ANTIOCH (1098–1268)

EMPIRE

Antioch

Aleppo

Andravida

Antalya

CYPRUS (1192–1489)

Krak des Chevaliers

COUNTY OF TRIPOLI (1102–1268)

EMPIRE

EMPIRE

Tunis

1248

1270

Damascus

Acre

KINGDOM OF JERUSALEM (1099–1291)

Mediterranean Sea

Damietta

Jerusalem

EMPIRE (1171–1250)

Alexandria

FATIMID EMPIRE (to 1171)

EMPIRE (from 1250)

AYYUBID

Cairo

MAMLUK

1 the crusades, 109–1500

Christian held, 1095

Muslim held, 1095

Pagan territory, 1095

added to Christian control definitively by 1500

added to Muslim control definitively by 1500

temporary Christian advances against Islam, 1096–1500

boundary of western and eastern Christian churches, 1400

The First Crusade, 1096–9

– – – The Second Crusade, 1146–8

········· The Third Crusade, 1189–91

–·–·–► The Fourth Crusade, 1202–4

–··–► The Fifth Crusade, 1228–9

later and other crusades to the Holy Land, with date

Crusade of Nicopolis, 1395

Crusade of Varna, 1444

general direction of other important crusades

limit of area of Templar houses before dissolution of order in 1312

core area of Cathars

provided good locations for settlement and the development of trade. This can even be said, in a perverse way (because it turned on a Christian empire), about the Fourth 'Crusade' (1202–1204), which was diverted on to the rich prize of Constantinople.

It is striking how far the crusaders and Muslims cooperated, even to the extent of ransoming each other as in the case of King Louis IX of France who was captured in Egypt in 1249. The customs of knightly warfare were hard to break, even in the fight against the infidel.

The crusaders built many castles and other fortifications. In the Kingdom of Jerusalem alone some 162 fortified sites have been identified. However, one lost battle could easily lead castles to fall like dominoes – as indeed happened after the Battle of Hattin in 1187.

PART III | **THE MILITARY RENAISSANCE 1500–1650**

the **italian** wars

The rediscovery of classical Greek and Roman thought, known as the Renaissance, affected warfare as well as painting, literature and architecture. Fifteenth-century Italy had the most sophisticated culture in Europe. Its well-developed economy also supported the most mature military institutions. Wealthy city states blended military professionalism and civil administration to secure political stability, and for a while the military capability of great powers. Italy's disunity and wealth, however, were an irresistible temptation to her neighbours.

Italy lay at the crossroads of regionally distinctive military traditions. The French invaders had the best heavy cavalry and field artillery in the world. The offensive capability of Swiss pikemen, rare in medieval infantry, inspired imitation by German Landsknechts. Spanish armies who traditionally relied on infantry quickly adopted the pike, and replaced their crossbows with the arquebus or *Hackenbusche*. The arquebus was the key weapon of the military renaissance. Requiring little training, it was readily transferable across national borders, unlike the pike, which the French never mastered. It revolutionized the soldier's equipment and killed regardless of social class or armour. The rapid spread

1 Renaissance Italy lay between competing power centres: France, Spain, Turkey and the empire. Foreign armies used the peninsula as a proving ground, testing novel combinations of shock and fire weapons in numerous battles (map right). Strategy remained rudimentary, however, driven by French obsessions with Lombardy and Naples.

1 the italian wars

✕ battles	▲ sieges

Charles VIII's invasion 1494–5
→ to Naples   ┈┈▶ return
╱╱ French controlled Alpine passes

*Map labels:*

Imperialist reinforcements from Germany via the Brenner Pass

SAVOY
VENETIAN REPUBLIC
DUCHY OF
Novara 1495, 1513 ✕
Milan
Bicocca 1522 ✕
Agnadello 1509 ✕
Marignano 1515 ✕
Pavia 1525 ✕
Verona 1516–17
Treviso 1509 ▲
Venice
Turin
Mt Genevre
Po
Ceresole 1544 ✕
Po
MANTUA
Po
MILAN
FERRARA
GENOA
Genoa
Fornovo 1494 ✕
PARMA
Col de Tende
MODENA
Ravenna 1512 ▲
MONACO
LUCCA
FLORENCE
Florence 1529–30
SAN MARINO
PAPAL STATES
Pisa 1495–1509 ▲
URBINO
PISA
Ligurian Sea
Siena 1552–9
PIOMBINO
SIENA
Corsica (GENOA)
Rome 1526
KINGDOM OF NAPLES
Garigliano 1503 ✕
Gaeta
Cerignola 1503 ✕
Tyrrhenian Sea
Sardinia
Naples 1527–8
Adriatic Sea

2 Pavia confirmed the invulnerability of fortifications defended by artillery, and the superiority of Spanish arquebusiers over French gendarmes (map right). The result was so decisive that Pavia would be the last major battle in Italy until Ceresole, 20 years later.

of mass-produced handguns fuelled the growth of armies, paid for by loans and higher taxes. The proportion of infantry carrying firearms rose steadily, from 30 per cent at Venice in 1548 to 60 per cent in the Spanish army of 1600. Commentators in the 1590s thought hand-to-hand combat a rarity.

The battles of the Italian Wars show the development of the new European tactical consensus, as the arquebus transformed the dominant mode of combat from shock to attrition. The opening battle at Fornovo (6 July 1495) recalled the chivalric past. French gensdarmes rode down similar Italian heavy cavalry, disordered by an unexpectedly flooded stream. Cerignola (April 1503) saw the first combination of arquebus and fieldworks to checkmate heavy cavalry, but at Ravenna (11 April 1512) cannon appeared to be the antidote to Spanish trenches. Field artillery played a decisive battlefield role for the first time, although it was the French heavy cavalry who clinched victory by penetrating the Spanish defences to take their infantry in the rear. Novara (6 June 1513) and Marignano (13/14 September 1515) revolved around Swiss attempts to forestall the deadly combination of field artillery and heavy cavalry, but Bicocca (27 April 1522) vindicated the Spanish defensive school. Prosper Colonna, a typically cautious *condottiere*, placed pikemen close behind his entrenched arquebusiers, to win the handgun's first major victory. Pavia (24 Feb 1525) confirmed the tactical dominance of firearms, this time in the open. Furious cavalry charges failed to break Spanish pikemen supported by arquebusiers, who shot down the French nobility around their king. So decisive was the Spanish victory that the French exchanged their crossbows for the arquebus.

europe and the **ottoman** empire

1520 to 1571

1354
Ottomans capture Gallipoli –
first foothold in Europe

1389
Battle of Kosovo: Ottomans
defeat Serbs

1456
Ottomans defeat Hungary
at Belgrade

1514
Battle of Çaldiran: Ottomans
defeat Safavid Persians

1526
Mohacs (29 August): Ottoman
raid of Hungary

1566
Suleiman dies of dysentery
during siege of Szigeth

1571
Battle of Lepanto (7 October):
a coalition of Christian naval
powers ends Turkish maritime
challenge

The main threat to the military renaissance lay outside Europe. The Ottoman empire more than doubled in size during the early 16th century and under Suleiman the Magnificent (1520–66) overran Hungary. Turkish corsairs raided as far west as Spain. Distance limited Ottoman expansion, however, while their military institutions stagnated.

The Ottoman empire followed a different military model to Western Europe. The Sultan ruled a monolithic state. His refusal to recognize other rulers as equals provoked conflict with Christian and Muslim powers alike. Turkish armies reflected this centralization of authority. Turkish tactics combined the defensive power of infantry and guns with the fluidity and resilience of nomad light cavalry. They changed little between Kosovo in 1389 and Kerestes in 1596. The Turks adopted firearms, but these were neither essential nor a Turkish monopoly. The system worked as well against the Hungarians at Mohacs who had guns, as against the Persians at Çaldiran (23 August 1514) who did not.

The Sultan's absolute power of life and death and the inspiration of Islam forged a discipline unknown in other armies, whose disunity was a major factor in Ottoman success. Treachery contributed to the Mameluke defeat at Mercidabik (24 August 1516). Less than half the Hungarian army turned up for Mohacs, while Hungarian renegades accompanied Suleiman to Vienna in 1529. The most crucial defection was that of France. Habsburg–Valois rivalry diverted Charles V from defending Vienna, and destabilized the Mediterranean. Turkish galleys were short-range vessels with large crews and fragile hulls. A French alliance allowed them to winter in Marseilles, and raid the Spanish and Italian coasts, turning the Habsburg flank when the Danubian front stabilized in the 1530s. The capture of Malta would have perpetuated the Turkish naval presence in the Western Mediterranean. However, the island's new fortifications and hard fighting by the Knights of St John, the last of the Crusading Orders, halted the Ottoman advance in 1564. At the Battle of Lepanto (7 October 1571), the largest naval action since Actium, a coalition of Christian naval powers ended the Turkish maritime challenge.

1 The Ottoman empire (map right) expanded rapidly in the early 16th century, exploiting weak and divided opposition. After the 1520s increased distances from the centre of power at Constantinople to the frontiers prevented further expansion, while tactics and fortifications developed in Italy proved superior to stereotyped and inflexible Turkish methods of war.

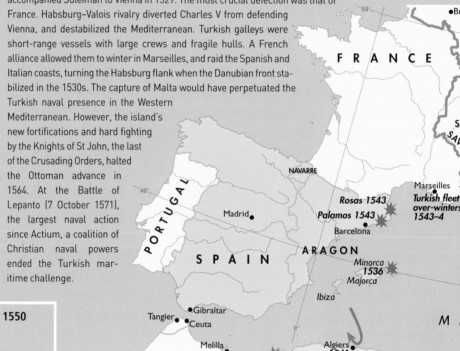

Brussels
FRANCE
Rhineland
SWITZERLA
SAVOY
Mila
NAVARRE
Marseilles
Piacenza
Genoa
Rosas 1543
Turkish fleet
over-winters
1543–4
Nice
1543
GENO
Madrid
Palamos 1543
El
154
Barcelona
Corsica
Genoes
ARAGON
PORTUGAL
Minorca
1536
Majorca
Sardinia
SPAIN
Ibiza
Med i
Gibraltar
Tangier
Ceuta
Melilla
Algiers
1541
Bizerta
SULTANATE OF
MOROCCO
Oran
1563
Bugia
1555
Bona
ALGERIA
Ottoman vassal
from 1537
TUNISI
Ottoman va
from 157
Jerba
1560

1 the ottoman empire, c. 1550

Ottoman Empire c. 1550

battles
✗ Ottoman victory   ✗ Christian victory

sieges
⬇ Ottoman capture   ⬇ successful Christian defence

✳ Ottoman raids
◼ Venetian fortified towns
➡ Christian counter-attacks

Selim I's expedition to Persia, 1514
➡ route   area of concentration

Selim I's expedition to Egypt, 1516–17
▸▸▸ route   area of concentration

Geography and political centralization limited Ottoman expansion. The Sultan's personal household troops were the basis of Turkish invincibility, and he could only fight on one front. As the empire grew, the campaigning season, when grass was available, grew shorter. Vienna was saved by its distance from the centre of Ottoman power in Constantinople. Turkish armies could not fight in winter; horses died, and Janissaries mutinied. A predominantly cavalry force easily overran the open spaces of Hungary and Syria, but suffered heavy losses in the mountains of Styria and Armenia. Bastioned fortifications defied the Turks' energetic but unscientific siege techniques. Rhodes surrendered for want of gunpowder, and Famagusta through treachery. Abortive sieges at Vienna and Malta mark the maximum reach of the Ottoman empire. Suleiman died of dysentery during the siege of Szigeth (Aug–Sep 1566), ending the most serious external threat to Europe for 400 years.

2 Ottoman armies used similar tactics against Hungarians, Mamelukes and Persians, supplementing the standard wagon laager of steppe warfare with cannon and professional infantry (map right). This firebase broke up enemy attacks, and provided a rallying point for the swarms of Turkish light cavalry.

0   1 km
0   1 mile

SULTAN SELIM
c.60,000 men

Turkish camp

Zaveyeh

SHAH ISMAIL
c.50,000 men

Persian camp

Dize

N

2   battle of çaldiran

Turkish forces
- Sultan Selim
- Timariot cavalry
- Janissaries
- Spahis
- Spahis irregular infantry

Persian forces
- Persian cavalry

POLAND

LUSATIA   SILESIA

BOHEMIA

MORAVIA

HUNGARY

Innsbruck

Vienna *1529*

AUSTRIA

STYRIA

Buda *1529*

TRANSYLVANIA

MOLDAVIA

JEDISAN

KHANATE OF CRIMEA

ÇERKES

death of Suleiman the Magnificent Szigeth 1566

Senj CROATIA

Mohács *1526*

Belgrade *1521*

WALLACHIA

Black Sea

GEORGIA

Zara

Trau

DALMATIA

Spalato

Kosovo *1389*

Nicopolis *1396*

Erzerum *1552*

AZERBAIJAN

REP. OF RAGUSA

Cattaro 1538

Scutari

Çaldiran *1514*

Tabriz

Rome

Constantinople

PERSIA

Naples

NAPLES

Valona 1537

Brindisi

Otranto *1480*

ALBANIA

Chios gained from Genoa, 1566

ANATOLIA

EMPIRE

Corfu *1537*

Preveza *1538*

Lepanto *1571*

Lipari Is. *1544*

Palermo

Levkas

Cephalonia

Action

Samos

Tenos

Merjdabik *1516*

Reggio *1534, 1541*

Sicily

Zante

Navarino

MOREA

Nauplia

Corone

Naxos gained from Venice, 1566

Modon gained from Venice, 1500

Monemvasia

Cyprus

Nicosia *1551*

Famagusta *1570–1*

Rhodes gained from Knights Hospitallers, 1522

SYRIA conquered 1517

Malta *1564*

Cerigo gained from Venice, 1540

Crete

Sea

ARABIA

Younis Khan *1516*

Alexandria

Ridanieh *1517*

49

IPOLITANIA
ttoman vassal from 1551

warfare in india and china

1526
Battle of Panipat: Babur conquers Delhi sultanate and founds Mughal empire. Seizes control of Hindustan

1550
Mongol threat re-emerges. Japanese pirate attacks on China increase

1644
Ming dynasty toppled

The largest states of the early modern world lay in the Far East. Both Ming China and Mughal India were regional superpowers. They possessed gunpowder weapons, but these only reinforced existing military patterns, preventing the type of change seen in the West.

Chinese and Indian military establishments ran into millions, but structural weaknesses limited effectiveness. The Hindu caste system prevented *sowars* doing menial jobs usually undertaken by troopers. The Mughal army with which Babar seized control of Hindustan in 1526 was a lean outfit, hardened by campaigns in Central Asia.

Ming China, with its bureaucratic tradition, had permanent training camps to prepare provincial units for expeditions or service on the northern border, but standards of training and equipment declined in the 16th century. Attempts to recruit competent leaders by examination failed, since educated Chinese despised military service. Unpaid garrisons took up banditry or farming. Raids from Mongolia imposed a stifling burden. The aggressive forward policy of the early 15th century cost three times the Emperor's annual revenue, but subsequent withdrawal behind the Great Wall deprived the Ming of influence and vital intelligence. Famine and banditry destabilized late Ming society to the point where only an external force could restore order. The Manchu, like the Mughals, were seen as an army of occupation. Socially conservative, they had no taste for destabilizing military innovation.

The Chinese had invented gunpowder weapons in the late 13th century, but the speed and strategic flexibility of their nomadic opponents outweighed theoretically superior weaponry. In the disastrous T'umu campaign (July–August 1449) 20,000 Mongols wiped out a Ming army of half a million and captured the emperor.

1 the confucian triumph

— Grand Canal
■ national capital
⊙ provincial capitals
✕ battle
→ Cheng Ho's expeditions 1405–33

Ming frontier defences
〰 Great Wall
□ border garrisons
◼ guard units

Yung-lo's expeditions
‑‑→ 1410
•••→ 1414
–•–→ 1424

Ming offensives
••••→ in Korea 1593
→ disasters against Nurhaci, 1619

⊗ Korean naval successes
⊗ Japanese naval successes

Japanese offensives
→ pirate raids 1540–65
□ invasions after 1550
→ in Korea 1592
••••→ in Korea 1597

Litzu Cheng's revolt
□ focus of revolt 1539–40
‑‑‑ raids
→ advance on Peking

consolidation of Manchu rule
‑‑→ 1645
–‑‑ 1646
•••→ 1647–50

naval battles
A Tanhangpo Jun 1592
B Pusan Aug 1592
C Kadok July 1597
D Chin Do July 1597
E Noryang Nov. 1598

2 the mughal empire, 1525–1605

✕ battle
⚓ siege
♛ fortress

borders
⎯ the Mughal Empire, 1605
⎯ Babur's Afghan Kingdom

campaigns
⎯ Babur 1516–17 and 1523–9
- - - Mughal attempts to expand beyond the Empire's natural limits

2 The Mughal conquests followed the usual pattern of Indian invasions, small numbers of vigorous outsiders overwhelming disorganized masses of defenders (map right). Despite the personal interest of Babur and Akbar in cannon, the Mughals failed to institutionalize the artillery arm, preferring to import guns and hire Turks and renegade European specialists.

1 The Ming period began with the new regime consolidating its control in China and in the southwest, which the Mongols had incorporated into China for the first time (map left). The first half of the 15th century was one of rapid expansion – great sea voyages and invasions of Mongolia and of Annam. Thereafter China went on the defensive, protected by vast armies along the rebuilt Great Wall. In the following century the Ming were beset by attacks from resurgent Mongols and Japanese pirates.

Firearms played a more significant role in Mughal victories. At Panipat (20 April 1526) and Khanwa (16 March 1527) Babur fortified his front with cannon and matchlockmen, but he depended as much on generalship as superior technology.

Eastern fortifications depended on medieval qualities of inaccessibility and massive physical strength. Lavish sieges were resolved by accident or treachery, despite monster guns cast on site. The most striking example was in China, where a bandit general found Peking accidentally undefended, and panicked the last Ming emperor into suicide. The Great Wall, given its modern form by the later Ming, bears little resemblance to Western fortresses, but like them formed an effective system of defence in depth. It withstood the Manchu, until a Ming general let them through.

Ships and sea power were culturally alien to the Mughals, who disciplined piratical Westerners by trade embargoes, but the early Ming had the world's foremost navy, with nine-masted junks, cannon and thousands of sailors. Expeditions sailed to East Africa and Arabia, returning with exotic luxuries and diplomatic envoys. Late Ming officials obsessed by the Mongol threat cancelled further voyages to save money, and prohibited boats with more than one mast. Japanese pirates and Western traders moved into China's coastal power vacuum.

51

the **wars** of religion

1562 to 1598

1562–63
French Protestants' struggle for freedom of worship and the right of establishment begins first civil war

1572
Massacre of Saint Bartholomew's Day

1577
Catholics persuade Henry III to repeal the edict of toleration

1585–89
War of the Three Henrys

1598
Wars conclude with Edict of Nantes in France and with the Treaty of Vervins with Spain

The French Religious Wars arose from a triangular struggle between the Crown and two factions, the Catholic League and Protestant Huguenots. Both sought to control a royal government weakened by the struggle with the Habsburgs, and a by succession of minors.

The Huguenots lacked the siege guns to complete victories won by their superior cavalry, but held too many towns themselves for the League to take them all. Protected by salt marshes or mountains, Huguenot redoubts at La Rochelle and in the Cevennes only fell to a revived royal government in the late 1620s. The crushing Huguenot defeat at Moncontour (3 October 1569) should have ended the war then, but the local nature of the struggle reduced the significance of pitched battles. Warlordism was endemic. Local gentry perpetuated instability for amusement and profit. The primacy of religious over national feeling encouraged and legitimized foreign intervention, which sustained the combatants whenever domestic support faltered.

The infrequency of battles in the later Italian Wars devalued traditional heavy cavalry. They were useless for sieges, and worn out by campaign duties like reconnaissance or raiding. The old French companies of *gensdarmes*

1 huguenots and the league

- ■ Catholic strongholds
- ■ Huguenot strongholds
- ✕ Catholic victories
- ✕ Huguenot victories
- ▲ Catholic sieges
- ▲ Huguenot sieges
- ✳ Catholic outrages
- ✳ Huguenot outrages

foreign interventions
- → by Spain
- → by Protestant powers

2 duel of wits: normandy, 1592

advances of:
- Dutch
- Henry of Navarre
- Duke of Parma

defended towns   field works
- ✳ Protestant
- ✳ Catholic

English Channel

Rue
Mar.–Apr.: besieged by Parma

Bresle

Amiens

DUKE OF PARMA
16 Jan. (30,000)

Dieppe

Béthune
Eaulne

Feb.–Mar.: Henry raids Parma's communications

27 Mar.: Henry re-establishes siege of Rouen

Scie
Varenne

HENRY OF NAVARRE (7,000)

Aumale

4 Feb.: cavalry skirmish at Aumale

Durdent
Saâne

Bellencombre

9–12 Feb.: Neufchatel besieged by Parma

30 Apr.–16 May: skirmishes

Yvetot

26 Feb.: Parma halts after sortie at Rouen

16–17 May: Parma reduced to 15,000, withdraws

24 Mar.–7 Apr.: Parma besieges Caudebec

Caudebec

Le Havre
held by Catholics

Seine

21 Apr.: Parma raises siege

Rouen

HENRY OF NAVARRE
29 Apr. reinforced to 26,000

DUTCH SQUADRON
on Lower Seine

F R A N C E

20–21 May: Parma escapes over bridge of boats and marches to resupply Paris

Seine

---

2 Individual campaigns displayed high standards of generalship and manoeuvre (map above). Henry IV was unable to force Parma to fight at a disadvantage, but refused to do so himself, despite his personal preference for reckless cavalry charges.

1 The Wars of Religion lacked stable fronts or clear lines of operation (map left). Like 20th-century ideological conflicts they took their shape from atrocities, local rivalries and foreign interventions. Widespread gangsterism and mutual distrust prolonged hostilities that served little rational purpose.

from the Hundred Years War were in decline before the Religious Wars, as great nobles opted for the comforts of civilian life. In their place appeared less heavily armoured cavalry carrying firearms, known as *Reiters* from the area of their origin. German heavy cavalry had often been worsted by French *gensdarmes*, and readily adopted the *pistala*, a single-handed arquebus that appeared in the 1540s. Such cavalry had a dual capability: they could ride arquebusiers down in the open, or shatter unsupported pike formations with their pistols. *Reiters* were vulnerable while reloading, and their skirmishing tactics encouraged unenthusiastic soldiers to fire uselessly at long range.

Infantry had become the dominant arm in Italy, but cavalry could still exploit the tactical discontinuity between marching and fighting order. Infantry could resist cavalry when suitably arrayed, but faced disaster if caught on the march by more mobile horsemen. Imperialist cavalry destroyed two-thirds of a French army retiring from St Quentin (10 August 1557). France had more open country than Italy, and the haphazard circumstances of civil war suited cavalry equipped with firearms. Most of the battles of the Religious Wars were cavalry actions, with the infantry hardly engaged. The Wars of Religion served to reverse the numerical decline of French cavalry. From 46 per cent in 1495 to 16 per cent in the Metz campaign of 1552, a quarter of the forces engaged at Ivry in 1590, when Henry of Navarre smashed the Leaguers' army, were cavalry. Except for a few Spanish lancers, most of these were armoured pistoleers, now the standard European heavy cavalryman. After a thousand years the man-at-arms had lost his predominance. One of Henry of Navarre's first acts as Henry IV was to disband the surviving *compagnies d'ordonnance*.

The prosperous towns and dank swamps of the Netherlands provide a surprising setting for the next step in the military renaissance. The burghers of the Low Countries not only fought the most powerful military machine of the day, the Spanish Army of Flanders, to a standstill; they also developed a new style of army, the prototype of professional military forces today.

The Dutch Revolt is a fine example of the advantages of the defensive. The obstinate resistance of every Dutch town gained time for the strategic balance to shift against Spain through the action of allies and the development of Dutch sea power, which enriched the Dutch while the Army of Flanders mutinied for want of pay. Delay brought all the country's resources into play: its numerous defensible towns, dykes, ponds and difficult passages, and the inaccessible national redoubt of Holland, so waterlogged that ships sailed across flooded fields to relieve Leyden (October 1573). The Duke of Alva, Spanish Viceroy in the 1560s, alienated popular support by his policy of terror. Wherever his victorious soldiers went, they swelled the ranks of his enemies. The 'Spanish Fury' at Antwerp (October 1576) even drove the loyal Roman Catholics of the southern provinces to rebel.

The War in the Netherlands had its own rules. Lack of space reinforced the contemporary preference for sieges. Battles were uniquely scarce, after early demonstrations of the crushing superiority of Spanish arms. At Jemmingen (21 July 1568) Alva's veterans lured the rebels out of their trenches, and shot them down like wild fowl. At Gemblours (31 January 1578) Spanish cavalry killed or captured 5,000 retreating rebels, unable to defend themselves on the march. A conciliatory Viceroy exploited Gemblours to pacify the southern provinces, but the action was atypically decisive. Like other civil wars the Dutch Revolt was fought out at a local level. Small garrisons squabbled over individual villages, with no fixed front line. 'La Guerre aux Vaches' generated widespread insecurity, and was perhaps more typical of the 16th-century experience of war, than battles and marches.

s' Hertogenbosch

N

ditches

2 The 17th century experience of war in Western Europe was of sieges rather than battles. Superior siege techniques swung the balance in favour of attackers by the mid-1620s. Both sides could predict the progress of a siege, often resulting in surrender before a practicable breach had been made.

2 **siege of s' hertogenbosch, 1629**

⌐ Spanish defences   ▭ Dutch entrenched camps
⌐ Dutch line of circumvallation (face outwards)
⌐▭ Dutch line of contravallation (face outwards)
◇ Dutch approaches

1 the dutch revolt, 1566–1609

1 the dutch revolt, 1566–1609

battles
- ✕ Spanish success
- ✕ Dutch success

sieges
- ▲ Spanish success/failure
- ✳ Spanish massacre
- ▲ Dutch success

Dutch defensive lines
- •••••• Oude Hollandsche Waterlinie
- ▪▪▪▪▪▪ River Ijssel 1605–6

regions
- *I* Catholic redoubt in North East until 1590's
- *II* Dutch inner redoubt
- *III* Dutch outer redoubt
- *IV* open cavalry country in Catholic south

support
- ⟶ Spanish
- ⟶ Protestant

1 The Dutch matched the Netherlands' strategic resources against superior Spanish tactics (map right). Numerous towns and inundations prolonged resistance, while the long frontier with Germany and the North Sea coast were always open to foreign assistance, but closed to the Spanish. Maurice of Nassau's offensives followed the fortified river lines that determined the final borders of the rebel Republic.

The years of attrition paid off in the 1590s. Dutch forces became strong enough to launch a counter-offensive, while half the Army of Flanders was absent fighting Huguenots. The great rivers were more than military obstacles. The Dutch used barges to shift siege guns rapidly on internal lines, reducing enemy fortresses in short sharp sieges: Zutphen in seven days, Deventer in 11, Hulst in five and Nijmegen in six. Maurice of Nassau consolidated the Netherlands' southern border, eliminated the Roman Catholic enclave in the northeast, and pushed the Dutch border 50 miles east of the River Ijssel. In 1598 the Dutch counter-offensive reached its culminating point along the modern frontier. The Army of Flanders returned, English help dwindled, and the Dutch army made little headway in the hostile open countryside of what is now Belgium.

the **thirty years' war**

1618
Revolt of Protestant nobles in Prague

1623
Imperialist victory at Stadtlohn

17 September 1631
Swede Gustavus victorious against Catholics at Breitenfeld

July 1632
Gustavus defeated at Alte Veste

16 November 1632
Battle of Lützen; Gustavus dies in action

6 September 1634
Spanish army defeats the Swedes at Nordlingen

17 May 1648
Turenne destroys last Imperialist army at Zumershausen

The Thirty Years' War began in Central Europe, but religious divisions and hostility between the Habsburgs and the French and Dutch broadened the conflict.

The unlimited aims of the Holy Roman Emperor Ferdinand II, intent on enforcing religious uniformity in Germany, made the war 'a fight between God and the Devil' with no third way. Gustavus Adolphus threatened Habsburg Silesia to draw the Imperial General Tilly away from Magdeburg, Sweden's only ally, but Tilly's army stormed Magdeburg anyway, killing five-sixths of the population. Despite Sweden's marginal location, Gustavus created the modern military hierarchy, grouping companies in battalions permanently affiliated to regiments, some of whose successors exist in the modern Swedish army.

Gustavus' victory at Breitenfeld (17 September 1631) destroyed Tilly's army, but a single battle was insufficient to knock out the Empire and its Spanish allies. Gustavus did not march directly on Vienna after Breitenfeld. Despite his personal taste for action, Gustavus was cautious, only fighting at an advantage, or from behind entrenchments. He expanded his base into the Rhineland, simultaneously reducing Imperial resources. His ensuing campaign in South Germany, however, degenerated into an indecisive raid on Bavaria, when he failed to storm Ingolstadt's bastions. Gustavus had an army of Napoleonic proportions, but as the leader of a coalition Gustavus lacked Napoleon's freedom to manoeuvre regardless of the interests of his allies. Wallenstein's advance against Nuremberg in July 1632 forced Gustavus to respond with a fraction of his strength (20,000 out of 150,000), or risk another atrocity like Magdeburg. Wallenstein avoided action, starving the Swedes out of their trenches. Gustavus attacked over ground unfavourable to combined arms tactics, and suffered his first defeat at the Alte Veste. Wallenstein persisted with a strategy of diversion. Raiding into Saxony, he compelled Gustavus to postpone an invasion of Austria.

1 Strategists of the Thirty Years' War manoeuvred to dominate areas of logistical importance, rather than to gain tactical advantage (map right). Despite the Swedish army's superiority on the battlefield, Gustavus Adolphus pursued similar logistical objectives to his enemies, seeking to build up an economic base in North Germany.

1 | **gustavus adolphus' campaign in germany, 1619–32**

Protestant states
Catholic states

Gustavus Adolphus' campaigns
➝ 1630–1
–➝ 1632 in south Germany
···➝ 1632 leading to Lützen

Imperial/Bavarian campaigns
➝ Tilly
–➝ Wallenstein

battles
✕ Imperial/Bavarian (Catholic) success
✕ Swedish (Protestant) success

sieges
▲ Catholic
▲ Protestant

intervention from outside Germany
➝ Catholic
➝ Protestant

*Map labels:*

DENMARK
Elbe
Stralsund 1628
Demmin 1631
Neu Brandenburg 1631
Gustavus lands at Usedom, 4 July 1630
Danish 1625–6
Werben Aug. 1631
BRANDENBURG
POLAND
Berlin
Frankfurt am Oder 1631
Tilly's Magdeburg Campaign 1631
1 Tilly moves east to block Gustavus' advance on the Oder
2 Gustavus moves west to consolidate his base in Mecklenburg, Tilly follows too late to save Demmin
3 Tilly invests Magdeburg and Gustavus threatens Frankfurt to draw him away
4 Gustavus takes Frankfurt, allowing Tilly to concentrate on Magdeburg, which he storms on 20 May
Magdeburg 1631
Dessau 25 Apr. 1626
Stadtlohn 6 Aug. 1623
Lutter 24–7 Aug. 1626
NETHERLANDS
Rhine
Breitenfeld 17 Sep. 1631
Leipzig
SAXONY
Dresden
Oder
SMALL
Lützen 16 Nov. 1632
Spanish 1620
Höchst 20 June 1622
Mainz 1631
Frankfurt am Main 1631
Mannheim 1622
Heidelberg 1622
Wurzburg 1631
RHINE PALATINATE
Wimpfen 6 May 1622
Alte Veste 31 Aug.– 4 Sep. 1632
Nuremberg 1632
UPPER PALATINATE
White Mountain 8 Nov. 1620
Prague 1631
MORAVIA
BOHEMIA
Zablati 10 June 1619
1632: Wallenstein threatens Gustavus' base in central Germany to draw him away from Bavaria
Huguenots and Swiss 1622
STATES
Rain 15–6 Apr. 1632
BAVARIA
Munich
Danube
Hungarian 1620
Vienna
AUSTRIA
HUNGARY
SWISS CONFEDERATION
Spanish 1634

1 The later course of the Thirty Years' War showed the primacy of politics over religion, and logistics over tactics (map below). A French Cardinal struggled to stop Catholic Spain intervening in Protestant Germany and Holland. Turenne's militarily brilliant campaigns were finally decisive, because Germany was too exhausted for the war to continue.

The ensuing Battle of Lutzen (16 November 1632) destroyed the last Imperial army, but Gustavus' chance death in action prevented an immediate advance on Vienna. Deprived of the Swedish Hercules, Cardinal Richelieu, the French chief minister, adopted a logistical strategy, attacking the communications between scattered Habsburg possessions in Italy, Germany and the Netherlands. The 'Spanish Road', by which reinforcements reached the Army of Flanders from the Habsburg Duchy of Milan, was a remarkable example of Renaissance military logistics. The troops followed routes surveyed by military engineers, skirting troublespots like Calvinist Geneva. Henry IV cut the original Spanish Road through Franche Comté, and Dutch seapower threatened the maritime route through the English Channel, but the Spanish found another route through the Grisons valleys. A Spanish army reached south Germany to defeat the Swedes at Nordlingen (6 September 1634), but French occupation of Alsace permanently cut the Spanish Road, dashing Habsburg ambitions for a unified Catholic Europe. Political plurality continued to ensure Europe's economic and military development, unconstrained by the command style of economy that crippled Europe's monolithic competitors in the East.

2 cardinal richelieu and the spanish road, 1633–48

battles
✗ Imperialist success
✗ French/allied success
✗ Swedish success

Habsburg communications
‑ ‑ ‑ sea links open to Dutch interdiction
→ Mediterranean Sea links
     original Spanish Road followed from 1567
· · · · Spanish Road avoiding French advances in Franche-Comté

French advances into Germany
→ 1645
‑ ‑→ Turenne, 1646
· · ·→ Turenne, 1648
→ French attempts to cut Spanish Road

Swedish raids through Bohemia
→ 1642
‑ ‑→ 1645

57

the **spanish war of succession**

13 August 1704
Battle of Blenheim

1704
English capture Gibraltar

1706
Eugene's victory at Turin, French evacuation of northern Italy. Marlborough's triumph at Ramillies

11 July 1708
Battle of Oudenarde

11 September 1709
Battle of Malplaquet: Allies suffer heavy defeat

1713
France, England and Holland sign Peace of Itrecht; Charles VI continues to war

1714
Charles VI agrees to treaties of Rastatt and Baden

Only the most skilful generals could achieve far-reaching success within the constraints of early 18th-century warfare. The Duke of Marlborough did so during the War of the Spanish Succession, by deception and variations of standard tactical procedures.

Marlborough's Blenheim Campaign was kept secret even from his allies. The march to the Danube wrong-footed hostile Franco–Bavarian forces and kept Britain's key ally, Austria, in the war. Logistical preparations even extended to replacement shoes. Marlborough extracted supplies from towns along his route by a smooth mixture of threats and promises. Payment was assured by Britain's sound war finances, symbolized by foundation of the Bank of England in 1694. His tactical victory at Blenheim broke the aura of French invincibility, and secured major Allied war aims: the Spanish Netherlands and Naples fell into Allied hands.

At Blenheim, Marlborough diverted the attention of the Franco–Bavarian armies to their flanks, then broke through the unstable centre. Almost two-thirds of the defeated armies became casualties, the highest attrition of any 18th-century battle. Marlborough used the same grand tactics at Ramillies (23 May 1706). Diversions on the flanks preceded a central break-through, while improvised cavalry reserves moved under cover to

---

1 marlborough's march to the danube (may–june 1704), and subsequent campaigns

→ Marlborough's march to the Danube
⇢ diversions
⋯• Marlborough's new communications
⇢ Marlborough's 1708 campaign
→ Allied troops moving to join Marlborough
→ French reaction
• towns falling to Allies after Ramillies
↓ sieges
⇠ French evacuation of Flanders after Oudenarde
⋯ *Ne Plus Ultra* lines forced by Marlborough, 26 July–4 August 1709

troop concentrations
▒ Marlborough
▒ Allies
▒ French

major battles
✕ Allied success
✕ French success

VILLEROI 46,000 men

SPANISH NETHERLANDS

Oudenarde 11 Aug. 1708

Lille 1708

Valenciennes 1712

Denain 24 July 1712

Brussels

Mons 1709

Malplaquet 11 Sep. 1709

Scheide

OVERKIRK 50,000 men

Maastricht

Ramillies 23 May 1706

Sambre

19 May

Bonn

Ruhr

Rhine

26 May

Koblenz

MARLBOROUGH 21,000 men

HOLY ROMAN EMPIRE

Ohm

Fulda

Werr

Saal

HANOVERIANS 5,000 men

Mainz 3 June

Main

DANES & PRUSSIANS 14,000 men

Nuremberg

DE COIGNE 10,000 men

7 June

A L S A C E

12 June

FRANCE

Oise

Aisne

Meuse

Marne

Paris

Marne

Aube

Seine

Yonne

L O R R A I N E

Moselle

Meurthe

Meuse

V o s g e s

TALLARD 36,000 men)

Strasburg

1 July

Rhine

BADEN & EUGENE 64,000 men

S c h w a r z w a l d

18 July

Danube

Schwäbische Alb

29 July

22 June

Ulm

Blenhei 13 Aug

Augs

BAVARIA 26,00

Lech

50°

48°

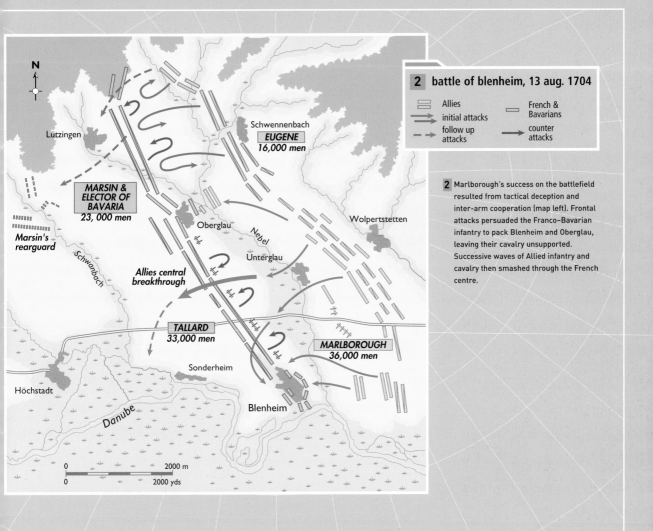

Lutzingen

Schwennenbach

EUGENE
16,000 men

2 battle of blenheim, 13 aug. 1704

Allies

initial attacks

follow up
attacks

French &
Bavarians

counter
attacks

**MARSIN &
ELECTOR OF
BAVARIA
23, 000 men**

*Marsin's
rearguard*

Oberglau

Nebel

Unterglau

Wolpertstetten

*Allies central
breakthrough*

2 Marlborough's success on the battlefield
resulted from tactical deception and
inter-arm cooperation (map left). Frontal
attacks persuaded the Franco–Bavarian
infantry to pack Blenheim and Oberglau,
leaving their cavalry unsupported.
Successive waves of Allied infantry and
cavalry then smashed through the French
centre.

Schwanbach

**TALLARD
33,000 men**

**MARLBOROUGH
36,000 men**

Sonderheim

Höchstadt

Danube

Blenheim

0   2000 m
0   2000 yds

1 A protégé of Turenne, Marlborough was one
of the few commanders able to overcome the
strategic limitations of his day (map left).
The ambiguous nature of Marlborough's
manoeuvres deceived both allies and the
enemy, but demanded sound logistical practice,
which earned him the affection of his troops.

the decisive point. However, Marlborough's methods became predictable. Marshal Villars inflicted heavy losses on the Allies at
Malplaquet (11 September 1709). He devastated Bavaria to force the
enemy to fight. When they occupied a strong position across his own
communications at Blenheim, he achieved surprise by attacking rather
than tamely withdrawing.

Marlborough could risk offensive battles because tactical developments were in his favour. French successes in the 1690s had made them
complacent. The remorseless advance and controlled fire of Allied battalions demoralized their opponents.

Even Marlborough could not avoid the frustrations of siege warfare. In
10 campaigns he fought four battles, two actions and 30 sieges.
Fortresses in Western Europe were too close together to be ignored, and
armies lacked the numbers to mask them as Napoleonic generals would
do a century later. The siege of Lille in 1708 required 80 heavy guns, 20
mortars and 3,000 wagonloads of stores. The siege lasted 120 days, and
cost the Allies five times the casualties of the Battle of Oudenarde (11 July
1708), which had made the operation possible.

1700
Denmark, Saxony–Poland and Russia form an alliance and attack Sweden

20 November 1700
Swedes defeat Russians at Narva. Denmark knocked out of the war by Sweden

1701
Swedes invade Polish Courland

1702
Swedes enter Warsaw and depose Augustus II

1706
Swedes force Saxony to make peace at Altrastadt

January 1708
Charles XII, King of Sweden, invades Russia

8 July 1709
Peter (the Great) destroys Charles army at Poltava . Brandenburg-Prussia, Hanover and Denmark join Russia in a struggle for Sweden's Baltic empire.

While Western Europe experimented with the balance of power, the East saw a strategic revolution. The export of the military renaissance to Russia created a new power from nothing. A well-armed Russia ended forever the nomadic incursions that had terrorized Europe throughout the Middle Ages. Turkey, the most recent intruder from the steppe, rejected modern military techniques, to the advantage of a resurgent Austria.

Russia was the first Asian country to import the military renaissance wholesale, forming European-style regiments in the 1630s. They made up two-thirds of the Russian Army by 1682, replacing the *streltsi*, an obsolescent corps of rebellious musketeers. German loan words, such as *soldat* or *junker*, reveal the foreign inspiration of Russia's military expertise. Peter the Great crushed the *streltsi* with exemplary cruelty, before accelerating military and social change to meet a strategic challenge from Sweden. Charles XII, the youthful king of Sweden, compensated for his small army with the most aggressive tactics in Europe. His cavalry gave up armour and charged at a gallop, when even Marlborough's horse trotted into contact. Swedish infantry advanced to 40 paces from the enemy without firing, fired two volleys and closed with the bayonet.

A Russian defeat at Narva (20 November 1700) showed their inability to withstand such shock tactics. Russian infantry ran about like stampeded cattle, while the Swedes, outnumbered five to one, took so many prisoners they let them go. Peter's response was to raise 50 new infantry regiments. When Charles XII invaded Russia in January 1708, advancing over the frozen rivers, the Russians avoided battle. They wore out the Swedes, destroying the countryside ahead of them. Charles' hopes of exploiting internal opposition to Peter were disappointed; the new Russian regiments could at least suppress dissidents. At Poltava (8 July 1709) Peter destroyed Charles' attenuated army, much to the Swedes' surprise. Other powers quickly recognized the emergence of a new military power. In the 1730s a Russian army marched into Germany, and defeated a French force at Danzig. Russian and Chinese forces met in Central Asia, ending the freedom of the steppe nomads. The forcible imposition of Western military institutions upon Russia exacted a terrible price. Brutally suppressed risings became a feature of the regime. The only reliable arm of government was the army, recruited more effectively and repressively than anywhere else. The military renaissance in the West tamed the man on horseback, but in Russia's militarized society it imposed new chains.

1 the eastern front, 1683–1721

→ Austrian Allied relief of Vienna, and counter-attacks
→ Russian campaign in Moldavia, 1711
- - ▶ Russian raids
•••••• Russian defences, 1708–9
▒▒ Russian winter quarters, 1708–9
→ Swedish campaigns
••••▶ Swedish campaign in Russia', 1708–9
▒▒ Swedish winter quarters, 1708–9
- ▶ Swedish retreat after Poltava
→ Turkish campaigns
- - ▶ Turkish raids

battle victories
✕ Austrian
✕ Russian
✕ Swedish
✕ Turkish

sieges
● Austrians besieging Turkish city
● Turks besieging Austrian city
● Danes besieging Swedish city
● Swedes besieging Danish city

1 Sweden's aggressive empire-building made it many enemies. When Sweden was attacked by Russia, Denmark and Saxony–Poland in 1700, Charles XII launched a series of brilliant campaigns, which saw him defeat Denmark, devastate Poland and invade Saxony before catastrophic defeat at Poltava ended his invasion of Russia (map right). The Swedish army's tactical pre-eminence was no substitute for the strategic strength that Peter the Great of Russia was able to mobilize.

NORWAY
(Danish)

SWEDEN

KARELIA

Trondhjem

Christiania

Nystad
Åbo
Helsingfors
St Petersburg

Gangut
6 Aug. 1714 ✕

INGRIA
Narva
20 Nov 1700 ✕

Revel

ESTONIA
Hummelsdorf
18 July 1702 ✕

Errestfer
7 Jan 1701 ✕

1701

RUSSIAN

Frederikstad
1718

Stockholm

Russian raids on Swedish coast

Pskov

Moscow

Gothenburg

LIVONIA
Riga

COURLAND

Dyneburg

Vitebsk

Smolensk

Tula

EMPIRE

Helsingborg
Feb 1710

Aarhus

DENMARK
Frederiksborg
Copenhagen

1700

Malmö

Baltic
Sea

1700

1708
Holovsin
4 July 1708 ✕
1708

Wilno

Minsk

Lesnaya
9-10 Oct 1708 ✕

Kursk

Gadebusch
1712

SWEDISH
POMERANIA

Königsberg

PRUSSIA

LITHUANIA

Hamburg

Stralsund
1713

Stettin

Gdansk

1709

1709
Kharkov
1709

Hanover

PRUSSIA

Elbe

Berlin

Poznan

Thorn

Vistula

1703

Pultusk
13 Apr 1703 ✕

Warsaw

Brest-Litovsk

HETMANATE
Kiev

8 July 1709 ✕
Poltava

Cossacks

Fraustadt/Wschowa
1706

SAXONY

Leipzig

Dresden

SILESIA

Lodz

Breslau

Oder

1702

1706

Kliszow
2 July 1708 ✕

POLAND
(in personal union with Saxony)

Lvov

Winnica

Dniester

1711

Dnieper

1709

Zaporogian Cossacks

Frankfurt

BOHEMIA
Prague

Cracow

MORAVIA
Brünn

Tartars

Stuttgart

Danube

1683

BAVARIA

Munich

Vienna
AUSTRIA

Pozsony

Buda

1686
Pest

Debrecen

Kolozsvár

Jassy

MOLDAVIA

Pruth
July 1711 ✕

KHANATE
OF
CRIMEA

Bakhchisaray

Salzburg

Graz

HABSBURG POSSESSIONS

HUNGARY

1687

Zenta
11 Sept 1697 ✕

Szeged

Temesvár
1716

TRANSYLVANIA

Brassó

WALLACHIA

1711

Black Sea

Milan

Venice

VENETIAN REPUBLIC

Trieste

Zágráb

(Military administration)

1689

Bucharest

Varna

Bologna

Zara

Spalato

Belgrade
30 Aug 1689
16 Aug 1717 ✕

Bosna Saray

1738-9

Danube

Ruschuk

1711

Burgas

Florence

PAPAL

Mostar

Nish

1689

Sofia

OTTOMAN

Rome

STATES

KINGDOM

REPUBLIC
OF RAGUSA

MONTENEGRO

Üsküb

Philippopolis

Adrianople

Constantinople

Angora

Naples

OF

NAPLES

Bari

Taranto

AND

SICILY

Salonica

Janina

EMPIRE

63

naval warfare under the ancien régime

1652 to 1762

1652–54
Anglo–Dutch War

1691
Act of Parliament required the Royal Navy to exceed the combined strength of its nearest rivals, the French and the Dutch

28 May–2 June 1692
spectacular naval victory for British at Barfleur

24 August 1704
Battle of Malaga: French withdraw to avoid combat

1739
war of Jenkins's Ear: struggle between England and Spain, growing out of commercial rivalry

22 February 1744
Battle of Toulon

20 May 1756
Battle at Minorca: Admiral Byng defeated, then executed by his own men

17 August 1759
Battle of Lagos: British under Admiral Boscawen defeat the French

Improved sailing warships and professionalization of Europe's navies introduced the classic age of fighting sail. The Anglo-Dutch War of 1652–54 saw more naval actions than the preceding 150 years, a trend continued in a series of maritime wars which defined the modern concepts of naval strategy. Fleets of sailing warships bound together European and colonial rivalries, causing the first 'world wars'.

A 1691 Act of Parliament required the Royal Navy to exceed the combined strength of its nearest rivals, the French and Dutch. By 1762 the Royal Navy had emerged as the most powerful in the world with 84,000 men and 300 ships Government dockyards supported the growing fleets, becoming the largest industrial enterprises in the world.

Naval architecture reflected different national strategies. The British built slower, stronger ships to enhance sea-keeping; the clean scientific lines of French ships made them faster, but less durable. Shallow coastal waters hand-icapped the Dutch when heavier rates appeared with 100 or more guns. They fell behind in the naval arms race.

Spanish and Portuguese monopolies of trade with the Indies and America had provoked English, French and Dutch incursions since the 16th century. Viewed by the occupying powers as pirates and smugglers, the interlopers gained respectability as officially sponsored companies and expeditions replaced the early buccaneers.

Security of merchant shipping was a dividend of sea power. Land transport was prohibitively expensive, so goods travelled by sea. Navies defeated in battle reverted to the medieval strategy of attacking trade. After Barfleur, heavy units of the French Navy participated in a systematic *guerre de course*, taking over 4,000 vessels. The Brest fleet captured 90 ships from one convoy off Cadiz in 1693. The English organized convoys from the 1660s to deter state-sponsored Dutch and French privateers, and freelance corsairs operating off North Africa and the West Indies. Parliamentary legislation, such as the 'Cruisers and Convoys Act' of 1708,

2 European sailing navies created global oceanic empires, inspiring and spreading conflict (map below). Admirals were innocent of Mahanian doctrines of sea power, but had a clear understanding of its practical value. They sought to protect their own trade, while damaging that of the enemy, launched amphibious operations around the world and blockaded enemy ports to prevent them doing the same.

1 Naval warfare was a way of breaking the strategic stalemate ashore, but fleets were often too large for decisive defeat, and fleets in being imposed a new deadlock (map above). The frequent Anglo-Dutch battles of the 1650s made way for long periods without fleet actions.

SWEDEN

NORWAY
(Danish)

St Petersburg
(from 1703)

Gangut
6 Aug. 1714

SCOTLAND

Marstrand
21 June–6 July 1719

North
Sea

Battle of the Sound
8 Nov. 1658

Karlskrona

Oeland
11 June 1676

COURLAND

IRELAND

Bay
–1689

ENGLAND

Battle of Sole Bay
7 June 1672

Copenhagen

Kjoge
4 Oct. 1710

LITHUANIA

Baltic
Sea

WALES

Kentish Knock
8 Oct. 1652

Downs
21 Oct. 1639

Gabbard
12–13 June 1653

DENMARK

SWEDISH
POMERANIA

Rugen
8 Aug. 1715

POLAND

Chatham

London

Texel
8–10 Aug. 1653

NETHERLANDS
Amsterdam

BRANDENBURG

SAXONY

Oder

SILESIA

mouth

Portsmouth

Rotterdam

Flushing

Four Day Fight
11–14 June 1666

Rhine

SMALL

Elbe

BOHEMIA

MORAVIA

Portland
28 Feb. 1653

Dover
29 May 1652

Barfleur
29 May 1692

Dungeness
10 Dec. 1652

STATES

Brest

Paris

French
occupation

Danube

Vienna

Lorient

Beachy Head
10 July 1690

BAVARIA

AUSTRIA

HUNGARY

Quiberon
20 Nov. 1759

FRANCE

SWISS
CONFEDERATION

Rochefort

SAVOY

Venice

V E N E T I A N

1 maritime rivalries,
1650–1760

naval bases

⚓	Britain
⚓	Denmark
⚓	France
⚓	Netherlands
⚓	Russia
⚓	Spain
⚓	Sweden
⚓	Venice

battles

as winners	as losers	
✕	●	Britain
✕	○	Denmark
✕	○	France
✕	●	Netherlands
✕	●	Russia
	○	Spain
✕	○	Sweden
	○	Turkey
✕		Venice

── borders
── border of Holy Roman Empire

REP. OF GENOA

Marseilles
Toulon

FLORENCE

SAN MARINO

PAPAL

Toulon
22 Feb. 1744

A R A G O N

Minorca
20 May 1756

SARDINIA

STATES

SICILY

Ebro

Port Mahon
(1708–56)

Cartagena

Mediterranean
Sea

Naples
(except 1714–35)

NAPLES

R E P U B L I C

REP. OF
RAGUSA

OTTOMAN

Corfu
8 Aug. 1716

EMPIRE

Lipari
11 Feb. 1675

Alicudi
8 Jan. 1676

Palermo
2 June 1676

Cape Passaro
11 Aug. 1718

Augusta
22 Apr. 1676

Matapan
19 July 1717
20–22 July 1718

2 sea power and the
globalization of war

── European trade routes
--→ French interventions in Spain and Italy
── Spanish Caribbean trade routes

naval bases

⚓	British/British ally	⚓	Spanish
⚓	French	⚓	disputed
●	captured by British expeditions		

**naval expeditions dependent
on sea power, with year**

→ British
→ Dutch (Lyme Bay)
→ French

reflected the sensitivity of overseas trade. Active counter-measures included Blake's attack on Tunis in 1655, followed by a short-lived occupation of Tangiers. Vigorous action in American waters against the Brethren of the Coast persuaded some buccaneers to move as far away as Madagascar. Jean Bart, the great practitioner of *guerre de course* in the 1690s, hoped to divert sufficient Anglo–Dutch resources to allow a new French challenge for control of the sea. Dispersal of French warships as commerce raiders, however, allowed the British to strengthen convoy escorts, and patrol the Western Approaches. The Royal Navy swept French ships off the sea, taking 2,200 in two years (1710–12). The collapse of French trade in the 1740s helped end the War of the Austrian Succession. Great Britain, her own trade intact, was the only power not to face financial ruin during the Seven Years' War.

mid 18th-century europe

1741 to 1750

10 April 1741
Battle of Mollwitz: Prussians defeat Austrians

1742
Austrian troops overrun Bavaria and lay siege to Prague. Peace made with Prussia

1743
Peace made with Saxony, who joins Austria as ally

1742-43
France under Marshal Belle-Isle retreat from Prague

1743
Victory of George II of Britain over the French at Dettingen

1745
Bavaria forced out of the war.

1748
Treaty of Aix-la-Chapelle signed

Eighteenth-century warfare was formal, but not static. Professional officers endlessly refined the skills of their men. International competition for power encouraged European armies to improve continually. However, logistical constraints on the conduct of war remained unresolved.

Peacetime armies optimized infantry firepower by constant drill. The British perfected a walking fire technique that nearly brought them victory at Fontenoy (10 May 1745). The Prussians streamlined their soldiers' coats, gave them paper cartridges and iron ramrods, and taught them to fire five rounds a minute. Trained musketry dominated the battlefield. The proportion of cavalry in European armies continued to decline: from a third in 1650, to a quarter in 1750 and one-sixth in 1810.

French officers, disgusted with the slaughter at Malplaquet, turned away from conventional linear tactics. Maurice de Saxe was the only reformer to put his ideas into practice. At Fontenoy he defeated British offensive fire tactics with Malplaquet-style fieldworks and a sophisticated artillery fire plan, including a dedicated reserve of 12 guns, a unique idea in the 1740s. At Roucoux and Lauffeld, Saxe took the offensive.

The inspiration for Saxe's skirmishers came from irregular troops, known as Croats, on their military frontier with Turkey. The appearance of Croats in Alsace inspired the Legion de Grassin, a French irregular corps that fought at Fontenoy. The British also learned about light troops outside Europe. Native North Americans, used to wood fighting, were tactically superior to local militia and regular troops imported from Europe. In 1755 Native North Americans destroyed a numerically superior British force at the Monongahela. Subsequently, the British formed irregular corps like Roger's Rangers, who beat the Native North Americans at their own game. British regulars in North America lightened their equipment, cut down their hats and learned to fight from cover.

Enhanced tactical mobility did not benefit strategy. Physical limits on manoeuvre remained the same. Large armies could not disperse to subsist, as detachments lacked the command structure and mixture of arms to fight

2	**battle of lauffeld, 2 july 1747**

Allied troops
⬜ British   ⬜ French
⬜ Austrian/Dutch

2 Some generals tried to play strength against weakness. The French Marshal, Maurice de Saxe, doubled his line at Lauffeld to attack the exposed part of a defending line with heavy columns. In a precursor of Frederick's celebrated oblique order, the French cavalry moved around the open Allied flank.

CUMBERLAND

Maestricht

Meuse

Kesselt

Klein Spaeven

Vlytingen

Lauffeld

Gross Spaeven

French move around allied left

N

French left wing moves behind right to form columns of assault

SAXE

0   2 kms
0   2 miles

1 The Austrian branch of the Habsburg dynasty was founded by Charles V's brother Ferdinand, elected king of Bohemia and Hungary in 1526. For 200 years, the Habsburgs disputed possession of Hungarian territory with the Ottomans. After the Turkish defeat at the siege of Vienna (1683), the Habsburgs extended control rapidly down the Danube, consolidating their gains by the Treaties of Carlowitz (1699) and Passarowitz (1718). Austria lost Silesia to Russia in the War of the Austrian Succession (1740–48) and failed to recover it in the Seven Years' War (1756–63). Croat irregular troops, long used to guard the frontier with the Turks, proved highly effective against the Prussians – their guerrilla tactics helped ensure the Prussians did not make inroads into Bohemia.

separately. Nor could they advance rapidly by a single line of operation. Inadequate roads delayed convoys, and low agricultural productivity inhibited requisitions. The numerous horses that moved an army ate immense quantities of fodder, so campaigns began when the grass grew in April. By the time one side had won a battle it would be too late to do more than pick up a fortress or two, before winter allowed the beaten army to recover. The Allied reconquest of the Spanish Netherlands after Ramillies (23 May 1706) was a rare opportunity to exploit a victory at the start of the campaigning season. Nevertheless, wars did cause major political shifts. Turkey was excluded from Europe and French ambitions were curbed, despite the limited capabilities of 18th-century armies.

1 the growth of the habsburg empire

- hereditary Habsburg lands, 1525
- acquisitions, 1526
- acquisitions, 1648–99
- acquisitions, 1699–1772
- acquisitions, 1772–1805
- boundary of the Holy Roman Empire, 1789
- military frontier

the **first colonial wars**

25 July 1746
French naval victory at Negapatam allows them to seize Madras

1754
War breaks out between British and French colonists in North America

1756
Nawab of Bengal occupies Bengal

1757
Britain gains control of Bengal

1759
Britain defeats French fleet at Quiberon Bay and Lagos. Britain takes Quebec

14 January 1761
Battle of Panipat: Afghans inflict defeat on Marathas

1761
the French surrender base at Pondichery to British

1763
Peace of Paris, France loses Canada

The Mughal Empire collapsed when internal decay invited external attack. Increasing intolerance of non-Muslims alienated the Rajputs and inspired Sikh militancy. Mughal generals seized power for themselves, such as the Nizam at Hyderabad. After the last great emperor, Aurangzeb, died in 1707, the Marathas of the Deccan took control of northern India, even taking Portuguese bases at Bassein and Chaul. An army of Afghan heavy cavalry inflicted a disastrous defeat on the Marathas at Panipat (14 January 1761). However, the Afghans lacked the numbers or political support to control India and withdrew, leaving chaos from which the British would profit.

French and British coastal enclaves in India needed control of the sea for supplies and military reinforcements. Their proximity provoked numerous naval actions. Linear tactics prevented loss of ships, yet as in European waters inconclusive battles had disproportionate effects. A French naval victory at Negapatam (25 July 1746) allowed them to seize Madras, but British reinforcements under Boscawen saved their nearby base at Fort St George. The British then besieged the French base Pondicherry, until the monsoon drove Boscawen off station. In the 1750s an outnumbered British squadron inflicted enough damage in three 'indecisive' actions, to compel the French admiral to withdraw to distant Mauritius to refit. Pondicherry surrendered in 1761, having no hope of relief by sea. Naval power allowed the British to move forces between the Carnatic and Bengal. When the Nawab of Bengal occupied Calcutta in 1756, the British mounted a joint operation from Madras to retake it. A squadron of battleships then pushed 21 miles up the river Hooghly, to bombard the French factory at Chandernagore (23 March 1757). Victory in India opened new strategic possibilities for the British. The 1762 expedition to Manila sailed from Madras. Calcutta developed a naval dockyard, building European-style warships in local teak.

Europeans revolutionized Indian land warfare. In the 1730s the French introduced light field guns, and trained their factory watchmen to fight with musket and bayonet, their cipahis defeating a Mughal successor army at St Thomé (3 November 1746). The British imitated the French, depending heavily on Indian troops to extend and consolidate British rule beyond the range of their fleets. At Plassey (23 June 1757) Colonel Robert Clive defeated 50,000 Mughal-style troops with 3,200 men, two-thirds of them sepoys. Traditional Indian armies had no tactical answer to well-drilled bayonets and mobile field guns firing case shot. Only the Marathas' strategy of retreating into ground unsuitable for artillery and harassing British communications had any success. By 1805 the East India Company employed 150,000 sepoys. Britain had become a major Asian land power, combining European military techniques with Indian numbers. The new style of Indian soldier would be a mainstay of British imperial power.

2 battle of laswari, 1 november 1803

▱ British cavalry at start of action
▱ British cavalry during infantry battle
→ British attacks
▭ Maratha 1st position
▬ Maratha final position, refusing right flank

2 The destruction of the Army of Hindostan followed the political defeat of its Maratha owners. Unlike traditional Indian armies, de Boigne's regiments could change front during a battle and their well-served field guns inflicted heavy losses on their British opponents before the 2,000 surviving sepoys surrendered.

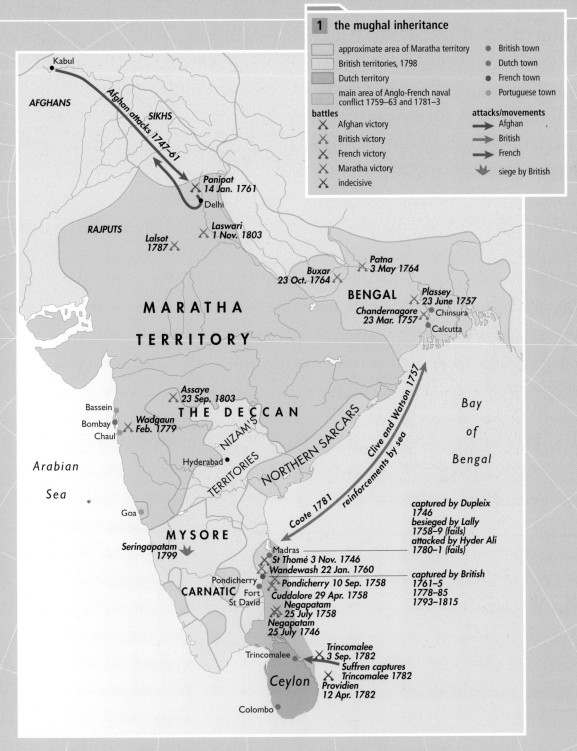

1 the mughal inheritance

- approximate area of Maratha territory
- British territories, 1798
- Dutch territory
- main area of Anglo-French naval conflict 1759–63 and 1781–3

- British town
- Dutch town
- French town
- Portuguese town

battles
- ✕ Afghan victory
- ✕ British victory
- ✕ French victory
- ✕ Maratha victory
- ✕ indecisive

attacks/movements
- → Afghan
- → British
- → French
- ↓ siege by British

Kabul

AFGHANS

Afghan attacks 1747–61

SIKHS

Panipat 14 Jan. 1761

Delhi

RAJPUTS

Lalsot 1787

Laswari 1 Nov. 1803

Buxar 23 Oct. 1764

Patna 3 May 1764

BENGAL

Chandernagore 23 Mar. 1757

Plassey 23 June 1757

Chinsura

Calcutta

M A R A T H A

T E R R I T O R Y

Assaye 23 Sep. 1803

Bassein

Bombay

Chaul

Wadgaun Feb. 1779

THE DECCAN

NIZAM'S

TERRITORIES

Hyderabad

NORTHERN SARCARS

Clive and Watson 1757

reinforcements by sea

Arabian Sea

Goa

Coote 1781

Bay of Bengal

MYSORE

Seringapatam 1799

captured by Dupleix 1746
besieged by Lally 1758–9 (fails)
attacked by Hyder Ali 1780–1 (fails)

Madras

St Thomé 3 Nov. 1746
Wandewash 22 Jan. 1760

Pondicherry

Fort St David

CARNATIC

Pondicherry 10 Sep. 1758

captured by British 1761–5
1778–85
1793–1815

Cuddalore 29 Apr. 1758

Negapatam 25 July 1758

Negapatam 25 July 1746

Trincomalee

Trincomalee 3 Sep. 1782

Suffren captures Trincomalee 1782

Providien 12 Apr. 1782

Ceylon

Colombo

1 There were four competitors to replace the Mughals: Afghans, British, French and Marathas. Anglo–French commercial rivalry concealed the strength of the outsiders, short-sightedly seen as allies or puppets. Sea power was crucial to British success, allowing them to shuttle reinforcements between Bombay and Bengal, while French lack of naval bases settled indecisive sea battles against them.

frederick the great and the prussian expansion

1756 to 1763

1756
Prussians invade Saxony and begin Seven Year War

1757
Prussians inflict 50 per cent losses on a stronger Austrian army at Leuthen (6 December)

1759
British victorious at battle of Minden (1 August)

1759
Battle of Kunersdorf (13 August)

1763
Frederick II makes terms with Saxony and Austria, begins reforms in Prussia

1764
Treaty of Alliance between Prussia and Russia

The genius of Frederick the Great and the training of his soldiers preserved Prussia from the combined efforts of Austria, France and Russia. Prussian battalions were so reliably drilled that Frederick the Great's armies could march across the enemy front, wheel into line, and go straight into an attack. This processional deployment formed the basis of Frederick's famous 'oblique order'. Trained to charge long distances at a gallop, Prussian cavalry set the standard for mounted tactics, until rifled small arms rendered them obsolete in the late 19th century. The Prussians were the first totally professional army.

Frederick's opponents soon countered his tactics. At Kolin (18 June 1757) Austrian light troops hung about the Prussian flank, provoking a premature advance. At Zorndorf (25 October 1758) encircled Russians faced about to convert the battle into another frontal attack, with ghastly results: 35 per cent Prussian losses against 53 per cent Russian. All armies had improved rates of fire, making frontal attacks terribly costly. Artillery had also improved. New casting techniques made guns lighter but more effective. The Russians and Austrians reformed their artillery in the early 1750s. Their new guns outclassed the Prussians in number, range and weight of fire, and massacred Prussian infantry at Prague and Kolin. Frederick strengthened his own artillery, deploying 12-pounder fortress guns at Leuthen. He broadened the capability of his gunners with field howitzers and horse artillery. Frederick's horse artillery formed a mobile reserve of firepower, foreshadowing Napoleon's use of reserve artillery.

The Seven Years' War does not fit the stereotype of 18th-century limited warfare. Prussia faced dismemberment if defeated. Frederick's pre- emptive occupation of Saxony drew in France, expanding a Central European conflict into a world war. Frederick's internal position and the tactical superiority of his army enabled him to attack his geographically dispersed enemies one at a time. He defeated a French army at Rossbach (5 November 1757), then marched 170 miles in 12 days to beat the Austrians at Leuthen. Frederick's early victories paralysed opposing generals. They were slow to exploit his absence, or their own successes. An Austro–Russian army failed to occupy Berlin, and end the war, after their victory at Kunersdorf (12 August 1759). Frederick, on the other hand, could not follow up his victories, as he always needed the troops elsewhere. Strategic weakness forced him into offensive battles, accepting heavy casualties to keep the

1 Frederick's well-drilled Prussians (map right) 'walked round the Austrians like a washerwoman at a tub', and smashed through the resulting angle in the Austrian line. Oblique order was not an infallible recipe for success. A similar attack at Kolin, seven weeks later, failed with heavy losses.

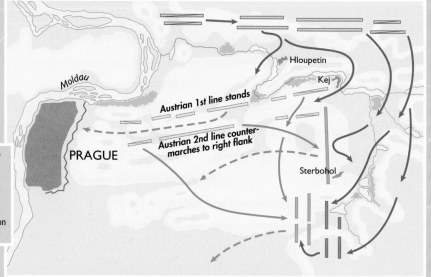

2 battle of prague, 16 may 1757

Prussian cavalry 1st and 2nd position
Prussian turning movement
Austrian reaction
Austrian cavalry 1st and 2nd position
Austrian infantry 1st and 2nd position
Austrian retreat

Moldau

PRAGUE

Hloupetin

Kej

Austrian 1st line stands

Austrian 2nd line counter-marches to right flank

Sterbohol

enemy at bay. However, he had little choice. Prussia lacked the fortifications that limited offensives in traditional seats of war, and Frederick could not risk losing territory by defending obstacles until outmanoeuvred. As long as he controlled Prussia's revenues and received British subsidies, Frederick could hire fresh mercenaries, while even a Prussian defeat wrecked the opposing army. Despite his tactical genius, however, Frederick came to regard battles as an expedient of the unimaginative. He was saved, accidentally, by the political breakdown of the opposing coalition.

1 Threatened by a numerically superior coalition, Frederick sought to defeat his enemies separately (map below). He manoeuvred on internal lines and exploited the tactical superiority of his army in offensive battles. Later opponents of geographically dispersed alliances, such as the Wehrmacht or IDF, would also combine a strategic defensive with offensive tactics.

1 the miracle of the hohenzollerns, 1756 – 63

fortresses
- Austrian
- Prussian
- Swedish
- captured by Austrians
- captured by Russians

battles
- Austrian victory
- Austro-Russian victory
- French victory
- Prussian victory
- Russian victory

advances
- Frederick's movements during the 1757 Rossbach/Leuthen campaign
- Austrian advance
- French advance
- Russian advance
- Swedish advance

the **american** revolutionary war

1772 to 1782

1765
the British Parliament's Stamp Act rouses violent colonial outcry

1773
Boston Tea Party

17 June 1775
Battle of Bunker Hill – costly British victory

March 1776
British give up Boston

July 1776
Declaration of Independence

17 October 1777
Battle of Saratoga: first great American victory in the war

1781
Battle of Cape Henry (5–9 September)

1781
Cornwallis surrenders at Yorktown (19 October)

The American War of Independence is commonly seen as defying the military conventions of the day. The strategy and tactics of the war, however, were not unusual. British defeat revealed the shortcomings of maritime power confronted with popular resistance on a continental scale while distracted by a strategic threat closer to home.

The British war machine of the 1770s was soundly financed, with a competent army experienced in colonial warfare and the largest navy in the world. It was defeated by a popular revolt that printed worthless paper money, created an army from nothing, and never possessed a navy beyond privateers. The initial weakness of the rebels was to their advantage, as the British government underestimated the response required. North America was simply too large to occupy with the troops available. British strategic mobility was low. They could make amphibious descents upon New York or Charleston, but once ashore lacked transport, and moved at the speed of a foot soldier. British defeats became disasters, while defeated American forces had space to withdraw, protected by difficult terrain.

Political factors constrained British conduct of the war in ways familiar today. Opposition to the war within Britain was vocal. Counter-insurgency forces faced the choice between ineffective half measures and extremes that alienated moderates. Revolutionary militia dominated the countryside, their political role in suppressing Loyalist dissent exceeding their value on the battlefield. The militia symbolized the dispersal of political authority in the United States. This made for poor strategic direction of the American war effort, but increased British difficulties in suppressing a many-headed revolt. Their capture of Philadelphia, the seat of Congress, lacked the political resonance of occupying a European capital.

Washington's success in keeping his army together deprived the British of victory, but French intervention won the war. The Royal Navy had too few resources to intimidate the rebels, or isolate North America, as it had in the Seven Years' War. Ships were rotten and the best admirals politically disaffected. Many ships remained in home waters to

1 **maritime vs continental power, 1776–82**

→ Allied (French/American) 1776–80
⇢ Allied 1781
→ British 1776–80
⇢ British 1781

battles
✗ Allied success
✗ British success

blockades
⛵ Allied
⛵ British

sieges
↓ American success
↓ British success

Guildford C
H
15 Mar.

Great Smoky Mts

Cowpens
17 Jan. 1781

Cornwa
1780–

Blue

Camden
16 Aug. 1780

Augusta
29 Jan. 1779

SOUTH
CAROLINA

Savannah

Charleston

GEORGIA

Savannah
Sep.–Oct. 1779

Ca

D'Estain
Sep. 177

Quebec 1775

NOVA SCOTIA

St Lawrence

Montreal

Kennebec

Halifax

44°

D
1777 Burgoyne
unsupported is forced
to surrender at
Saratoga

NEW
HAMPSHIRE

64°

40

1777
St Leger defeated
on Mohawk River

B

Lake
Ontario

Oswego

Mohawk

Saratoga
17 Oct. 1777

Bunker Hill
17 June 1775

April 1776 British evacuate Boston

MASSACHUSETTS   Boston

Aug 1776 Howe moves on New York

Hudson

NEW
YORK

1777 Clinton raids
up Hudson

C

RHODE
ISLAND

CONNECTICUT

Newport

French expedition July 1780

New York
Long Island
27 Aug. 1776

72°

1

Trenton
25 Dec. 1776

PENNSYLVANIA

Philadelphia
Brandywine
11 Sept 1777

68°

A

1777 Howe sails south to take Philadelphia

Barras' squadron (Fr) evades British blockade

Washington marches south to trap
Cornwallis at Yorktown

3

DELAWARE

MARYLAND

James

RGINIA

Cornwallis Apr.–May 1781

Yorktown
1781

Cape Henry
5 Sep. 1781

Aug.–Oct. 1781

De Grasse's fleet (Fr)
summoned from the West Indie

2

36°

76°

Atlantic

Ocean

1 The American colonies formed an
enormous theatre of war. The few
British regulars were unable to
suppress the numerous local irregulars,
although the Royal Navy allowed them
to strike at will at coastal areas. The
British were defeated when a French
fleet cut off supplies and
reinforcements from Cornwallis'
isolated army at Yorktown.

ORTH
ROLINA

Wilmington

on 1780

8–9

deter a combined Franco–Spanish battle line that outnumbered the
British 140 to 120. The French had no European diversions, and
usurped the Royal Navy's amphibious monopoly, sending an expedition to assist the Americans. In August 1781 Washington moved superior numbers of French and American troops against Cornwallis'
army at Yorktown. He urged the French fleet to concentrate off
Chesapeake Bay, to cut Cornwallis' communications with British
forces at New York. In the crucial battle off Cape Henry (5–9
September 1781) 24 French ships prevented 19 British from raising
the siege. Sea power compelled Cornwallis to surrender (19 October
1781). The end of the land war allowed the British to focus on the
naval war and a reinforced West Indies Squadron broke the mould of
linear naval tactics at the Battle of the Saints (12 April 1782). Admiral
Rodney broke the French line, and captured five ships, pointing the
way for British naval successes in the 1790s.

1757
Prussians defeat French at Rossbach

1792
Louis XIV declares war on Austria

1792–94
conquest of the Low Countries and the left bank of the Rhine

1793
threatened with invasion, the French government issues a levée en masse

18 May 1794
Battle of Tourcoing: French mount a 60,000 strong force against the allies

1796
Jourdan and Moreau invade Germany

The French Revolution profoundly changed the art of war. It released social forces that combined explosively with late 18th-century military trends. Unlike other 'military revolutions' these were not technological in origin, but tactical.

French army officers despaired of rivalling the precision of the Prussian drillmasters who had defeated them at Rossbach (1757). Instead they exploited the native flexibility of the French soldier by integrating skirmishers with the line of battle. Skirmishers screened the movement of columns unable to use their own weapons, and prepared the advance with accurate individual fire. Aimed fire was more dangerous than that of men jammed together in close order, while skirmishers presented a less vulnerable target. Dispersed skirmishers could thus achieve fire superiority over formed troops armed with similar weapons. This system became official French Army doctrine in 1791 and by 1815 it had spread to all European armies, forming the basis for a new tactical consensus. The French Army's system of all-arms divisions further enhanced tactical articulation.

Battles were less deadly, but there were more of them: 713 battles took place in Europe between 1790 and 1820, compared with 2,659 for the period 1480 to 1790. Enthusiastic French armies suffered more casualties than the regular troops they defeated. Their losses were replaced by compulsion. Threatened with invasion in August 1793, the government in Paris proclaimed a *levée en masse*. Half a million Frenchmen were under arms by the end of the year, in 11 separate armies. Such numbers were hard to maintain, falling to 227,000 in 1799. Battlefield strengths rarely exceeded those of the Seven Years' War; Tourcoing (18 May 1794) was exceptional. Nevertheless, the increased total size of armies made it essential to feed them at the enemy's expense. A ring of annexed territories and puppet republics surrounded France by 1796, a system fundamental to Napoleon's Empire.

French expansion was slow, until Napoleon focused Revolutionary energies. Republican armies often failed to cooperate. When Jourdan and Moreau invaded Germany in 1796, the Austrian Archduke Karl beat them in detail, and chased them back to the Rhine. However, the conquest of the Low Countries and the left bank of the Rhine in three years (1792–94) compares strikingly with Louis XIV's decades of fighting fruitlessly for the same objectives. The contrast suggests the decisive potential of Revolutionary warfare, when it was directed in a coordinated manner.

The new tactical methods exploited a profound shift in political attitudes. War was no longer the exclusive concern of kings or governments. It demanded popular participation, and soldiers who could be trusted not to desert when dispersed to forage or skirmish. Other European armies distrusted light infantry as socially subversive, and wished to avoid the economic dislocation caused by living off the country. They were slow to make the same demands of their soldiers and populations as the French.

1 French revolutionary wars, 1792–96

— France, 1789

centres of Republican terror with numbers of executions

Chouan and Vendéen resistance

→ foreign intervention

→ French offensives with date and commander

✕ French victories

annexed and puppet states

1 Austria and Prussia invaded France in 1792, but the Duke of Brunswick's half-hearted campaign ended after an indecisive action at Valmy. After executing King Louis XVI in January 1793, the Republic declared war on Britain, Holland and Spain too (map opposite left). To the surprise of the Allies, the French republican armies repelled each invasion and exported their revolution to the Low Countries, the west bank of the Rhine and northern Italy.

2 The campaigns of the 1790s saw both sides disperse their forces over wide frontages, ready to concentrate for battle (map top right). At Tourcoing the French defeated the Allies in detail, acting on interior lines to concentrate against York's forces. However, both sides' losses were about eight per cent: decisive victories proved elusive.

3 In 1796 Archduke Karl of Austria exploited his central position to defeat two French invasions of southern Germany (map below). Jourdan was driven back and compelled to seek an armistice after the Battle of Würzburg.

2 battle of tourcoing, 18 May 1794

- Allied forces engaged, 18 May
- Allied delayed advance and retreat, 19 May
- French offensive forces and moves
- French blocking forces and moves

N

Courtray

Lys

CLERFAYT 16,000 men

SOUHAM 60,000 men

Lannoy

Roubaix

YORK 24,000 men

Tourcoing

Menin

ARCHDUKE KARL 25,000 men

Pont a Marque

Lincelles

Lille

Allied advance from South : planned but not carried out

Wervicke

Allies' delayed advance from North and retreat over Lys 19 May

0   5 km
0   5 miles

3 archduke karl's german campaign, 1796

movement of armies

- French advance, July–August, 1796
- French retreat, September–October 1796
- Archduke Karl's advances between northern and southern wings of campaign

battles

- ✕ French victory
- ✕ Austrian victory
- ✕ indecisive
- 🏰 forts

Düsseldorf
21 Sep.

Kassel

Weser

Jourdan

Cologne

Bonn

Rhine

Jourdan

Lahn

Koblenz

10 July

Frankfurt

Offenbach

Mainz

Aschaffenburg

Schweinfurt

Erzgebirge

Cheb

Mosel

Bamberg

Würzburg 2–3 Sep.

Bayreuth

Jourdan

Pilzen

Main

Ludwigshafen am Rhein

Jourdan

Erlangen

24 Aug.

Mannheim

Heidelberg

Nuremburg

Ansbach

Amberg 24 Aug.

Naab

Böhmer

Saarbrücken

HOLY

ROMAN

Neumarkt 22 Aug

EMPIRE

Heilbronn

Wald

Karlsruhe

Pforzheim

Regensburg

FRANCE

Malsch 10 July

Moreau

Stuttgart

Neresheim 11 Aug.

Ingolstadt

Geisenfeld 1 Sep.

Isar

Passau

Strasbourg

Offenburg

Schwäbische Alb

Donauwörth

Ulm

Landshut

Colmar

Emmendingen 19 Oct.

Black Forest

24 Aug.

Passage of the Lech 24 Aug.

Breisach

Freiburg

Siegmaringen

Tuttlingen

Danube

Moreau

Biberach 2 Oct.

Augsburg

Lech

Dachau

Munich

Inn

Landsberg

Rhine

Moreau

Stockach

Memmingen

Iller

Rosenheim

Salzburg

Mulhouse

Huningen

25 Oct. Basel

Schaffhausen

Lake Constance

Kempten

the **napoleonic wars I**

1796
Bonaparte's first campaign in Italy

1797
Treaty of Tolentino; Napoleon defeats Austrians at Neumarkt and Unzmarkt

1797
French occupation of Venice

1798
Bonaparte's Egyptian campaign; Mamluks defeated at battle of Pyramids

1799
Austria (supported by Britain, Russia, Naples and Portugal) declares war on France

1800
French army crosses Alps in the Marengo campaign, and gains a narrow victory over the Austrians

The Armies of the Revolution contained the seeds of Napoleon's success. General Bonaparte's first campaign in Italy in 1796 showed his grasp of the potential of divisional organization and skirmishing tactics. In his first campaign, Bonaparte showed the originality of his genius, defeating larger, better-equipped armies with two strategies that became Napoleonic trademarks: The Strategy of the Central Position, and The Envelopment or *La Manoeuvre sur les Derrières*.

The first allowed inferior numbers to divide a superior enemy army, and defeat its wings in detail. It worked best against allied armies, more concerned with their own safety than for their ally. When the Austrians fell back behind the Po and Ticino, Bonaparte used his now superior numbers to implement the more ambitious *Manoeuvre sur les Derrières*. Screened by the River Po, Bonaparte gained the Austrian rear between Piacenza and Lodi, precipitating an immediate Austrian withdrawal from Lombardy. The French advanced 100 miles in two weeks, and seized Milan with enormous quantities of loot, resolving their own logistical difficulties. The crossing of the Alps in the Marengo campaign of 1800 was an even more impressive demonstration of The Envelopment. The Austrians had regained Northern Italy, and were pressing against the French frontier on the Riviera. Bonaparte, now the French head of state, crossed the Alps behind the Austrians. The French re-occupied Milan, cutting Austrian communications, while maintaining their own through Switzerland.

1 bonaparte's italian campaign, 1796

troop concentrations on the eve of Bonaparte's attack

- Sardinian
- French
- Austrian

→ French advance, 12 Apr.–4 May

Sardinian army at armistice, 4 May

Austrian cordon and troop concentrations, 8 May

→ Bonaparte's Lodi manoeuvre

French security detachments during the initial attack and Lodi manoeuvre

French dispositions to cover siege of Mantua

→ Austrian attempts to relieve Mantua

Austrian fort

battles
✕ French victory

1 In April–May 1796 Napoleon led the outnumbered French Army of Italy to victory over the Austrian and Piedmontese forces, striking at their dispersed armies and driving them from Lombardy (map right). In August, he repeated the strategy of using a central position to defeat superior forces in turn. French losses averaged less than 10 per cent in these battles, while the Austrian armies lost a quarter of their effectives.

AOSTA 18,000 men
KELLERMAN 18,000 men
COLLI 25,000 men
BONAPARTE 40,000 men
BEAULIEU 30,000 men
BEAULIEU 24,000 men

Dego 17 Apr.
Montenotte 12 Apr.
Savona
Lodi 10 M

Valle di Susa
Turin
Asti
Alessandria
Pellice
Alba
Cuneo
Stura di Demonte
Belbo
Genoa
REPUBLIC OF GENOA
Gulf of Genoa

A   L   P
Lake Maggiore
Lake Lugano
Lake Lecco
Varese
Adda
Berg
MILAN
Milan
Novara
Vercelli
Pavia
Po
Piac
Cervo
Sesia
Agogna
Sesia
Dora Baltea
Po
P I E D M O N T
Curone
A   P   P   P
FRANCE

HELVETIC REPUBLIC

St Gotthard Pass

Simplon Pass

14 May • Martigny

Matterhorn

Great St Bernard Pass

Little St Bernard Pass

Aosta 17 May

2 Napoleon returned from Egypt in 1800 to find the French all but driven out of Italy (map right). He led his army over the Alps to place his men across the Austrians' lines of communication and defeated Melas's counter-attack at Marengo. Casualties were relatively light, but the Austrians were compelled to abandon Piedmont once again.

VUKASSOVICH 10,000 men

CISALPINE REPUBLIC

Lake Maggiore

Lake Lugano

Lake Lecco

Varese

Bergamo

Rhône

Cervo

Sesia

Ticino

26 May

Novara

30 May

Milan 2 June

4 June

Oglio

Cremona

SAVOY

Mont Cenis Pass

Orco

Dora Baltea

Vercelli

Sesia

Agogna

Pavia

Po

Piacenza 7 June

Casteggio 9 June

Valle di Susa 10,000 men • Turin

PIEDMONT

Pellice

Asti

Alessandria

Marengo 14 June

MELAS 34,000 men

PARMA

Ceno

Tanaro

Alba

Belbo

Po

Nure

Arda

Curone

APPENINES

Cuneo

Stura di Demonte

4,000 men

MELAS 30,000 men

Orb

Savona

Genoa

British blockade

OTT 21,000 men to Antibes, 4 June

LIGURIAN REPUBLIC

HABSBURG EMPIRE

Chiese

Lago d'Iseo

REPUBLIC

Brescia •

Lake Garda

Adige

OF

Peschiera

Verona

VENICE

Lonato 3 Aug.

Castiglione 5 Aug.

Cremona

Mincio

BONAPARTE 50,000 men

• Mantua

Po

MANTUA

Parma •

Enza

Secchia

A

Modena •

MODENA

NINES

At Lonato and Castiglione in August 1796 Bonaparte faced encirclement by an Austrian pincer movement. A less energetic commander might have been lost, for the Army of Italy appeared to be at the culminating point of its advance: the siege of Mantua tied up 15,000 French soldiers, occupation duties absorbed another 10,000, leaving only 27,000 in the field. Bonaparte used his central position to attack each Austrian column separately in a three-day battle. Abandoning the siege of Mantua, he concentrated every available man, even enveloping the Austrians left on the second day at Castiglione. Bonaparte retained no specific strategic reserve, the divisional system allowing him to call on any available body of troops as necessary.

The culminating point of the 1800 Italian campaign came at Marengo. The outmanoeuvred Austrians could still supply their army by sea through Genoa. Bonaparte needed a tactical victory to confirm his strategic success. Fifty thousand French advanced on a 50-mile front, between the Alps and the sea. They prevented the Austrians escaping, but gave them a numerical advantage on the battlefield. However, the French had the advantage of the tactical defensive and the divisional system. Fresh troops came into action during the battle, to gain a narrow victory.

2 the marengo campaign, may–june 1800

Austrian troop concentrations

	14 May
	14 June

➤ French reserve army advance

⚑ extent of French reserve army advance, with date

➤ subsidiary French advance

● French garrisons

✸ French sieges

➤ Austrian advance

✹ Austrian siege of Genoa

battles ✕ French victory

1805 to 1807

1804
General Bonaparte becomes Emperor

20 October 1805
27,000 Austrians surrender at Ulm

December 1805
battle of Austerlitz, Vienna captured and Napoleon's army occupies south Germany

1806
Prussia declares war on France

18 October 1806
battle of Jena-Auerstadt: Napoleon victorious against Prussians

4 June 1807
battle of Friedland: Russians seek peace after heavy losses

Napoleon Bonaparte became Emperor of France in 1804. Lacking legitimacy, except the bayonets of his followers, he had to ensure their continued support. He plundered Europe for the benefit of the French army, perpetuating international instability. The Grande Armée began as the Army of England, but in 1805 it turned upon Napoleon's continental rivals, Austria and Russia.

The Grande Armée advanced with seven corps to the Danube. The Austrian high command fatally underestimated the threat. General Mack occupied an exposed position at Ulm in Bavaria, a French ally. He expected a direct advance through the Black Forest. Meanwhile, the mass of the Grande Armée swung north of Ulm, reaching the Danube between Ulm and the Austrian base at Vienna. Twenty-seven thousand Austrians surrendered on 20 October 1805. Napoleon's 2:1 numerical superiority made his success a rare example of a bloodless triumph.

The Allies were unable to defend Vienna, its arsenals falling into French hands. Napoleon caught up with a combined Austro–Russian army at Austerlitz, 70

1 the march to the danube, 1805

troop concentrations
French, 25 September
Bavarian, 25 September
Austrian, 6 October

French/Bavarian movements to:-
6 October
9 October
16 October
Austrian troops escaping

I BERNADOTTE

Rhine

Frankfurt am Main
Mainz

Main

SMALL

Würzburg

Bamberg • Bayreuth

II MARMONT

FRENCH EMPIRE

GERMAN

PRUSSIAN • Nuremburg
• Ansbach

III DAVOUT
• Mannheim

Frankische Alb

NAPOLEON
207, 000 men

Neckar

TERRITORY

IV SOULT
Speyer

Regensburg •

VI NEY

Rhine
• Karlsruhe

Heilbronn

STATES

Danube

Strasbourg

Stuttgart

Lannes
Ney

Donauwörth

Ingolstadt

KIENMAYER
16,000 men

V LANNES GUARDS MURAT (CAV)

Black Forest

diversons by reserve cavalry

Schwäbische Alb

Ulm

Augsburg

FERDINAND
44,000 men

Lech

Isar

Munich •

• Freiburg

Rhine

Danube

JELLACIC
16,000 men

L. Constance

Iller

BAVARIA

Inn

miles north of Vienna. There, nine years into his career Napoleon fought his first conventional set-piece battle. Napoleon outwitted the Allies, but their defeat required hard fighting. The French owed their final success to the tactical superiority of their veterans. This second defeat, in the heart of his country, persuaded the Austrian Emperor to make peace. Napoleon had knocked Austria out of the war in just three month's fighting.

The Grande Armée occupied South Germany after Austerlitz, to oversee creation of the French-dominated Confederation of the Rhine. In response Prussia occupied Saxony and Hesse-Kassel, north of the Main. They made a dangerous flank march across Napoleon's front to regain the Elbe, their divisions strung out along a single road unlike the French, who moved by several roads on a broad front.

Napoleon's tactics brought on the double battle of Jena-Auerstadt. The Prussians outnumbered Davout's Corps on the right at Auerstadt 2:1 but he beat them off. Bernadotte's Corps then intercepted the Prussian withdrawal near Apolda, converting it into a rout. The devastating consequences of the French victory made clear the implicit message of Marengo: an army losing its lines of communications and suffering a decisive defeat would be ruined.

The large French army quickly overran the small kingdom of Prussia, but resistance continued in Poland and East Prussia, with Russian help. Strategic success eluded Napoleon in the roadless wastes of Eastern Europe. The Grande Armée had to fight bloody frontal actions against the traditionally obstinate Russians, whose unpredictable movements sometimes enabled them to seize the initiative. For the first time Napoleon had failed to gain the type of rapid decisive victory that he needed. The Treaty of Tilsit (July 1807), signed on a raft on the River Niemen, was the high-water mark of his empire.

2 **battle of austerlitz, 2 december 1805**

troop concentrations

French, 25 September

Bavarian, 25 September

3 **battle of wagram, 4–6 july 1809**

→ French manoeuvres

Lauriston's 112 gun battery

→ Austrian flank attack

- → Austrian retreat

1 Napoleon opened the 1805 campaign with a far larger army than he had previously commanded, outnumbering the enemy by 2:1 (map left). His Grande Armée carried little baggage, invading enemy territory at harvest time and marching far faster than the Austrians anticipated. Before they realized what was happening, the French had slipped past Ulm and Ferdinand's army was obliged to surrender.

2 At Austerlitz Napoleon tempted the cumbersome Austro–Russian army to attack his right flank, weakening its own centre (map above right). Napoleon broke through the middle of the Allied army, which broke up with 30 per cent losses. It was militarily and politically decisive: Austria sued for peace.

3 The Austrians demonstrated just how much they had improved at Wagram: although defeated by 6 July, with 45,000 casualties, it had been a 'near run thing' and Napoleon's loss of 34,000 cut deeply into the ranks of his veterans (map right). The Grande Armée would never be quite the same again.

1783
Battle of St Vincent: Sir John Jervis outmanoeuvred a Spanish fleet of superior numbers

28 May–1 June 1794
the Glorious First of June

14 February 1797
battle of St Vincent

21 October 1805
Battle of Trafalgar: Nelson's 27 ships against a 33-strong Franco–Spanish fleet; 18 Franco–Spanish ships were taken or sunk

Sea warfare in the 1790s underwent no revolution comparable to that ashore. Occasional battles and invasion scares punctuated years of blockade and privateering in a pattern familiar from the 1690s. A century of Anglo–French naval rivalry was about to reach a climax.

The French Revolution showed the irrelevance of the Nation in Arms concept to organizing a fleet in wartime. Eighty per cent of French naval officers emigrated, leaving ships and dockyards in chaos. France's main naval ally, Spain, could never recruit enough trained seamen to man her extensive inventory of well-constructed ships. Half-trained crews could not match the rapid broadsides of well-drilled British seamen-gunners. The Allies' tactical inferiority encouraged a preference for pursuing strategic aims while avoiding a decisive battle. The Glorious First of June (1 June 1794) appeared to justify this approach. The British had the better of the fighting, but the French secured a vital grain convoy, saving the Revolution.

The Battle of St Vincent (14 February 1797) underlined the tactical value of British seamanship. Sir John Jervis exploited a gap in a Spanish fleet to achieve local superiority of numbers. Outnumbered 2:1 overall, he captured four ships, breaking off the action before numbers began to tell. Nelson repeated Jervis' tactical concentration at the Nile, against a French squadron at anchor, reversing the strategic balance of power in the Mediterranean.

Atlantic Ocean

Ballinamuck 1796

To...

U N I T

Dublin
Liver

Bantry Bay 1796

K I N

Glorious First of June 28 May–1 June 1794

50

Plymouth
Port

Villeneuve's return from West Indies (July 1805) and failure to join French fleet at Brest

Isle de Groix 23 July 1795

21 Brest

Lorient
3

Belle Is. 17 July

Ferrrol squadron joins Channel fleet

Cape Finisterre 22 July 1805

Aix Roads 10–11 Apr. 1809

Rochefort

8

Ferrol **12**
Corunna

Bordeaux

Vigo

Santander
1813

P O R T U G A L

Douro

1807
Lisbon
Tagus

Madrid

S P A I N

Ebro

40

CAT
Bar

Madeira

Cape St Vincent 14 Feb 1797

6
Cadiz 12 July 1801
Cadiz
7
Gibraltar
British
Trafalgar 21 Oct. 1805
Algeciras 6 July 1801

Cartagena
6

M

Nelson's return from West Indies and junction with Channel fleet

1797 Canary Islands
Tenerife

M O R O C C O

A L

Trafalgar was the culmination of this series of British successes. Nelson concentrated all his 27 ships against 23 of the combined Franco-Spanish strength of 33. He attacked in two divisions to break the enemy line, cutting off the centre and rear. Eighteen Franco–Spanish ships were taken or sunk.

Napoleon's plan for the Trafalgar campaign was to concentrate his fleets in the West Indies. This threat to a vital economic region might draw off enough British ships to give the combined fleets numerical superiority in the Channel. However, Napoleon's naval forces lacked the Grande Armée's professionalism, and he did not allow for the greater friction of war at sea, with its variable weather and erratic communications. His subsequent attempt to return to the Mediterranean gave Nelson the chance to put an end to French strategic machinations, by destroying the French fleet in combat.

The Continental System was Napoleon's admission of defeat at sea. The extent of his empire allowed him to reverse the British blockade by excluding them from European ports. The British responded by developing markets outside Europe. Maritime supremacy brought prosperity. The British subsidized opposition to Napoleon, while mounting expeditions against the periphery of the empire, at Copenhagen, Sicily and Spain. The Royal Navy's aggressive combat strategy had given the British strategic freedom. The limited risk strategy of the French had lost them the ability to pursue even restricted strategic goals at sea.

1 naval warfare, 1791–1814

naval bases with numbers of operational battleships
- 9 French and Allies
- 6 Spanish

naval bases with date of occupation
- 1813 British

naval interventions ashore
- French
- British

naval movemets
- French
- British

naval actions
- French victory
- British victory
- Russian victory

8 British blockading squadrons, March 1805 with number of battleships

British naval concentration to cover English Channel, August 1805

direction of prevailing winds

1 The Revolution permanently weakened the French navy, which was further handicapped by spending most of its time in port. British squadrons, deployed to blockade enemy ports, maintained their efficiency, enabling the Royal Navy to take tactical risks unthinkable against the French navy of the mid-18th century.

the **peninsular war**

1808 to 1814

1808
British expeditionary force lands in Portugal

1809
John Moore dies at Corunna; British win at Oporto and Talavera

1810
Massena invades Portugal; Wellington holds the line at Torres Vedres

1811
Battle of Albuera (16 July)

1812
Battles of Ciudad Rodrigo, Salamanca (22 July) and Badajoz; Wellington forced back to Portugal (October)

1813
Battle of Vitoria effectively ends war

The Napoleonic military system failed comprehensively in Spain. The country is large, divided by mountain ranges that run across the path of a French invader. There was no agricultural surplus like that in Central Europe, meaning that large armies starved. Good roads were few, hampering strategic combinations. Fortresses like Badajoz and Ciudad Rodrigo dominated such communications as there were, and could not be bypassed, giving sieges an unusual significance. A conservative people, suspicious of outsiders, found ideals of liberty and fraternity unattractive, depriving the French of the political support they had received in Italy and Germany.

Elsewhere in Europe, occupation of the capital soon brought a country to order. Spanish central government was weak and local particularism ensured that resistance continued regardless of the fall of Madrid. Even so the centres of Spanish patriotic resistance would have fallen to French repression, or the more imaginative pacification measures pursued by Suchet in Catalonia, had it not been for British intervention.

1 Napoleon's attempt to impose his brother as King of Spain triggered a war of attrition in the peninsula (map left). Although Spanish field armies proved brittle, the French had little answer to the ensuing guerrilla war which pitted them against another nation in arms. The British exploited their maritime superiority to sustain an army ashore, a force poised to take advantage of French weakness when Napoleon invaded Russia.

Britain's army was small, but it stopped the French finally crushing the guerrillas. They in turn prevented the French concentrating against the British. The British commander Sir Arthur Wellesley, later Duke of Wellington, exploited British financial and maritime strength to organize a supply train of Spanish muleteers and feed his army. He avoided alienating the local population by foraging, as the French had done. When Napoleon withdrew his best troops for Russia, Wellington went on the offensive, using sea power to switch his base from Lisbon to ports in northern Spain.

Unlike Napoleon, Wellington did not depend on grand strategic combinations. His methods derived from an older tradition, based on direct control of formations by the commander. Like Frederick the Great, Wellington relied on his personal eye for country to exploit enemy mistakes. Marmont had outmanoeuvred him in July 1812, forcing Wellington to retreat from Tordesillas on Salamanca. As the two armies raced side by side for a strategic river crossing, Wellington detected a gap in the French column, isolating their leading division. Within minutes he had organized an overwhelming attack on the head of the French column, not dissimilar to Frederick's demolition of the Austrian left at Leuthen. At Salamanca, however, both armies were moving, showing how dynamic battlefields had become with the general adoption of the divisional system.

Wellington had not cut off Marmont's retreat, so his victory was less decisive than Napoleon's strategic masterpieces at Marengo or Jena. Despite his humiliating defeat, Marmont was able to regroup his army and drive Wellington back to the Portuguese frontier in October 1812. Wellington lacked Napoleon's unlimited reserves of manpower, so he could never risk throwing his army across the enemy's rear. He depended on a Frederician strategy of attrition to wear down French strength, assisted by the country and the guerrillas.

2 battle of albuera, 16 may 1811

Anglo-Portuguese troops
◻ ◪ initial positions
◻ ◪ final positions
◻ Spanish troops
French troops
◼ ◪ initial positions
◼ ◪ final positions
- - -▶ approach march
━━▶ turning movement
━━▶ retreat

diversion by one French brigade

Albuera

Ohicapierna

Nogales

Soult's turning movement by three brigades

N

0   1 km
0   1 mile

2 Marshal Soult's attempt to raise the siege of Badajoz was bloodily repulsed at Albuera (map above), but not before French cavalry had wiped out one British infantry brigade and driven off much of the Spanish contingent.

3 At Salamanca, Wellington duped the French into attacking in the mistaken belief he was retreating (map right). Marmont's army was caught out by the British assault; he and his successor were both wounded and the leaderless French army disintegrated.

3 battle of salamanca, 22 july 1812

Anglo-Portuguese troops
━━▶ lines of attack
- - -▶ concealed march of Pakenham's division and two cavalry brigades
French troops
- - -▶ approach march
━━▶ counter attacks
⬭▶ final position and retreat

Salamanca

Santa Marta

Calvarrasa de Abajo

Carbajosa

Calvarrasa de Arriba

Aldea Tejada

Las Torres

Lesser Arapil

Los Arapiles

Greater Arapil

N

0   2 km
0   2 miles

1 the peninsular war, 1808–14

✹ Spanish insurrections, May 1808
   spread of Spanish revolt
🏰 Spanish fortress
🏰 Portuguese fortress
🚩 French garrisons, 1808
- - - Moore's campaign, 1808–9
▪▪▪ line of Torres Vedras
▬ approximate extent of French control, January 1812
━━▶ Wellington's campaign, 1813–14

battles and sieges
✕ British victory
✕ French victory (discounting numerous defeats of smaller Spanish units)
✕ Spanish victory

1812
Napoleon invades Russia (7 June); battle of Borodino (7 September); retreat from Moscow (begins 19 October); disastrous French crossing of Berezina (26–28 November)

1813
Battle of Lützen (2 May); battle of Bautzen (20 May); Napoleon defeats allies at Dresden (26 August); Napoleon defeated at 'Battle of the Nations' at Leipzig (16–19 October)

1814
The "five days" (10–14 February); Allies enter Paris (30 March); Napoleon abdicates and is exiled to Elba.

1815
Napoleon lands in France (1 March). 'Hundred Days' begins; Waterloo campaign (11–21 June); battles of Ligny, Quatre-Bras and Waterloo; Napoleon abdicates for second time (22 June)

All the factors that vitiated Napoleon's war in Spain applied in Russia. After two months his forces had lost 150,000 men from sickness and desertion. The Russians, aware of Napoleon's weaknesses, ordered a lengthy retreat, leading the Grande Armée into the infamous long marches, which sapped their strength.

The Battle of Borodino (7 September 1812) marked the climactic point of 20 years of Revolutionary and Napoleonic violence. The Russians lost more men at Borodino than any other modern army suffered in one action, until the first day of the Somme in July 1916. Nevertheless, the battle failed to shake the Russians' resolve. The French had no alternative but retreat.

The battle of Maloyaroslavets persuaded Napoleon to withdraw by the Smolensk road, which had been swept bare of supplies during the advance. Fresh Russian forces, released from the South after peace with Turkey, threatened Napoleon's line of retreat, preventing him from wintering at Smolensk. The Cossacks prevented the French resting or dispersing to forage, while infuriated peasants murdered French stragglers. The Grande Armée's veteran cadres were lost.

Napoleon rejoined the remnants of the Grande Armée in April 1813. His last campaign in Germany began with a string of classic victories. The next 12 months, however, saw the initiative pass to his enemies. The Allies, recognizing Napoleon's superior battlefield skills, concentrated against his subordinates. Gradually the Allies closed the circle around Napoleon, who fell back on Leipzig.

Understanding how Napoleon's military success at Ulm, Jena and Wagram had depended on their political disunity, the Allies realized that, acting together, they could achieve numerical superiority without adopting radical ideas about the Nation in Arms. In the brief Waterloo campaign (11–21 June 1815) Napoleon took the initiative, invading Belgium to knock out his most inveterate

1 the retreat from moscow, 1812

- French troop concentrations, October 1812
- Russian troop concentrations, October 1812
- ■ French supply depot
- ✕ French tactical success
- ✕ Russian tactical sucess

French movements to
- ⟶ 14 November
- ⤍ ⤍ 21 November
- ⋯⋯ 14 December

Russian movements to
- ⟶ 14 November
- ⤍ ⤍ 21 November
- ⋯⋯⟶ 14 December

Riga under siege
ESSEN 14,000 men
MACDONALD 25,000 men
STEINGELL 13,000 men
10,000 men 14 Dec.
Dvina
Ney crosses frontier 14 Dec.
Dvinsk
Drissa
WITTGENSTEIN 40,000 men
Tilsit
12,000 men 5 Dec.
R U S S I A N
Kovno
Neris
Polotsk
18–19 Nov.
ST CYR 25,000 men
Vitebsk
87,000 men 2 Nov.
NAPOLEON 95,000 men - 29 Oct.
Moscow
Borodino
Mozhaisk
Moskva
Vilna 9 Dec.
Smorgoni
Berezina 26–28 Nov.
VICTOR 37,000 men
Vyazma (Russian road block) 3 Nov.
Tsarevo
PRUSSIA
Napoleon abandons army
Maledechno
Smolensk
Orsha
Tarutino 18 Oct.
Maloyaroslavets 24 Oct.
Grodno
Nieman
Borisov
Krasnoi (Russian road block) 15–17 Nov.
KUTUZOV 110,000 men
first snow 4 Nov.
Minsk
Mohilev
37,000 men 9 Nov.
Kaluga
Lomza
Belostok
Berezina
E M P I R E
Napoleon burns pontoons
Desna
Oka
Volkovysk
GRAND DUCHY OF WARSAW
TCHITCHAGOV 38,000 men
Bobruisk
Dnieper
50,000 men 21 Nov.

1 The Russians forced Napoleon to retreat over the route of his original advance after he evacuated the smouldering ruins of the Russian capital. The countryside had already been stripped bare and his soldiers found nothing left to plunder. Foraging parties fell prey to Cossack patrols that hovered like vultures around the French columns.

enemies, the Prussians and the British. Outnumbered almost 2:1, Napoleon naturally tried to seize a central position between them. Napoleon's attempts to drive the Allies apart caused the double battle of Ligny/Quatrebras. One wing of the French held off Wellington, while Napoleon tried to crush Blücher. However, the Prussians were allowed to retreat and joined Wellington. The late Prussian arrival at Waterloo proved decisive. The appearance of the Prussians drew off Napoleon's reserve, leaving no infantry to support Ney's cavalry charges against the British centre. Blücher's flank march gave him the central position. He used his interior position to extend Wellington's left flank and to envelop Napoleon's right. The direction of the Prussian advance combined with Wellington's pursuit of the columns of Old Guard to precipitate a rout, decisively ending one of the few truly revolutionary periods in the history of war.

2 the battle of the nations, 16–19 oct 1813

→ Allied movements, 16 Oct.
→ French movements, 16 Oct.
⇢ Allied advances, 18 Oct.
⇢ French breakout, 18 Oct.

3 battle of ligny and quatrebras, 17 june 1815

▦ Anglo–Dutch advance Guard
▦ Prussian corps
▦ French corps

→ Allied counter attacks
⇢ French attacks afternoon / evening
⇢ D'Erlons counter march

2 Leipzig was the largest battle of the Napoleonic wars, on a scale that even the Emperor could not control (top right). Some 185,000 French and allied troops held off nearly 300,000 Russian, Austrian, Prussian and Swedish soldiers until the premature demolition of the Lindenau bridge turned a fighting retreat into disaster. French losses were around 30,000 with another 30,000 captured; their opponents lost over 50,000 men.

3 At the twin battles of Quatrebras and Ligny, Napoleon sought to crush the Prussians while Marshal Ney dealt with the British advance guard (middle right). The Prussians were beaten and withdrew, but Ney's assault at Quatrebras was too late in the day to be decisive.

4 From his headquarters at La Belle Alliance, Napoleon could see little of the British position (bottom right). Clumsy infantry tactics and the frittering away of a whole corps in the battle for Hougomont left Napoleon exposed to the Prussian flank attack that afternoon. Too late, he flung his Imperial Guard into a final assault on the British, only to see it broken.

4 battle of la belle alliance, 18 june 1815

▦ Anglo–Dutch corps
▦ Prussian corps
▦ French corps

⇢ Prussian approach and attack
⇢ British reserves

the **crimean war**

The Tsar's ambitions in the Balkans culminated in a Russian naval attack on a much weaker Turkish squadron at Sinop (30 November 1853). Newly developed shell guns caused a 'massacre', and inspired an Anglo–French alliance to keep the Russian fleet out of the Eastern Mediterranean. Their natural war aim was to destroy the Russian Navy's dockyard at Sebastopol in the Crimea, although there were subsidiary operations in the Baltic and White Sea.

The Allies could nourish their forces from the sea, while the Russians withered at the end of lengthy land communications. Fleets provided superior operational mobility, transporting Allied armies directly across the Black Sea, before Russian troops on the Danube could reach the Crimea on foot. It was impossible to blockade Russia, but Allied gunboats interdicted coastal traffic through the Sea of Azov which sustained Russian forces in the Crimea. Improving communications had other consequences. The telegraph paralysed French commanders with contradictory orders from Paris. Newspapers inflamed public war fever, spurred governments to ill-considered action, and compromised operational security. The world's first war correspondent (William Howard Russell) made the British Commander-in-Chief a scapegoat for governmental neglect and muddle, but did heighten awareness of the human cost of war.

Crimean battles failed to match Napoleonic paradigms of brilliant manoeuvre or decisive success. All arms coordination was poor. Battles became slogging matches where increased firepower swelled casualty lists.

The Alma saw the first major use of muzzle-loading rifles in battle. The Allied monopoly of the Minié rifle sufficed, with a 3:2 superiority of numbers, to drive the Russians out of a strong defensive position in a frontal attack. The Allies lacked transport and cavalry to move inland to envelop the Russians, or mount an effective pursuit. The Russians took shelter behind improvised defences at Sebastopol, armed them with guns from the Russian fleet, and baffled the Allied armies for almost a year. Rifle pits and earthworks thrown up by Sebastopol's civilian population proved more effective than formal defences. Trench warfare had made its unwelcome début. Mutual attrition was costly. The Royal Navy landed 140 32-pr guns during the siege: 32 were destroyed, and 73 condemned as worn out. Crowding large numbers of men together caused heavy losses from disease.

Battles at Balaklava (25 October 1854), Inkerman (24 October 1854) and the Traktir Bridge (16 August 1855) underlined the Russian inability to face Allied firepower in the open. At

1 battle of the alma, 20 sept. 1854

☐ Russian	vineyards
☐ British	battery entrenched
▨ French	battery in open
☐ Turkish	

line of retreat to Sebastopol

N

Bourliouk

Alma

Alma

Almatamak

Black Sea

0 — 1000 metres
0 — 1000 yards

1 Little changed from 1812, the Russian army occupied a strong position at the Alma which it defended with traditional stubbornness (map left). Russian counter-attacks drove back part of the British army, but many Allied regiments had muzzle-loading rifles which gave them a tremendous advantage. The Russians withdrew after serious casualties, but the numerically weak Allied cavalry failed to convert retreat into rout.

Transylvanian Alps

WALLACHI

Bucharest

Oltenitza
4 Nov. 1854
Silistria

Ma
18.

Shumen

BULGARIA

Taganrog

Berdyansk

**Allied naval operations
cut Russian supply lines
Jun 1855**

Sea of Azov

1853

ug 1854

Odessa

Kinburn

Dnieper

Inhulets'

Dniester

22 Apr 1854   16 Oct 1855

Mar 1854

Danube

**Russian
reinforcements
Oct 1854**

Arabat

Kertsch

Kuban'

**Feb
1854**

Eupatoria
17 Feb 1855

**Alma
20 Sep 1854**

Simferopol

**Sebastopol
May 1855**

Nov 1854

Balaklava

25 May 1855

7–13 Sep 1854

B L A C K   S E A

C a u c a s u s

Nov 1853

Sinop Nov 1853

Batum

E M P I R E

ul

32°

36°

40°

2   the black sea, 1853–55

- → Allied troop movements
- ⛵ Allied naval bombardments
- → Russian offensives
- ⚡ arrival of telegraph

battles
- ✕ Allied victory
- ✕ Russian victory
- ✕ Turkish victory

sieges
- ⬤ Allied
- ⬤ Russian

---

2 In 1853 Britain and France declared war on Russia following a dispute about who had custody over the Christian Holy Places in Ottoman-ruled Palestine (map above). Though the Anglo–French force was poorly equipped and undermined by disease and inter-allied squabbles, the Russian forces proved even more incompetent. Russian defeats at Balaklava and Inkerman in 1854 opened the way to the loss of the Black Sea base of Sebastopol in 1855. By highlighting Russian weaknesses, the war led to widespread reforms.

3 Unable completely to invest the port, the Allies fell back on traditional siege warfare, with the heaviest guns yet seen (map right). However, Russian earthworks proved very resilient and their defenders resolute. The Russian army's attempt to relieve the siege was beaten off in a battle most famous for the Charge of the Light Brigade and the 'Thin Red Line'.

Balaklava their cavalry refused to charge a single battalion armed with the new rifle. Inkerman was fought in a fog, but edged weapons caused only six per cent of the casualties. In the sixth and final bombardment, 183 Allied guns and mortars fired 28,176 rounds in three days, an unprecedented display of firepower. Russian casualties exceeded 1,000 a day, before the Malakoff redoubt fell, persuading the Russians to evacuate Sebastopol's smoking ruins (8–9 September 1855). The Allies had won, but their armies only left the Crimea after another seven months of naval and diplomatic pressure, including the first use of ironclad warships to bombard Kinburn (16 October 1855).

Sebastopol Harbour

N

Sebastopol

**MALAKOFF
MAMELON**

REDAN

*original
French attack*

*British
attack*

*decisive French
attack on Malakoff*

✕ Inkerman 5 Nov 1854

Tchernaya

*from Kamlesch
Bay*

*French
headquarters*

*British
headquarters*

*charge of the
Light Brigade*

*Traktir
Bridge*

*charge of the
Heavy Brigade*

**The Tchernaya
16 Aug 1855**

*93rd
Highlanders*

Kadikoi

Balaclava

*Marine
Heights*

Black Sea

0   2 kms
0   2 miles

3   the siege of sebastopol, oct. 1854–sept. 1855

- ▢ Russian
- ▢ British
- ▢ French
- ↯→ cavalry charges 25 Oct 1854
- ⚏ battery

Nationalism posed a particular threat to the multinational army of the Habsburg empire, the antithesis of a Nation in Arms. In 1858 France allied with Sardinia, the largest independent Italian state, to drive the Austrians from the peninsula.

Bonapartist mythology had helped the Emperor's nephew, Napoleon III, seize power. Like his uncle he needed to win a quick victory, but feared the Austrian army at Milan might overrun the outnumbered Sardinians before the French arrived. Steam power resolved both problems. Steamships carried French troops to Genoa. Other units went by rail to the foot of the Alps, and marched to the Sardinian railhead, pre-empting a plodding Austrian advance on Turin.

The Austrians fell back, thinking Napoleon III would envelop their left. Instead he turned to their right, boldly transferring his army 60 miles across the Austrian front by rail. Napoleon III achieved a double first, using railways not only to move his army to the theatre of war but to outmanoeuvre the enemy.

The Austrians retreated to the Ticino, where they surprised the Allies by defending the river line, although French troops had already crossed further north. The result was an asymmetrical battle, fought astride the Ticino. Neither side's losses were decisive, but the Austrian Corps withdrew eccentrically, unlike the Prussians after Ligny, becoming too scattered to resume action the next day.

The soldiers on both sides were conscripts, but many French soldiers re-engaged, becoming long-service professionals. Austrian recruits served only a short time. Their battlefield performance reflected this, with losses of only a twelfth reducing Austrian units to hopeless disorder. Men from non-German regiments deserted in droves. Both sides used muzzle-loading rifles, but masses of fruit trees obscured the battlefield and limited their effect. Austrian reservists only received their rifles on the way to the front. They did not know how to load, let alone compensate for the weapon's high trajectory when aiming. French tactics speeded up to counteract the increased fire power of rifles. French light infantry, Chasseurs and Zouaves, became shock troops, closing rapidly with the enemy to avoid their fire effect.

1 The campaign in lombardy, 19 may–2 july 1859

advances
- - -> French concentration, 28 April–8 May
——> Allied turning movement, 28 May–3 June and advance through Lombardy after Magenta
——> Garibaldi's operations and Sardinian advance to contact, 24 June
——> Austrian advance to contact, 2–4 June and 23–4 June
- - -> advance of French V Corps from Tuscany, 27 June–2 July
▯ Austrian fort

Valle di Susa

Turin

45

army positions, 19 May
Sardinian
French
Austrian

army positions, 23 June
Sardinian
French
Austrian

battles
✕ French victory
✕ Sardinian victory
✕ Austrian victory

2 The French infantry did not just rely on the Minié rifle, but on dash and élan: in sad contrast to the Austrian army whose non-German regiments tended to melt away at indecent speed. The Austrian attempt to crush the French bridgehead over the Ticino collapsed in the face of furious counter-attacks. The eventual arrival of the French flanking force led the Austrians to break off the action (map right).

2 Battle of Magenta, 3–4 june 1859

corps concentrations
French   Austrian

French advances
⇒ to 3 June
⇒ to 1400 hours 4 June
- - ⇒ 1600–1800 hours 4 June
⇒ Austrian advances

Castano
Buscate
Turbigo
II
Inveruno
Cuggiono
Ticino
Marcallo
Buffalora
I
II   Magenta
VII
Robecco
part of French III/IV corps from Novara, afternoon 4 June to reinforce the Guards
III/IV
GUARDS
Trecate
N
VII
III
Abbiategrasso

0 ————— 5000 metres
0 ————— 5000 yards

When the Austrians launched a counter-offensive to catch the Allies off balance at Solferino, the monolithic Allied deployment made a frontal 'soldier's battle' inevitable. Napoleon III went forward promptly. Austrian corps commanders failed to support their own brigades, let alone each other. The ground was open, allowing the French to use their new rifled field guns effectively for the first time. Massed in the Napoleonic style, they overpowered Austrian smooth-bore batteries before they came into action.

With moderate advantages in generalship and weaponry, aggressive French regulars smashed the Austrian centre at Solferino in a typical Napoleonic central breakthrough. The defeated army escaped over the Mincio. Casualties in the largest battle since Leipzig shocked the two emperors into agreeing peace terms.

1 The French army was the first to effect a strategic concentration by steam-power: shipping part of the army to Genoa while the other travelled by rail. Once in Lombardy, the French outflanked the Austrians with another rail move, forcing them back to the river Ticino (map below). Defeated at Magenta, the Austrians fell back, reaching the Mincio before counter-attacking on 24 June. Throughout the campaign, the Austrians were handicapped by the poor training of their conscripts who only received their new rifles on their way to the front.

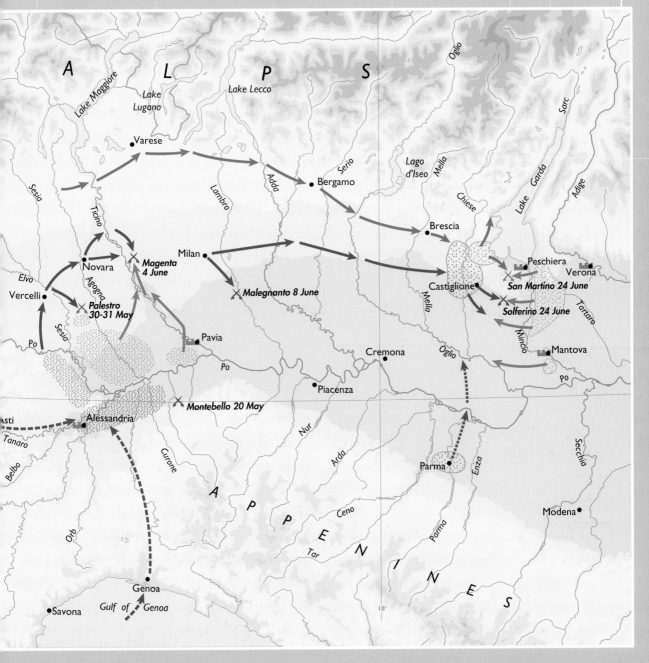

the **franco-prussian** war

1870 to 1871

1870
France declares war on Prussia (19 July); battle of Fröschwiller (6 August); French defeats at Vionville (16 August), Gravelotte (18 August); battle of Sedan (1 September); Prussian forces encircle Paris; siege begins (19 September); Strasbourg surrenders to Prussians (28 October); battle of Coulmiers (9 November)

1871
Paris surrenders (28 January); Peace of Frankfurt, France cedes Alsace-Lorraine to Germany (10 May)

Prussia's destruction of the army of the French Second Empire in the summer of 1870 began a new military era. Helmut von Moltke was chief of Prussian General Staff. His victory was strategic, for French tactics, morale and weapons were in many respects superior to those of the Germans.

Moltke used railways to occupy broad defensive positions, which served as jumping-off points for a converging invasion of France's eastern provinces. Allied forces from South Germany increased his numerical superiority: 450,000 against 180,000. Moltke laid down the general order of advance, leaving its execution to Army and Corps commanders, guided by their staff. Their movements led to a series of battles that the high command may not have intended but which they could exploit to their advantage. French commanders, starved of initiative by an over-centralized Napoleonic command style, failed to support each other.

The battle of Fröschwiller (6 August 1870) set the tactical pattern of the war. The French held a magnificent position, with splendid fields of fire for their Chassepot rifles, but the Germans trumped them with superior artillery. German frontal attacks and artillery fire pinned down the French, until neighbouring corps enclosed the French cen-

2 battle of fröschwiller, 6 aug 1870

- French
- German
- French charges
- German advances

2 The first major action set the pattern: Prussian infantry attacks were pressed home with great gallantry, supported by their powerful artillery (map left). Fierce French counter-attacks collapsed in the face of unprecedented firepower and the army retreated. Recriminations followed, with accusations of betrayal in the air. Within weeks, the cries of 'to Berlin' seemed very hollow.

re in a circle of fire. Some French infantry units lost three-quarters of their numbers in ferocious counter-attacks. The French rifle outranged the Dreyse, but German skirmish lines presented a dispersed target allowing them to close the range without disproportionately heavy losses.

French commanders were intellectually ill-prepared to command armies far larger than the corps they had led previously, and lacked effec-ive staffs to help them. The weight of responsibility paralysed the experienced Marshal Bazaine, who allowed his army to be surrounded at Metz. The Paris government ordered Marshal MacMahon, hero of Magenta, to relieve Bazaine with a turning movement that exposed his own communications. Moltke exploited his central position between the two Marshals to concentrate against MacMahon, forcing him to surrender at Sedan. MacMahon's predictable destruction shows the dangers of political demands that ignore military realities.

A republican government seized power after Sedan, with a conscious appeal to the Nation in Arms. By the end of the war the French had called up as many men as the Germans. However, French numbers proved no substitute for skill in raising the German siege of Paris. Past besieging forces had been vulnerable to attack by relieving forces. Now the tactical superiority of the defence, coordinated by telegraph, allowed the Germans to defeat separate attacks launched from unoccupied French territory. At Coulmiers, the only French victory of the war, the defeated Bavarians escaped with limited casualties, despite French superiority of numbers of more than 3:1.

The people of Paris and Strasbourg suffered starvation and bombardment. However, Bismarck limited his political ends, unlike Napoleon Bonaparte, who had threatened the very existence of his enemies.

1 Duped into declaring war by Bismarck, Napoleon III was told by his generals that the campaign could last a hundred years and they wouldn't need so much as a gaiter button. The truth was sadly different: French organization was such an oxymoron that 'muddling through' was a celebrated virtue. Their better-prepared opponents fielded an army twice the size, with breech-loading artillery that dominated the battlefields (map below).

1 the invasion of france, july 1870–january 1871

German armies, July 1870
French armies, July 1870
German advances, Aug-Sep 1870
German sieges
German armies, Nov. 1870–Jan 1871
German advances against Republican forces
German victory
French victory
French railways used by Germans

the **american civil war I**

1861
Major Robert Anderson surrenders Fort Sumter (13 April); Confederate victory at First Bull Run (21 July); blockade of South begins (July)

1862
Nashville falls to Union forces (25 February); Confederacy moves troops from Charleston, Mobile and New Orleans to surprise Grant at Shiloh (6 April); 'Stonewall' Jackson forces Union forces back across Potomac (May); battle of Antietam (17 September); Confederate victory at Fredericksburg (11–15 December)

1863
Lee defeats Hooker at battle of Chancellorsville (2–4 May); Grant's victorious Vicksburg campaign (May); Confederates defeated at battle of Gettysburg (1–3 July)

The Civil War was an ideological conflict, releasing deep antagonisms on both sides, fought across vast distances with poor communications. The improvised armies had similar weapons and levels of training, so neither side had a qualitative edge. Tactical equality and the defensive power of modern weapons forced both sides to entrench as thoroughly as had the Romans. American infantry learned to fight in open order, and avoid frontal attacks.

2 General Robert E. Lee led the Army of Northern Virginia from 1862–65, seldom passing up an opportunity to attack despite his numerical inferiority (map below). Chancellorsville was his most impressive victory: Lee divided his already outnumbered army to strike Hooker's army in the flank and drive it from the field. Tragically, his brilliant subordinate 'Stonewall' Jackson was killed at the moment of triumph, shot by mistake by a Confederate piquet.

2 battle of chancellorsville, 1–6 may 1863

- Confederate armies
- Union armies
- Confederate trenches
- Union trenches

The Union outnumbered the Confederacy overall, but the rebels' interior position allowed them to concentrate their smaller forces against successive Union attacks. Railways were essential lines of communication in the undeveloped South, where roads did not exist, and the cotton/tobacco-based agriculture was unable to sustain large armies from local resources. Civil War generals used railways to mount strategic concentrations far more ambitious than those attempted in Europe. In 1862, the Confederacy succeeded in moving troops 500 miles from Charleston, Mobile and New Orleans to surprise Grant at Shiloh.

The Battle of Chancellorsville (2–4 May 1863) epitomized Lee's methods. Although acting on the strategic defensive, Lee assumed the tactical offensive in response to Union advances on the Confederate capital Richmond, uncomfortably close to the frontline. Always outnumbered, Lee made maximum use of the defensive superiority of entrenched riflemen to free sufficient forces for his offensive counter-moves. He could conceal his movements in the tangled woods of North Virginia, but the boldness of his plan bordered on the reckless. The collapse of the Union commander's morale shows how a battle lost is a battle believed to have been lost. When Hooker ordered his troops to retreat, Lee's advance was faltering, while Union troops at Fredericksburg had driven back the Confederate covering force. In the absence of wireless communications, the success of an enveloping manoeuvre depended on inspired cooperation, in this case between Lee and 'Stonewall' Jackson. His death at Chancellorsville destroyed a battle-winning team, and may have cost the Confederacy the Battle of Gettysburg (1–3 July 1863).

The stalemate in the East was broken by General Ulysses S. Grant. Grant had shown a willingness to take risks in the Vicksburg campaign that baffled less able opponents. Against Lee, in the more confined spaces of North Virginia, Grant's tactics resulted in a series of bloody battles. In a month's fighting (3 May–3 June 1864), both armies lost half their strength. Grant then changed his line of operations, transferring his army across

1 the war in the east, 1861–63

PENSLYVANIA

Carlisle

Chambersburg

Gettysburg
1–3 July 1863

Cumberland

Hagerstown

WEST VIRGINIA

Antietam
17 Sep. 1862

Martinsburg

Harpers
Ferry

Frederick

Baltimore

MARYLAND

Kernstown
23 Mar. 1862

Winchester
25 May
1862

Leesburg

Moorefield

Strasburg

Front
Royal

Shenandoah Mountains

Shenandoah

Cacapon

Potomac

Washington

Alexandria

1st Battles of Manassas
21 July 1861
2nd Battle of Manassas
29–30 Aug. 1862

McDowell
8 May
1862

Harrisonburg

Cross Keys
8 June 1862

Port Republic
9 June 1862

Chancellorville
1–6 May 1863

Fredericksburg

Patuxent

Spotsylvania

Fredericksburg
13 Dec. 1862

Potomac

Rappahannock

Chesapeake Bay

Staunton

Gordonsville

Charlottesville

B L U E R I D G E M T S

James

North Anna

VIRGINIA

South Anna

Mattaponi

Gaines Mill
27 June 1862

Mechanicsville
26 June 1862

Richmond

West Point

Malvern Mill
1 July 1862

Petersburg

Harrison's
Landing

Williamsburg

Yorktown

Blackwater

James

Fort Monroe

Nottoway

Norfolk

1. The proximity of the two capitals led both sides to field their largest armies in the East (map right). Union maritime superiority enabled their armies to base themselves at the mouth of the James River in 1862 and 1864. The Shenandoah had a dual role: as a 'back door' to the North, it was the springboard for several Southern offensives; it was also the 'bread-basket' of the South until Sheridan laid it to waste.

Culpeper

GRANT
118,000 men

Wilderness
5–6 May

Rapidan

LEE
64,000 men

Fredericksburg

Potomac

3 The wilderness and the james river, 4 may–18 june 1864

✕ Confederate victory
✕ Union victory
〰 defensive lines
═ Union cavalry
🚂 troop movements by sea

Spotsylvania
9–19 May

North Anna
23–26 May

Yellow Tavern
11 May

Cold Harbour
3 June

Pamunkey

Richmond

White
House

Rappahannock

N

Drewry's Bluff
15 May

Butler's bridgehead
at Bermuda Hundred
and attempts to break
out 5–16 May

Williamsburg

Petersburg

Petersburg 15–18 June

bridge built
14 June

James

3. Hopelessly outnumbered, Lee resisted the onslaught by digging in and by a number of fierce counter-attacks, but the Army of the Potomac was now directed by a general of equally great determination and infinitely greater resources (map left). Grant bulldozed his way to Richmond and laid siege to Petersburg too. Casualties soared, but Sherman's timely capture of Atlanta helped Lincoln win the election. There would be no compromise peace.

the James River to cut Richmond's rail communications with the rest of the Confederacy. He prepared this major engineering feat in such secrecy that Lee did not know of the operation until six days after it began. Friction narrowly prevented Grant winning the war at a stroke. The leading Union column stopped short of the vital rail-way junction at Petersburg before Confederate reinforcements arrived. The stalemated armies settled in for a nine-month siege.

the **american civil war II**

1863
Battle of Chickamauga (19 September); Grant defeats Confederates at Chattanooga (23–25 November); siege of Knoxville (November–December)

1864
Grant's Wilderness Campaign (May); battle of Cold Harbor (31 May–12 June); battle of Mobile Bay (5 August); Sherman's Atlanta Campaign (August); Atlanta surrenders (1 September); Sherman's March to the Sea (November)

1865
Sherman marches through North and South Carolina (February); Grant breaks through Confederate lines around Richmond(March); Lee evacuates Richmond (2 April); Army of North Virginia surrenders at Appomattox Courthouse (9 April)

By 1862 a third of the US army was acting as an occupation force. Like other belligerents unable to occupy enemy territory effectively, the US army resorted to raids. The most spectacular was Sherman's march through Georgia to the sea. This not only inflicted economic damage on the areas traversed, but disrupted the railways that supplied Confederate armies.

Sherman realized he was fighting a hostile people, and deliberately made them feel the hard hand of war. Sherman's superior numbers and his willingness to feed them from the countryside achieved astonishing strategic mobility. He turned successive Confederate positions between Chattanooga and Atlanta, and by the end of the war had carried his army to Raleigh in North Carolina.

1 The Confederacy underwent a government-led industrial revolution during the war, but its economy was slowly strangled (map right). Imports were choked off as the US Navy seized its ports and Union forces controlled the Mississippi. Internal communications relied on a ramshackle rail net that was soon exposed to Union cavalry raids and ultimately ripped up by Sherman's army on its march to the sea. Conversely, the Union war economy was so powerful it was exporting weapons and even building battleships to foreign accounts during the war.

1 the destruction of the s

Union advances
← Grant's campaign in the west and Virginia
← Rosecran, Jan.–Sep. 1863
← Sherman, May 1864– Mar. 1865

2 The Confederates converted the hulk of the steam frigate *Merrimack* into an ironclad ram, intended to raise the blockade of Norfolk. Hopes that it might raid New York would never have been realized, her ancient powerplant and shallow freeboard restricting her to coastal waters, but she met her match in the bizarre shape of the *Monitor* off Hampton Roads on 9 March (map right). The *Merrimack's* short life ended when Norfolk was abandoned by the Confederates: drawing too much water to escape up the James, she had to be blown up.

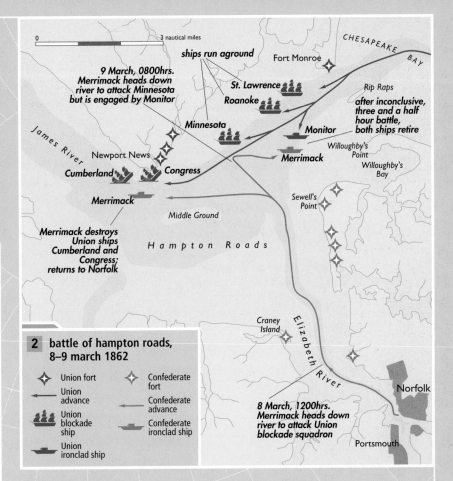

0   3 nautical miles

CHESAPEAKE BAY

Fort Monroe

ships run aground

St. Lawrence

Roanoke

Rip Raps

9 March, 0800hrs. Merrimack heads down river to attack Minnesota but is engaged by Monitor

Minnesota

Monitor

after inconclusive, three and a half hour battle, both ships retire

James River

Newport News

Merrimack

Willoughby's Point

Willoughby's Bay

Cumberland

Congress

Merrimack

Middle Ground

Sewell's Point

Merrimack destroys Union ships Cumberland and Congress; returns to Norfolk

H a m p t o n R o a d s

Craney Island

Elizabeth River

Norfolk

2 battle of hampton roads, 8–9 march 1862

✦ Union fort

◇ Confederate fort

← Union advance

← Confederate advance

🚢 Union blockade ship

🛳 Confederate ironclad ship

🛳 Union ironclad ship

8 March, 1200hrs. Merrimack heads down river to attack Union blockade squadron

Portsmouth

VANIA

NEW JERSEY

MARYLAND

DELAWARE

Washington

Chesapeake Bay

Sheridan Aug–Oct 1864

GINIA

Richmond

Hampton Roads ✕ 8–9 Mar. 1862

Petersburg June 1864–Apr 1865

...erate ...er

...mattox, ...865

Roanoke I. 1862

Raleigh

Fort Hatteras 1862

ROLINA

Fort Macon 26 Apr. 1862

Fort Fisher 13–15 Jan. 1865

r.

Wilmington

Fort Sumter 15 Jan. 1865 ...harleston

ATLANTIC OCEAN

...ulaski ...v. 1861

...1 Mar. 1862

St Augustine 9 Mar. 1862

◀--- Union naval attacks

← Union raids

← Confederate raids

Savannah Confderate blockade running ports

battles

✕ Union victory

✕ Confederate victory

sieges

✵ Union siege

✳ Confederate siege

The Confederacy was industrially weak, exchanging agricultural produce for foreign manufactured goods, including weapons. It was therefore vulnerable to naval blockade. Lack of roads and guerrilla raids on railways made rivers the most attractive lines of communication in the West.

Like the contemporary Royal Navy, The US Navy had command of the sea, which it exploited by supporting land operations along the coast and great rivers, or strangling the Southern economy through blockade. The US Navy carried Grant across the James River, linked up with Sherman at Savannah, and took the Atlantic coastal forts, to enforce the seaborne blockade. Significant naval actions arose from these activities. A Confederate attempt to lift the blockade of the James River led to the first clash between armoured warships at Hampton Roads. One of them, the *USS Monitor*, mounted two big guns in a revolving turret, a revolutionary design giving a flexible arc of fire, independent of the vessel's movement. The Battle of Mobile Bay confirmed the difficulty of sinking armoured ships by gunfire or ramming. The sinking of USS *Tecumseh* by a mine, however, suggested one antidote to armoured ships.

Mobile Bay sealed off the last Southern port, not long before Sherman began his 'March to the Sea', but the collapse of the Confederate armies in the field overtook the Union's economic strategy. Grant's efforts to turn Lee's flanks at Petersburg covered the front with 37 miles of trenches. When Grant broke through the attenuated Confederate lines in March 1865, Lee was unable to disengage. American cavalry had never aspired to a battlefield role, but adopted the rifle to pursue strategic raids and reconnaissance. Dismounted action by Sheridan's cavalry delayed Lee's retreat long enough for Union infantry to force the Army of North Virginia to surrender at Appomattox (9 April 1865).

the **russo-turkish** war

1877 to 1878

1877
Russia declares war on Ottoman Empire (24 April); 150,000 Russians cross the middle Danube (June); siege of Plevna (July–December)

1878
Unratified Treaty of San Stefano (March) gives Russians extensive gains, largely reversed by Treaty of Berlin (July)

Russia invaded the Turkish Empire in 1877 to protect Bulgaria's Christians against their Muslim rulers, but underestimated Turkish resistance. They mobilized insufficient forces, turning a peace-keeping operation into a major war.

Turkish command of the Black Sea since 1855 forced the Russians to advance inland, over the River Danube and the Balkan mountains. Communications were poor. The single-track Romanian railway system north of the Danube was useless for troop movements. Bulgaria was economically backward, with appalling roads. Nevertheless, the Russians crossed the middle Danube with 150,000 men in June 1877. The Russians believed that the mere appearance of their troops south of the Balkans would terrify the Sultan into giving up Bulgaria. Count Gourko led 30,000 men across the mountains in a daring raid, creating panic in Istanbul. Turkish armies on either flank of the Russian advance were undefeated, however, while reinforcements poured into Thrace by sea. When Osman Pasha marched from Vidin to Plevna (Pleven), threatening the Danube bridgeheads, he threw the whole Russian army on to the defensive. The Russians had occupied a huge salient, 180 miles across, its most advanced point at the Shipka Pass. They could not retreat without exposing Christian Bulgarians to unspeakable reprisals. The Russians' pursuit of geographical objectives with insufficient numbers had cost them the strategic initiative, and forced them to attack Osman in a position of his own choosing.

Defensive victories like those of Osman's are rarely enough to end a war favourably. Osman failed to press his advantage, was shut up in Plevna, and starved out. The fall of Plevna in December 1877 released sufficient Russian troops to restore the momentum of their stalled advance. Crossing obscure Balkan passes on a wide front, the Russians surrounded 36,000 Turks at Shipka, and cut off their main army of 50,000 men from Istanbul. The mountains had proved a trap for their defenders. Sea power saved the Turks, moving the remains of their armies from Enez to Istanbul, covered by the guns of the British Mediterranean Fleet. Unwilling to provoke a European war, the exhausted Russians agreed terms.

2 The siege of Plevna anticipated some features of later wars, but the Russian tendency to attack superior numbers of entrenched Turks said as much about the need for reconnaissance as the advantages of field works (map below). With little artillery, and cavalry fit only for massacring civilians, the Turkish infantry was unable to exploit its victories or break through the Russian lines of investment when the food ran out.

2 siege of plevna, 19 july–10 dec. 1877

- Turkish trenches & redoubts
- telegraph linking Turkish positions
- Allied lines of investment after failure of direct assault
- Allied attacks of 22–30 July & 11 Sep.
- vineyards & orchards

0 ____ 2 kms
0 ____ 2 miles

(Map labels: Dolna Netropolie, ROMANIAN ARMY, Verbitza, Vid, Opanetz, Gorna Netropolie, Kyust, GOURKO'S CORPS, Turkish breakout attempt 6 Dec 1877, Bukova, ROMANIAN ARMY, Plevna, Grivitza, Stru, Vardar, Vid, Krishin, Radishevo, RUSSIAN IV & IX CORPS, DETACHMENT SKOBELEFF)

The Russo–Turkish War underlined the tactical lessons of the Franco–Prussian and American Civil Wars. Turkish infantry dug themselves in, while Russian cavalry fought as mounted rifle-men. Both sides used the latest breech-loading rifled artillery and small arms. More effective weapons increased absolute losses, but long-range firefights and larger armies led to lower percentage casualties. The rifle became the main cause of wounds, reversing the Napoleonic dominance of artillery. Positions were no longer carried at bayonet point, but by developing superior fire to that of the defenders. Armies dispersed to reduce losses, and dominated larger areas with their longer-ranged weapons. The Russians held the 44-mile line around Plevna with 100,000 men, half the number of Germans needed for a similar front at Paris seven years earlier. To penetrate such a line was widely regarded as a purely theoretical possibility.

1 Making imaginative use of mounted infantry, the Russian army raced through Bulgaria to seize the Shipka pass, but it was unable to advance south of the Balkan mountains because a Turkish army had dug itself in at Plevna (map below). The campaign was marked by widespread atrocities; Turkish irregulars (the infamous Bashi-Bazouks) preyed on Bulgarian Christians who conducted some 'ethnic cleansing' of their own against their Muslim neighbours, aided by the Cossacks.

1 the war in the balkans, 1877–78

Russian advances

- ← - - Russian advance to the Danube
- ← to the beginning of the siege of Plevna
- ⤼ Russian bridges over the Danube
- ← Turkish counter offensives

troop concentrations, 5 Aug 1877

- Russian
- Turkish
- Romanian

- ← Russian winter campaign after the fall of Plevna

Osman Pasha's march to Plevna   35,000 men

Plevna 50,000 men

12,000 men   35,000 men

23,000 men

62,000 men   MEHEMET ALI 75,000 men

Rustchuk 10,000 men

Shipka Pass

Stara Zagora   SULEIMAN 40,000 men

Turkish fugitives from Philippopolis and transfer to Constantinople

101

colonial wars

1830 to 1902

From 1830
Algeria conquered by France

1842
hostile Afghan mountaineers destroy British army at Gandamak (13 January)

1874
Battle of Amoafu: the British campaign against the Asante (1 February)

1876
Americans defeated by Plains tribes at battle of Little Big Horn

1880s
the French overcome Vietnamese and Chinese forces

1885
Battle of Abu Klea, Sudan (17 January)

1899–1902
Boer War

Colonial wars were the main source of military experience for the British, French, United States and even Russian armies in the 19th century. The colonial experience was at odds with 19th-century trends, encouraging recklessness and improvisation rather than professionalism and organization. Every colonial campaign was different. Western forces adapted to local conditions, or suffered catastrophic defeats.

Imperial forces could not match the mobility of their enemies. Operating in agriculturally undeveloped areas with poor roads or none, they had to bring their supplies with them, restricting strategic mobility. Difficulties of supply kept imperial forces small, and forced them to detach up to 90 per cent of their strength to protect their supply lines. Western tactical superiority made it safe to take such risks against opponents unlikely to exploit the advantages of internal lines. A battle usually favoured the imperial forces, so commanders preferred combat to manoeuvre. They needed a victory before disease, the weather or supply problems forced them to withdraw.

The Boer War employed almost 500,000 British soldiers, many of them reservists. For all its imperial setting, the Boer War was a total war for the Transvaal and Orange Free State who faced political annihilation if they lost. The war began with rapid advances by mounted Boer commandos, their mobility multiplying their initial numerical

1 The accelerating pace of military technology gave colonial powers an increasing advantage over irregular opponents. Formed armies that played the colonial forces at their own game came off worst: the Sikhs and Zulus were overcome, despite the occasional upset. Nomads, or the denizens of fever-stricken jungles, were harder to tame. European armies suffered heavy losses to tropical diseases, another reason to rely on locally recruited 'native' regiments. Colonial 'small wars' provided valuable experience for several European armies, but not every 'lesson' would prove applicable to regular warfare, or even other colonial campaigns (map right).

1 the world impact of colonial empires to 1900

British	Spanish	Belgian
French	Dutch	Japanese
Portuguese	Russian	Ottoman
Italian	USA	other countries
German	Danish	

ALASKA

DOMINION OF CANADA

NEWFOUNDLAND

UNITED STATES OF AMERICA

America's westward expansion doomed the Plains tribes, but the military forces employed over this vast area were very small. On one of the few occasions the tribes concentrated their forces they inflicted the shock defeat of the Little Big Horn (1876).

Algeria conquered by France in successive campaigns from the 1830

MEXICO

CUBA (occupied by USA)

Jamaica (Br.)

BRITISH HONDURAS

France's attempt to install a puppet regime in Mexico while the USA was torn with civil war led to a savage guerrilla campaign against Mexican insurgents. Napoleon's marshals eventually concluded the war was unwinnable and Emperor Maximilian was abandoned to his fate.

VENEZUELA

COLOMBIA

ECUADOR

BRITISH GUIANA
DUTCH GUIANA
FRENCH GUIANA

Amoafu, 1874: The campaign against the Asante place in dense jungle. Disea. greater enemy than the tribe

PERU

ACRE

BRAZIL

BOLIVIA

PARAGUAY

ARG.

CHILE

URUGUAY

The leading powers of South A. established armies on the Euro pattern and used them in the se manner to adjust their borders. Bolivia lost her coastline. Some modern navies too: by the 188 had a larger and more modern than the USA.

GREEN

advantage. British forces deployed too far forward, in a salient, making it easy to surround them. Fortunately for the British, the Boers failed to press on to seize the ports through which imperial reinforcements would enter South Africa. The commandos sat down around Ladysmith and Kimberley (October 1899), blocking the only routes for British relief attempts: the railways. The British took four months to build up enough forces to break through the Boer lines.

Neither General Sir Redvers Buller nor Field Marshall Lord Roberts inflicted sufficient attrition on the Boers to defeat them outright. A hard core of Bitter-Einders fought on after the fall of the Boer capitals at Pretoria and Bloemfontein. Logistically independent of the towns, they drew food and remounts from their family farms, and replaced weapons and uniforms at the expense of the enemy. The British had too few

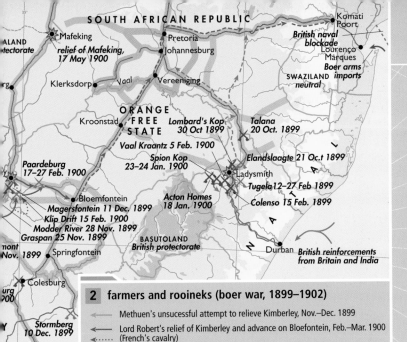

SOUTH AFRICAN REPUBLIC

Komati Poort

Mafeking
relief of Mafeking, 17 May 1900
Pretoria
Johannesburg
British naval blockade
Lourenço Marques
Boer arms imports

Klerksdorp
Vaal
Vereeniging
SWAZILAND neutral

ORANGE FREE STATE
Kroonstad
Lombard's Kop 30 Oct 1899
Talana 20 Oct. 1899
Vaal Kraantz 5 Feb. 1900
Spion Kop 23–24 Jan. 1900
Elandslaagte 21 Oc.t 1899

Paardeburg 17–27 Feb. 1900
Ladysmith
Tugela 12–27 Feb 1899
Colenso 15 Feb. 1899

Bloemfontein
Magersfontein 11 Dec. 1899
Klip Drift 15 Feb. 1900
Modder River 28 Nov. 1899
Graspan 25 Nov. 1899
Acton Homes 18 Jan. 1900

BASUTOLAND British protectorate

Springfontein
Durban
British reinforcements from Britain and India

Colesburg

Stormberg 10 Dec. 1899

2 farmers and rooineks (boer war, 1899–1902)

→ Methuen's unsuccessful attempt to relieve Kimberley, Nov.–Dec. 1899
→ Lord Robert's relief of Kimberley and advance on Bloefontein, Feb.–Mar. 1900
····> (French's cavalry)
◄--- Lord Robert's advance through the Transvaal
◄--- Buller's operations to relieve Ladysmith, Dec. 1899–Feb 1900
→ Buller's advance into the Transvaal, May–Aug. 1900

mounted troops to dominate the wide spaces of the veldt. They countered Boer mobility by building lines of blockhouses across the country, joined together by barbed wire. Mobile columns tried to pin the elusive Boer guerrillas against these obstacles with limited success. Wireless telegraphy was too clumsy to coordinate the drives. The war took a sinister turn with the concentration of Boer families in camps to prevent them helping their unreconciled kinsmen. Ignorance of hygiene led to many deaths, causing an outcry in the United Kingdom, and permanently embittering Anglo–Boer relations. British recruitment of Hands-Oppers or surrendered Boers to hunt their kinsmen threatened to tear Afrikaaner society apart. Combined with general warweariness this brought both sides to the peace table. Like many later guerrilla wars, the Boer War did enormous damage without producing a clear-cut victory.

Russian expansion into central Asia involved major campaigns in the 1880s, led by the hero of the Russo-Turkish War, General Skoboleff. The Caucasus, including Chechenya, was conquered too: setting the scene for today's conflicts in the region.

Both British invasions of Afghanistan met with defeat, despite the occupation of large parts of the country by Lord Roberts. The North-West Frontier remained an active training ground for British soldiers until 1946.

China was compelled to concede to western trading interests after losing a series of wars with Britain and France, but its modernized army presented a much more serious threat by 1900.

French campaigns in the 1880s overcome Vietnamese and Chinese forces

Non-European armies that adopted European methods proved relatively easy to defeat. The Sikh kingdom was defeated by Britain and its soldiers soon formed a vital part of Britain's army in India.

The abortive attempt to rescue General Gordon from Khartoum pitches a tiny British expeditionary force against the Sudanese. The desert column is lucky to escape downriver.

A deliberate campaign of genocide against the Ovambo tribe in 1906 marks Germany's late entry into the 'scramble for Africa'.

...fter its capture from the ...h, nine wars with local ...expand Cape Colony. ...two Boer republics are ...tablished in defiance of the British, but are ...eventually invaded and ...cupied 1899-1901. The Zulu Empire is invaded ...d conquered by Britain in 1879

2 The Boer War absorbed 500,000 British soldiers and echoes of it can still be heard in Army slang a century later. Once their capitals were occupied, many of the commandos fought on, relying on their mobility and the support of the civilian population to keep one step ahead of the British (map top). Mao's revelation that guerrillas are fish in the civilian sea was already familiar to Lord Kitchener who ordered it drained. Penned in by the blockhouses, with their families dying in British concentration camps, even the 'Bitter Einders' were compelled to surrender.

Maori resistance to British colonial rule was based on remarkably modern entrenchments (see below).

the **russo–japanese** war

The Russo–Japanese War was the first major conflict of the 20th century. The Japanese saw it as a war for national survival. They employed all the means at their disposal, showing how a small power can defeat a stronger but less-committed power.

The total destruction of the Russian fleet contrasted with the indecisive results of the war on land. The Japanese tipped the local balance of naval forces in their favour by a surprise torpedo boat attack on Port Arthur (8 February 1904), followed by a close blockade by their battleships. The Japanese achieved strategic surprise by attacking without first declaring war, but found it difficult to follow up. Russian mine warfare, pursued in defiance of international law, sank two Japanese battleships, forcing them to abandon their close blockade.

The Japanese could not devote all their energies to Port Arthur. They had to cover the siege against Russian troops in Manchuria, who

1 the russo–japanese war, 1904–05

←	Japanese army landings and advances to April/May 1904

subsequent Japanese advances and front lines to

←	June 1904
←	July 1904
←	October 1904
⊠	temporary Japanese naval base
✕	Japanese naval victory
←	Russian naval advances

1 The Russian navy had a squadron of modern battleships based at Port Arthur, but the Russian army in Manchuria was largely composed of reservists. Japan's army was modelled on the Prussians, its navy self-consciously imitated Britain's Royal Navy. The Japanese army laid siege to Port Arthur and held off the Russian army in Manchuria. Despite losing two of his six battleships on mines off the harbour, Admiral Togo blockaded the Russian fleet in Port Arthur until it was sunk at anchor by army howitzers (map right).

Map labels

M A N C H U R I A
Harbin
Mukden • • Fushun
• Liaoyang
Newchuang •
Liao
Yalu
Antung • • Wiju
• Takushan
Bo Hai
Pitzuwu
Jun 1904–Jan 1905 under siege
Elliot Is.
4TH ARMY
Korea Bay
• Dairen
Port Arthur •
2ND ARMY
3RD ARMY
8–9 Feb 1904 Japanese torpedo attack
1ST ARMY
Weihaiwei •
C H I N A
10 Aug 1904 Sortie into Yellow Sea
• Hungnam
Pyongyang •
• Wonsan
Chinampo •
K O R E A
Seoul •
Chemulpo •
• Kangnung
• Andong
Taejon •
Taegu •
Masan •
Fusan •
Korea Strait
Tsushima
28 Jun 1905 Tsushima
Takeshima

Sea of Japan

Jun 1904 Raid by Vladivostok cruiser squadron; Japanese troop transports sunk
Oki Is.
14 Aug 1904 Sea of Japan
• Matsue
• Hiroshima
J A P A N

May 1904 Approach of Baltic fleet
Quelpart
Fukuoka •

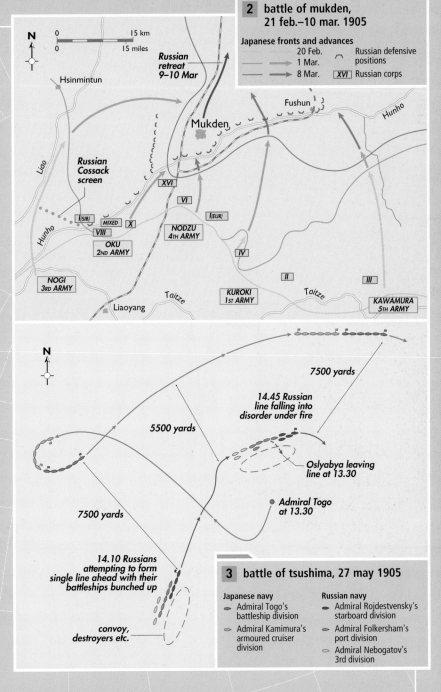

2 The Tsar and his senior officers indulged in racist jokes at the expense of the Japanese when war was declared. But the unthinkable happened: the Russian field armies were defeated and a first-class naval squadron was destroyed at Port Arthur. A non-European power had overturned three centuries of unbroken European expansion. On the sprawling battlefields of Manchuria, cosmic levels of incompetence exposed the Russian army as a 'rubber lion' in the parlance of the German General Staff (map right). It was effectively written out of Germany's war plans for future conflict in Europe.

3 Russia's Baltic Fleet sailed from Petersburg to Japan only to meet with annihilating defeat at Tsushima (map below right). Gunnery seldom produces fast results in naval actions although some Russian battleships were so overloaded, their main armour belts were submerged and their waterline protection consequently reduced. Japanese torpedo boats finished off damaged vessels and even laid mines in the path of escaping battleships, actions studied with grim interest by British and German naval officers.

2 battle of mukden, 21 feb.–10 mar. 1905

Japanese fronts and advances
20 Feb.   Russian defensive positions
1 Mar.
8 Mar.   *XVI* Russian corps

3 battle of tsushima, 27 may 1905

Japanese navy	Russian navy
Admiral Togo's battleship division	Admiral Rojdestvensky's starboard division
Admiral Kamimura's armoured cruiser division	Admiral Folkersham's port division
	Admiral Nebogatov's 3rd division

were steadily reinforced by the Trans-Siberian Railway. Needing a quick victory, the Japanese began a converging advance against the main Russian army. The Russians retreated after tied battles at Liaoyang and the Sha-Ho (October 1904). Outnumbered 3:2, Marshal Oyama persisted with his double envelopment strategy at Mukden, employing deception to even the odds. Troops released from the siege of Port Arthur massed behind the Japanese left, unknown to the Russians, while other troop movements on the other flank drew Kuropatkin's reserves away from the true point of attack. After two weeks' fighting Kuropatkin's troops were in a pocket around Mukden. The Japanese advance had reached its culminating point at Mukden. They had committed every man available without decisively defeating the Russian army, which regrouped still further up the railway line. The war would be ended, as it had begun, at sea.

The naval battle of Tsushima (27–28 May 1905) left the strategic situation unchanged, but dramatically confirmed Japanese command of the sea. Tsushima was the only fleet action fought to a finish by pre-dreadnought battleships. Tsushima was the product of decisively superior Japanese seamanship and gunnery which allowed Admiral Togo, hailed as the Japanese Nelson, to take the same sort of risks as his predecessor. Japanese battleships made 15 knots against the Russian nine. Togo easily crossed the Russian 'T', concentrating gunfire on the leading Russian ships. The big gun was still the dominant weapon at sea, despite mine and torpedo successes off Port Arthur. Tsushima's most significant lesson was psychological. It spelled the end of European supremacy at sea.

The Russo–Japanese War showed how easily a limited war might escalate. Both sides suffered enormous losses in week-long battles that made a mockery of distinctions between limited and absolute war. The Russians saw their fleet destroyed and revolution shake the Tsar's government. Even the pursuit of limited objectives needs effective preparation and organization, without which superior resources remain unrealized potential and losses reach catastrophic levels.

the **war** in the **west**

The First World War was not the inevitable result of an arms race, nor was it an accident. It was the product of political choices, but military developments over the previous quarter of a century ensured a plentiful supply of inflammable material.

Armies doubled in size after the Franco–Prussian War, outpacing the rate of population growth. Only Great Britain, secure in its naval supremacy, still relied on volunteers. The great powers resembled mistrustful travellers, brought together in a carriage by chance. If one of them put his hand into his pocket, his neighbour would get his own revolver ready to fire the first shot. However, no one army had the qualitative advantage possessed by the Prussians over the ill-led French Gardes Mobiles of 1870.

Industrial growth provided new weapons for nations now truly in arms. Practical rates of fire rose to eight rounds a minute, compared with two previously. Gunners could remain near their gun as it fired, sheltered by bullet-proof shields. The flat trajectories of field guns were ineffective against trenches, so howitzers reappeared, lobbing a heavier round to a shorter range. Automatic machine guns epitomized the effect of industrialization on war. Easily mass-produced, they created a large volume of accurate fire with minimal effort. Machine guns added to the vulnerability of horsed cavalry,

2 Intending to replicate Napoleon's manoeuvre at Ulm, the German armies plunged through Belgium to outflank French forces along the Meuse (map right). General von Kluck departed from the plan and wheeled his army south before reaching Paris. The French commander, General Joffre, kept his nerve and shuttled reinforcements to the Marne by rail and road.

1 From the 1890s the system of multi lateral diplomacy gave way to a system of alliance blocs (map left). Collaboration between the Powers still proved possible as the crises over Morocco, Bosnia and Albania showed between 1905 and 1913, but when Britain reached informal agreements on colonial issues first with France in 1904, and then with Russia in 1907, Europe divided into two armed camps. The subsequent arms race created a volatile international order, made worse by the rise of popular xenophobia and a growing fatalism about war. At the same time as the European powers recruited enormous armies of conscripts, weapons technology gathered pace, putting ever more lethal weapons into their hands. Only Britain remained apart, relying on its status as the world's leading naval power.

2 the miracle of marne, aug. – sep. 1914

- 🏰 fortress, with date of surrender
- ✕ battles, with date
- ▬ Allied front lines 5 September
- ▬ German front line 5 September
- ▬ ▬ German front line 12 September
- ➤ German advance to the Marne
- ⇢ German retreat to the Aisne

1 the drift to war

- 🚩 mobilizations, with date
- ☐ Entente Powers at outbreak of war
- ☐ joined Entente Powers during the war, with date
- ☐ Central Powers at outbreak of war
- ☐ joined Central Powers during the war, with date

troop concentrations, 1914
1 block per 100,000 combatants
- ☐ Entente and allies
- ☐ Central Powers and allies

naval bases
- ⊞ Entente and allies
- ⊞ Central Powers and allies

industrial strength
- ☐ 1 block per million tons of steel
- ▬ frontiers, 1914

already at a disadvantage in Europe's enclosed countryside. Motor vehicles would resolve the hiatus of the mobile army but, like wireless telegraphy and aircraft, were scarce and unreliable in 1914.

Absolute war had previously been moderated by political factors and the impossibility of a state deploying all its reserves at once. In 1914 offensive strategy, untempered by diplomacy, could deploy the whole of a nation's military resources instantaneously, by rail. Absolute war had become a realizable prospect, the only strategic aim the total defeat of one side. With both sides prepared to make every effort to avoid such an outcome, wars would be long and hard-fought, leading to the ruin of both sides.

The technical forces that revolutionized military weaponry also applied at sea. Precision-made heavy guns could deliver accurate long-range fire, centrally controlled by mechanical computers and range finders. Tsushima prompted development of the all big-gun battleship. HMS *Dreadnought* (1906), the first of the new type, gave a new twist to a naval race underway since the British Naval Defence Act of 1889. German Navy Laws of 1898 and 1900 refocused British naval concerns. They mended fences with France and Russia, and concentrated the Royal Navy in home waters, confirming German fears of encirclement. The British won the naval race, but the Agadir crisis confirmed Anglo–German hostility, entangling Great Britain in a European alliance for the first time in a century. The British army was small, but the empire possessed enormous resources, capable of balancing the industrial power of Germany. Britain's adherence to the *Entente* ensured that a renewed Franco–German war would be long.

1914 to 1915

15 August 1914
Russia invades East Prussia

20 August 1914
Germans defeated at Gumbinnen

26–31 August 1914
Battle of Tannenberg

9–14 September 1914
First Battle of Masurian Lakes

5 November 1914
Turkey joins Central powers

5–17 December 1914
Austrians defeat Russians at Limanowa

The German army, the leading military power of Europe, was obsessed by fears of a two-front war against Russia and France. Count von Schlieffen, Chief of the General Staff 1893–1905, hoped to defeat France before Russia, hampered by its size, could mobilize. The Schlieffen plan launched 90 per cent of Germany's mobile forces through neutral Belgium. The war on the Eastern Front started with one of those brilliant manoeuvres so noticeably absent in the west, the Battle of Tannenberg.

The Schlieffen plan was crucially flawed by its assumption that the enemy would behave as planned. Instead Joffre, the French Commander-in-Chief, regrouped his forces and the enveloping force was pierced by British forces (the BEF), when aerial reconnaissance revealed a gap between the German armies. In frustrating the Schlieffen Plan, Joffre had won the decisive battle of the war, and perhaps of the century.

On the other hand, the Battle of Tannenberg was the most striking German victory of the war. General Paul von Hindenberg took over the Eighth Army after the unscripted German defeat at Gumbinnen (20 August 1914), with Ludendorff as his General Staff officer. German I Corps trapped the whole Russian army in a pocket near Tannenberg. Their commander shot himself, and 100,000 prisoners surrendered. However, Tannenberg was the result of Russian command failures, not innate backwardness. The subsequent battle of the Masurian Lakes against the surviving Russian army in the north began well for the Germans, but bogged down by the end of September 1914. It cost the Eighth Army 100,000 casualties out of 250,000. Masurian Lakes, not Tannenberg, would be the pattern of the war in the east.

Germany was not Russia's only opponent. The Eastern Front formed a series of salients: Germany in East Prussia; Russia at Warsaw; Austria–Hungary in Galicia to the south. Poor communications prevented reserves moving swiftly to block gaps in the line. Pushed back into the Carpathians, Austria–Hungary appealed for German help. Hindenberg and Ludendorff flattened the Warsaw salient, but there were no more wholesale Russian surrenders. By year end, Russian gains in Galicia balanced losses in Poland.

The German General Staff, in their professional ivory tower, had started a world war to chastise an obscure Balkan kingdom. Their politically naïve invasion of Belgium placed Britain's economic and strategic potential at the disposal of the *Entente*. Germany faced a two-front war, with no clear idea of how to end it.

2 The Russian 1st and 2nd Armies failed to coordinate their invasion of East Prussia and, while Rennenkampf was bluffed into immobility, the Germans concentrated every man against Samsonov, who committed suicide when his surrounded army was compelled to surrender (map left).

2 tannenberg, 20–31 august 1914

XVII	German army corps 20 August
3R	German reserve division
ᐱᐱᐱᐱᐱ	German cavalry screen
→	German corps moving by rail
■-■▶	German other corps marching
•••▶	German attacks 26-29 August
XIII	Russian army corps 20 August
▬-▬▶	Russian advances 1st army-unopposed
➡	Russian advances 2nd army

Baltic Sea

Memel

GERMAN EMPIRE

Königsberg

Gumbinnen
20 Aug.

Kovno

Plan G

8TH ARMY
(200,000 men)

Tannenberg
26–31 Aug.

Masurian Lakes
9–14 Sep.

1ST ARMY

Minsk

Torun

Grodno

Poznan

2ND ARMY

4TH ARMY
RESERVE

Breslau

Warsaw

Lodz

9TH ARMY
RESERVE

Brest
Litovsk

PLAN A

R U S S I A N   E M P I R E

9TH ARMY
(from western front)

Cracow

1ST ARMY

5TH ARMY

4TH ARMY

3RD ARMY

3RD ARMY

Przemysl

Lemberg

Carpathian Mts

8TH ARMY

PLAN R

Budapest

2ND ARMY
RESERVE

Czernovitz

A U S T R O - H U N G A R I A N
E M P I R E

PLAN B

5TH ARMY

200,000

Belgrade

R O M A N I A

Sarajevo

6TH ARMY

SERBS
(190,000 men)

S E R B I A

1 the eastern front, 1914

German armies in August

- - -▶ movement by rail (Sep.)

──▶ counter attack to relieve Austrians

🏰 fortresses

✕ German victory

Austrian armies in August

──▶ advances and retreats in August

- - -▶ alternative plans

──── defensive line (mid-Sep.)

🏰 fortresses

Russian armies in August

──▶ advances in August

✕ Russian victory

- - -▶ alternative plans

🏰 fortresses

Serbian army in August

1 Along the far wider frontage of the Eastern Front,
manoeuvres were still possible on a grand scale (map left).
Russia surprised the Central Powers by assuming the
offensive before her mobilization was complete, invading
East Prussia and driving the Austro–Hungarian armies back
on the fortresses north of the Carpathians. The Austro-
Hungarian commander-in-chief changed his mind, first
committing the bulk of his armies against Serbia, then
withdrawing large forces to fend off the Russians.

trench warfare

The development of trench warfare in late 1914 is less surprising than the war of movement it replaced. Twentieth-century firepower made it possible to hold long fronts with only two men per yard, compared with the five needed in the 1870s. Armies had grown so large they could occupy the entire space available, creating an inviolable front without flanks. Only the Germans possessed weapons appropriate to trench warfare: howitzers, grenades, signal rockets. The French had neglected howitzers, and hastily stripped their fortresses of heavy guns for the frontline.

Joffre's tactics resembled those of D'Erlon at Waterloo. Massive columns advanced after concentrated artillery had blasted a path through the enemy position. The two regiments of each brigade followed each other in waves, so close together that 3,600 men formed a mass 1,300 yards wide and 185 yards deep. Surprisingly the concept almost worked. Petain's 33rd Corps reached the top of Vimy Ridge on 9 May 1915, but machine-gun fire from fortified villages held up progress on the flanks. Joffre's September attacks were on a wider front: 22 divisions broke through on a 10-mile front in Champagne. The

1 General Joffre conducted a succession of offensives in 1915, but hopes of a strategic breakthrough foundered against barbed wire, machine guns and concealed artillery (map below). French losses were catastrophic, although one officer showed that a thoroughly prepared attack could succeed: General Pétain led his 33rd corps to the top of Vimy Ridge in May 1915.

1 Joffre's strategy, 1915

1915 offensives
- → French
- → British
- → German
- ⇢ Joffre's strategic intentions
- ── strategic railways
- ━━ front line, 1915

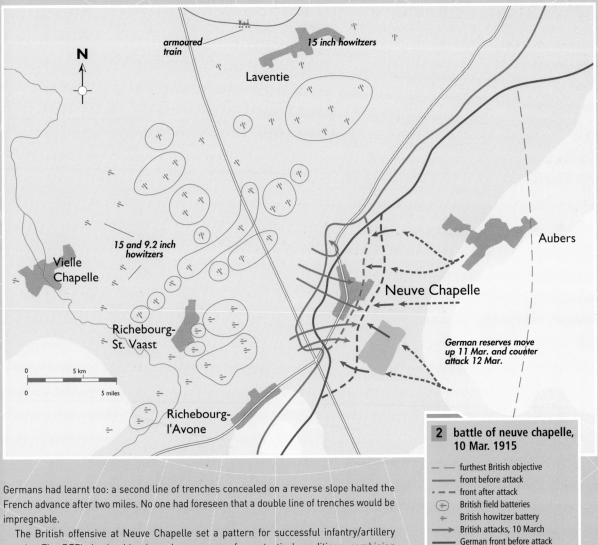

N

armoured train

15 inch howitzers

Laventie

15 and 9.2 inch howitzers

Vielle Chapelle

Richebourg-St. Vaast

| 0 | | 5 km |
| 0 | | 5 miles |

Richebourg-l'Avone

Aubers

Neuve Chapelle

German reserves move up 11 Mar. and counter attack 12 Mar.

2   battle of neuve chapelle, 10 Mar. 1915

- - - furthest British objective
─── front before attack
- - - front after attack
⊕ British field batteries
⊷ British howitzer battery
→ British attacks, 10 March
━━ German front before attack

Germans had learnt too: a second line of trenches concealed on a reverse slope halted the French advance after two miles. No one had foreseen that a double line of trenches would be impregnable.

The British offensive at Neuve Chapelle set a pattern for successful infantry/artillery attacks. The BEF's leadership showed awareness of new tactical conditions, combining methodical preparation and surprise. An unprecedented whirlwind bombardment by 340 guns cut the wire and wrecked the German front line. Tactical novelties included aerial photography, an orchestrated fire plan, and first official use of the term 'barrage'. Neuve Chapelle, like Vimy Ridge, showed how the German front line might be penetrated, starting a debate among the high command. Some hoped better planning or more firepower would produce a decisive breakthrough. Others preferred to wear the Germans down by a 'bite and hold' strategy, a strategy unacceptable to a public still expecting speedy victory.

The Germans launched only one offensive on the Western Front in 1915. They released clouds of chlorine gas at Ypres, in the first large-scale use of weapons of mass destruction. The Germans took half the Ypres salient, but suffered a resounding propaganda defeat. The unbelievable horror of a gas cloud attack confirmed perceptions of Hun beastliness first inspired by atrocities against Belgian civilians. Gas masks transformed soldiers into dehumanized monsters, but human qualities of morale and training remained essential for troops to survive gas warfare.

2 British experience at Neuve Chapelle showed the German line could be penetrated, but the defender's reserves could plug the gap before the attacker could move fresh troops forward (map above). Until this conundrum was solved, no major breakthrough was possible. The last cadres of the BEF were expended in these assaults; larger British operations would have to wait until the Kitchener armies were equipped and trained.

gallipoli

25 April 1915
Allied Landings at Anzac Cove

5–6 May 1915
Failed Allied attack on Cape Helles

6–8 May 1915
Second Battle of Krithia

29 June 1915
Last Turkish attack on Anzac cover

7 August 1915
British landing at Suvla Bay

18–20 December 1915
Allies evacuate Anzac Cove

9 January 1916
Remaining British troops evacuated from Cape Helles

The stalemate on the Western Front stimulated a search for alternative areas of operations. Over-optimistic expectations of sea power inspired an Anglo–French amphibious attack on Turkey, which had joined the Central Powers in October 1914.

The failure of both sea and land operations at Gallipoli underlined the gulf between strategic vision and operational reality during the First World War. The scheme depended on makeshift expedients: obsolete ships officially regarded as expendable; civilian trawlers impressed as minesweepers; half-trained divisions with incomplete artillery and staffs. A purely naval attack on the Dardanelles flew in the face of experience going back to 1807, and begged the question of what to do if the Turks refused to surrender on the fleet's arrival at Istanbul. Pre-Dreadnought battleships were to silence the Turkish forts at the mouth of the Dardanelles, the straits leading to the Sea of Marmara and the Bosphorus. Trawlers would then clear the minefields for the battleships to engage forts inside the Narrows. Shore bombardment failed to silence Turkish forts permanently. Flat trajectory naval guns were ineffective against the mobile howitzer batteries that hampered mine-clearing operations. When the fleet attempted to brazen it out on 18 March, unswept mines sank three old battleships, and damaged another two, almost a third of the force. The underwater threat ended the purely naval phase of the campaign. Two months later a U-boat torpedoed two more pre-Dreadnoughts, confirming the dangers of traditional naval power projection in the face of mines and submarines.

The naval bombardments lost any chance of strategic surprise. The Turks held the April landings on the Cape Helles beaches, until nightfall. The red stain in the sea was visible from the air. The début of Australian and New Zealand Dominion forces at Anzac Cove was more successful, but once ashore, the troops became entangled in razor-backed hills and scrub not apparent from a small-scale map. Rifle, barbed wire and spade dominated the battlefield as in the West, but at Gallipoli the Allies had no continuous line, no high ground for observation, no depth providing escape from enemy fire and no clean water. Over half the British and Dominion casualties, 145,000 out of 214,000, were from dysentery. The losses from disease associated with every 1914–18 'sideshow' condemn all of them as a way of winning the war on the cheap. The landings

Gulf of Saros

0   5 km
0   5 miles

Gallipoli

Suvla Bay

British 7 Aug. 1915

Allied bridgehead

evacuated 18–19 Dec. 1915

Sari Bahr

Anzac 25 Apr. 1915

Gaba Tepe

Dardanelles

N

British 25 Apr. 1915

Achi Baba

Krithia

Canakkale

4 knots current

X
Cape Helles W
S
Y

evacuated 8–9 Jan 1916

French 25–27 Apr. 1915

French 25 Apr. 1915

1 The assault on the Dardanelles, 1915-16

- - - Turkish minefields
- Turkish field artillery positions
- Turkish mobile artillery positions
→ Allied Naval attack, 18 Mar 1915
XWVS British/Dominion assault landings
French assaults and diversions
- - - Allied evacuations
✳ ✳ British and French naval losses

1 An unsupported naval attack in March gave notice of Allied intentions, so the improvised amphibious assault in April met with disaster. The attacking troops were shot down in the water, so much blood spilled it was visible from the air. Attempts to break out from the beachhead were defeated by the familiar combination of wire, machine guns and concealed artillery (map left).

2 In November 1914 the Ottoman empire joined the Austro–German alliance against the Allied powers in return for a promise that Macedonia would be restored to Turkish rule (map right). Early Turkish offensives were unsuccessful: an attack against Russia was repelled and ended with Russia seizing Armenia. Turkish efforts against the other western allies fared better. The landing by British empire forces at Gallipoli in April 1915 was repelled after nine months while a combined Anglo–French force stationed at Salonica in October 1915 was bottled up there until 1918. In 1916 an Anglo–Indian force was captured at Kut trying to secure Middle Eastern oil supplies. Kut was finally retaken in 1917; Baghdad fell in March 1918. Meanwhile, with the aid of a widespread Arab revolt against Turkish rule, British empire forces under Allenby had pushed through Sinai and on into Jerusalem.

2 **the war in the middle east, 1914–18**

Entente Powers

Central Powers

Advances

→ British   → Russian

⇢ Arab   → Ottoman

→ French

Offensives

— area of Arab revolt against Ottomans

— Ottoman frontline at time of surrender, 30 Oct. 1918

— railways

Map labels:

Black Sea · BULGARIA · Constantinople · Gallipoli · Dardanelles · April 1915 · Smyrna · Dodecanese to Italy · OTTOMAN · Angora · EMPIRE · Erzinjan · 1916–18 · Batum · Kars · RUSSIAN EMPIRE · Baku · Sep. 1918 · ARMENIA · AZERBAIJAN · Tabriz · Caspian Sea · Adana · Alexandretta · Aleppo · Nisibin · Mosul · Kirkuk · Hamadan · Teheran · PERSIA · SYRIA · Oct. 1918 · Homs · Samarra · Sultanabad · 1916–17 · Mediterranean Sea · Cyprus annexed by Britain 1914 · Oct. 1918 · Beirut · Damascus · Baghdad · Kut el Amara · Apr. 1916 · Amara · Apr. 1916 · Oct. 1918 · Megiddo · MESOPOTAMIA · Jan.–Mar. 1917 · Jerusalem · Gaza · Amman · PALESTINE · 1917 · Basra · Alexandria · Port Said · 1917 · 1914–15 · El Akaba · KUWAIT · Kuwait · Cairo · 1914 British protectorate · Sinai · EGYPT · ARABIA (NEJD) · HASA annexed by Arabia 1913–14 · Persian Gulf · QATAR · Red Sea · HEJAZ · Medina · Yenbo · Empty Quarter (Rub' al Khali) · Jedda · Mecca · Taif · ASIR

at Suvla in August once more showed the futility of amphibious assaults with untrained troops. Only the flawlessly planned and executed evacuation of December 1915/January 1916 showed the impressive capabilities of the staffs, when operating beyond the constraints of bullet, wire and spade. The rapid technical response to the demands of modern amphibious operations suggest what more careful preparation might have achieved: small cheap monitors replaced battleships for fire support; modified destroyers took over minesweeping; motorized barges or 'beetles' replaced the ships' boats traditionally used for landing troops. The British would not resolve the deeper problems of political/military relations that underlay the disaster until the Second World War.

1914 to 1918

28 August 1914
Battle of Heligoland Bight

1 November 1914
Battle of Coronel

8 December 1914
Battle of Falkland Islands

24 January 1915
Battle of Dogger Bank

31 May–1 June 1916
Battle of Jutland

9 January 1917
Unrestricted submarine warfare
adopted by Germans

Events at sea were crucial to the outcome of the war. The Royal Navy possessed significant material and geographical advantages over the Imperial German Navy.

The British had 50 per cent more Dreadnoughts, with numerous cruisers, to blockade German ports, protect British commerce, and escort expeditionary forces. The British Isles physically obstructed German access to the Atlantic, except via the easily blocked Dover Straits, or the Iceland–Faroes gap. The Grand Fleet's concentration confined the German High Seas Fleet to the North Sea. Wireless permitted steam warships to concentrate independent of the weather, in response to enemy initiatives, while signal intercepts provided early warning of German intentions.

Like other outnumbered fleets, the High Seas Fleet remained in harbour, inspiring the first air attack on warships in harbour, by RNAS seaplanes on Christmas Day 1914. German cruisers bombarded civilian targets along the east coast of Great Britain in attempts to draw out part of the Grand Fleet. One raid brought on the first action between Dreadnoughts at the Dogger Bank. The refusal of the stricken German cruiser *Blücher* to surrender marked a return to the obstinate savagery of earlier naval wars.

The battle of Jutland, the only fleet action between Dreadnoughts, resulted from a complex German plan, combining U-boats and Zeppelins, to trap part of the Grand Fleet. But the Grand Fleet was forewarned of the German moves by signals intelligence. Only nightfall and two very smart 180-degree turns saved the High Seas Fleet. Jutland was the last fleet action in the old style, the combatants in view of one another.

Meanwhile, German maritime trade was subject to a blockade of increasing rigour. A patrol line of cruisers and armed merchantmen intercepted ships passing between Iceland and Scotland, and redirected those carrying 'contraband' to British ports. Although the Admiralty had been planning economic warfare since 1906, there was no pre-concerted plan to starve Germany out. Food was not declared contraband until 1915, after the first unrestricted U-boat campaign began. The military effects of the blockade are unclear, although it has been blamed for the deaths of 750,000 German civilians.

N

Glasgow

Belfast

UNITED KINGDOM

Liverpool

Queenstown

Dover

Portsmouth

Plymouth

Le Havre

Cherbourg

Brest

FRANCE

2 Most U-boat sinkings were achieved in coastal waters, the submarines lying off familiar land falls just like 18th-century privateers (map left). Many attacks were carried out by gun, to save torpedoes, but the advent of 'Q' ships led most captains to make their attacks from underwater.

2 u-boat sinkings in the western approaches, 1917–18

- ships sunk by submarines, May 1917
- ships sunk by submarines, May 1918

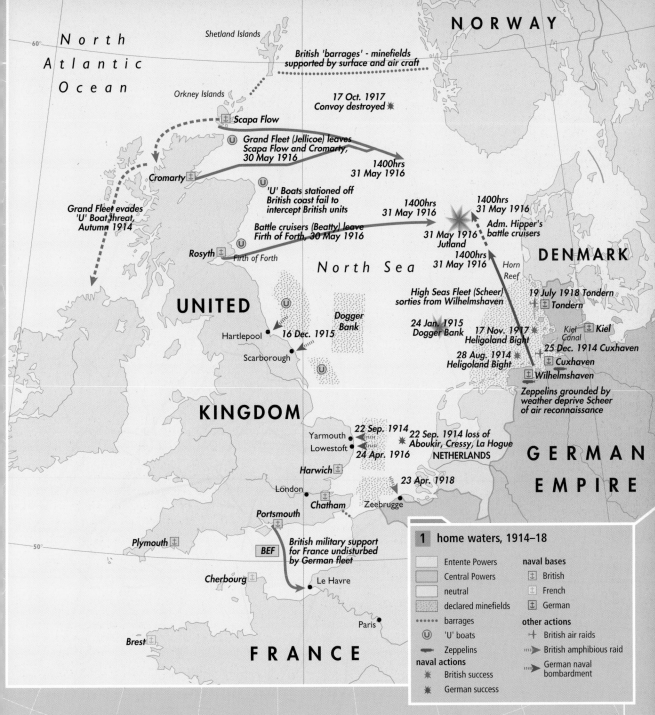

North
Atlantic
Ocean

NORWAY

Shetland Islands

British 'barrages' - minefields
supported by surface and air craft

Orkney Islands

17 Oct. 1917
Convoy destroyed ✳

Scapa Flow

Grand Fleet (Jellicoe) leaves
Scapa Flow and Cromarty,
30 May 1916

Grand Fleet evades
'U' Boat threat,
Autumn 1914

Cromarty

1400hrs
31 May 1916

'U' Boats stationed off
British coast fail to
intercept British units

1400hrs
31 May 1916

1400hrs
31 May 1916

Adm. Hipper's
battle cruisers

Battle cruisers (Beatty) leave
Firth of Forth, 30 May 1916

31 May 1916
Jutland

Rosyth

Firth of Forth

1400hrs
31 May 1916

DENMARK

Horn
Reef

North Sea

UNITED

High Seas Fleet (Scheer)
sorties from Wilhelmshaven

19 July 1918 Tondern

Tondern

Dogger
Bank

24 Jan. 1915
Dogger Bank

17 Nov. 1917
Heligoland Bight

Kiel
Canal

Kiel

Hartlepool

16 Dec. 1915

25 Dec. 1914 Cuxhaven

28 Aug. 1914
Heligoland Bight

Cuxhaven

Scarborough

Wilhelmshaven

KINGDOM

Zeppelins grounded by
weather deprive Scheer
of air reconnaissance

22 Sep. 1914

Yarmouth

22 Sep. 1914 loss of
Aboukir, Cressy, La Hogue

Lowestoft

24 Apr. 1916

NETHERLANDS

GERMAN

Harwich

23 Apr. 1918

London

Chatham

Zeebrugge

EMPIRE

Portsmouth

British military support
for France undisturbed
by German fleet

Plymouth

BEF

Cherbourg

Le Havre

Paris

Brest

FRANCE

In February 1917 German naval and military leaders agreed they could not win the war by conventional means, and insisted on a resumption of unrestricted submarine warfare. This tactic brought Great Britain to the brink of ruin in April 1917, the only month when U-boats sank the target of 600,000 tons. The carnage prompted the Allies to re-allocate shipping, ration civilian food supplies and reintroduce convoys. Convoy escorts, transferred from futile seek-and-destroy missions, found targets for their new hydrophones and depth charges. Of 88,000 ships convoyed by 11 November 1918, only 436 were lost. Convoys with air cover lost no ships to U-boats at all. The Germans on the other hand lost half their submarine flotilla, with the pick of their crews. The losses contributed to morale problems in the High Seas Fleet whose mutiny precipitated Germany's political collapse in 1918.

1 Public opinion in Britain expected the German fleet to be annihilated in a 20th-century Trafalgar, but the Kaiser forbade his battleships to risk themselves at sea. From its bleak anchorage at Scapa Flow, the British Grand Fleet dominated the North Sea, ensuring an economic blockade of German ports that denied her war economy key resources (map above). In 1916 both fleets tried to trick each other on to minefields or submarine ambushes, preparatory to an engagement: the result was Jutland.

1915
Russians evacuate East Prussia (January); battle of Gorlice-Tarnow; Austrians break Russian line (May 2–13); Russian forces pull out of Poland (July); Germans capture Brest-Litovsk (26 August); Serbia falls to German and Austrian forces (November)

1916
Brusilov offensive (4 June–17 October) shatters Austrian defensive line; Romania declares war on Central Powers (27 August); Turkey declares war on Russia (30 August); Bucharest falls to Central Powers (6 December)

1917
February Revolution in Russia; Tsar Nicholas II abdicates; Kerensky counter-offensive by Russia (26 June–19 July); Germans take Riga (3 September); Bolsheviks seize power in Russia (7 November)

1918
Treaty of Brest-Litovsk

1 Timed to coincide with the Anglo-French offensive on the Somme, General Brusilov's attack led to a widespread collapse of the Austro-Hungarian front. German troops had to be integrated with the dual monarchy's enfeebled divisions.

Falkenhayn, Chief of the German General Staff since the failure of the Schlieffen Plan, believed Russia was too large to defeat in a single offensive. He wanted a limited campaign of attrition; the Gorlice-Tarnow offensive of May 1915 was to be a victory for firepower and organization, not manoeuvre.

Falkenhayn transferred eight divisions from France to the Carpathian front, deploying 700 guns, one to every 60 yards of front. This sufficed to smash the shallow Russian front line in a four-hour bombardment. No-man's-land was two miles across, much wider than in France, allowing German infantry to approach the Russian trenches unseen, and capture the shell-shocked defenders. For the first time aircraft strafed headquarters and billets in the Russian rear. In a fortnight the Germans advanced almost 100 miles. Falkenhayn exploited north and then east, cutting the Russians' lateral railway through Brest-Litovsk. The offensive petered out in the autumn mud, as the Russians slipped away eastwards. Events had justified Falkenhayn's scepticism about achieving a strategic decision against a numerically stronger enemy prepared to retreat into Russia's endless wastes.

Falkenhayn had not crippled Russia's offensive strength as he hoped. Winter 1915/16 provided a breathing space for Russian industry to make up shortages in rifles and munitions. Material deficiencies persuaded some Russian commanders to seek subtle alternatives to simply piling up masses of shells and men. In June 1916 General Brusilov achieved surprise by attacking on a wide front, with no apparent preparations to alert the enemy. After a 24-hour bombardment, Russian infantry patrols tested the defences. Often the Russians surprised Austrian defenders in their dugouts. The Brusilov offensive finished the Austro–Hungarian Army, which never recovered from losing a

1 The Brusilov offensive, June–Oct. 1916

—— railways
—— borders, 1914

front lines
—— 4 June
- - - 10 June
····· mid-July

Russian army
☐ army units, with commanders, (divisions numbers at 4 June)
▷ army unit headquarters
□ headquarters Southwestern Front (commander Brusilov)
- - - army boundaries
➤ attacks

Central Powers army
☐ Austrian army units, with commanders
☐ Austro-German unit, with commander
- - - army boundaries

1 The dictated peace – the treaty of Brest-Litovsk

western border of Russian territory, 1914

Central Powers territory in 1914

frontline at Armistice 15 Dec. 1917

furthest extent of Central Powers occupation, 9 Jan. 1918

area of Russia occupied by Central Powers at armistice, 15 Dec. 1917

area of Russia occupied by Central Powers at peace treaty, 3 Mar. 1918

area of Russia independent after Dec. 1917

serious Russian mutinies in Aug. 1917

principal towns where Bolsheviks took power, Nov. 1917–Feb. 1918

2 The harsh terms of the peace treaty dictated to Russia by the victorious Germans in 1918 suggest how ghastly the consequences might have been for western Europe had the Kaiser's armies met with victory there. Ironically, the Germans toyed with removing Lenin and his regime, but eventually supported the revolutionaries who were prepared to make peace on any terms.

independence of Finland recognized Dec. 1917

return of Lenin from exile

German drive on Petrograd forces Bolsheviks to sign peace treaty at Brest-Litovsk 3 Mar. 1918

Government moved from Petrograd Mar. 1918

42 Austro-German divisions left as occupation forces exposed to Bolshevik subversion

grain supplies from Ukraine prevent starvation in Vienna

SWEDEN · FINLAND · RUSSIA · GERMAN EMPIRE · POLAND · AUSTRO-HUNGARIAN EMPIRE · ROMANIA · SERBIA · BULGARIA · GREECE · OTTOMAN EMPIRE · GEORGIA · Caucasus

Baltic Sea · Black Sea · Sea of Azov

Petrograd 7 Nov. 1917 · *Moscow 15 Nov. 1917*

Stockholm · Abo · Helsingfors · Revel · Lake Onega · Petrozavodsk · Lake Ladoga · Novgorod · Vologda · Pskov · Dvinsk · Riga · Danzig · Königsberg · Vilna · Minsk · Vitebsk · Kostroma · Yaroslavl · Tver · Smolensk · Ivanovo · Kaluga · Mogilev · Nizhniy Novgorod · Warsaw · Brest-Litovsk · Lodz · Gomel · Orel · Tula · Penza · Cracow · Kursk · Tambov · Voronezh · Don · Zhitomir · Lemberg · Kassa · Kiev · Kharkov · Tsaritsyn · Debrecen · Vinnitsa · Poltava · Kolozsvár · Yekaterinoslav · Jassy · Kishinev · Nikolayev · Novocherkassk · Temesvár · Odessa · Rostov · Astrakhan · Brassó · Volga · Kuma · Bucharest · Simferopol · Danube · Ruse · Sebastopol · Novorossiysk · Sofia · Varna · Plovdiv · Burgas · Adrianople · Salonica · Constantinople · Tiflis

Vistula · Dniester · Dnieper · Don

third of its total manpower in a week. The Germans had to stabilize the front with more divisions from the West, despite the Battle of the Somme. Hindenberg and Ludendorff replaced Falkenhayn, completing the military subordination of Germany's political leadership.

The Brusilov offensive cost the Russians a million casualties, but led nowhere strategically. Another million Russian soldiers deserted. Military failure, however, was not the immediate cause of Russia's leaving the war. There were still 6.5 million troops at the front, when Russia's internal collapse justified pre-war claims that protracted war was economically unsustainable. Wartime inflation had eroded the price paid to Russian grain producers. Peasants refused to market their corn, causing hunger and revolutionary disturbances in the towns. The Germans quietly allowed the Russian Army to disintegrate from within, returning exiled dissidents, such as Lenin, to hasten the process. Peace was essential to the Central Powers, particularly Austria–Hungary, but unlike the Russians they still had an Army capable of imposing a 'peace of violence'. The Treaty of Brest-Litovsk was an example to Germany's other enemies of what they might expect, if forced to sue for peace.

verdun and the somme

21 February 1916–20 August 1917
Battle of Verdun

July–November 1916
Battle of the Somme

15 September 1916
First use of tanks, by British at Flers-Courcelette

24 October 1916
Battle of Douaumont

15 December 1916
Battle of Louvemont

February 1917
Germans withdraw to Hindenburg line

Falkenhayn needed to end the war in the West before the Allied blockade or the new British armies became effective. Verdun was the strategic hinge of the Allied line.

The Germans had 14 railways against a single narrow-gauge railway on the French side. Tactically Verdun was vulnerable to converging artillery fire, its woods and steep ravines concealing offensive preparations. Falkenhayn was relying on an unprecedented bombardment of two million shells to destroy not just the frontline, but the whole zone under attack. German air superiority and the absence of the usual advanced trenches ensured surprise, while the short bombardment left no time for French reserves to react. German troops advanced inexorably, seizing the outlying fort at Douaumont. For a few hours they held open the way to Verdun.

Lacking railways the French passed lorries full of troops and stores along La Voie Sacrée from Bar-le-Duc to Verdun, at 14-second intervals, while battalions of territorials continually shovelled gravel into the potholes. For the first time a great battle depended entirely on the internal combustion engine. The British relieved the French Tenth Army at Arras, releasing fresh divisions to be rotated through the mincing machine at Verdun. Falkenhayn could not halt the offensive, lest the 550,000 French troops drawn to Verdun launched a counter-attack.

German infantry attacks suffered heavy losses for little gain, as they tried to end the battle before the anticipated Allied offensive on the Somme. Its opening bombardment in June forced Falkenhayn to close down operations at Verdun. However, German positions on the Somme were particularly strong.

The British in 1916 possessed unprecedented material and mechanical resources, which may have dulled their tactical ingenuity. Organization of the rear areas, however, was a logistical masterpiece, including three broad-gauge railways, water and accommodation for 400,000 men and 100,000 transport animals, and 7,000 miles of telephone cable to control 1,500 guns. Allied air superiority ensured the preparations remained secret.

The disastrous failure of the initial British attacks on 1 July was tactical in origin. The BEF suffered the heaviest casualties ever suffered by one army in a single day's fighting. Contributory factors included a late start and the infantry-man's excessive load. However, many British soldiers were shot down as they went over the top, implying the enemy was waiting for them. Almost two million shells were fired during a seven-day bombardment, but one in three failed to explode. There were too few heavy guns. The British had no gas shells and infantry–artillery cooperation was poor.

The first day of the Somme showed the impossibility of piercing the German line, but the balance of losses shifted against the defenders as the BEF learned their trade. German commanders unwillingly accepted the need for a less rigid defence, after they had destroyed the last of the peace-trained German infantry in repeated counter-attacks. In February 1917 the Germans withdrew to the Hindenberg Line to spare their infantry another Somme battle.

1 The initial assault failed to take Verdun, but did capture Fort Douaumont. The offensive widened to take in the left bank of the Meuse, but the French line held and a battle of attrition ensued. A final German offensive took Fort Vaux, but with the Somme battles under way, no more troops could be spared to prosecute the offensive. French counter-attacks continued into 1917, retaking the symbolic ruins of the forts.

Map: Verdun, 1916

Meuse

0   5 km
0   5 miles

first use by Germans of improved flame throwers

VII CORPS

XVIII CORPS

I LANDWEHR CORPS
Consenvoye

III CORPS

Montfaucon
Brabant

72 DIV

IV RESERVE CORPS

XV CORPS

67 DIV
Hill 295
Mort Homme

51 DIV

Etain

Hill 304

Ft Douaumont

29 DIV
Avocourt

Ft Vaux

10 DIV

Ft Souville

first use by Germans of phosgene gas

VERDUN

II CORPS

main railway cut by German artillery

Clermont

La Voie Sacrée – the only road link with Verdun

narrow gauge Chemin de fer Meusien – the only rail link with Verdun

French Corps in reserve (at Bar-le-Duc, 50 miles from Verdun)

Souilly

I + XX DIV CORPS

2 **Verdun, 1916**

———— frontline at start of offensive, 21 Feb. 1916

✕ French forts

III CORPS German assault Corps

II DIV French formations

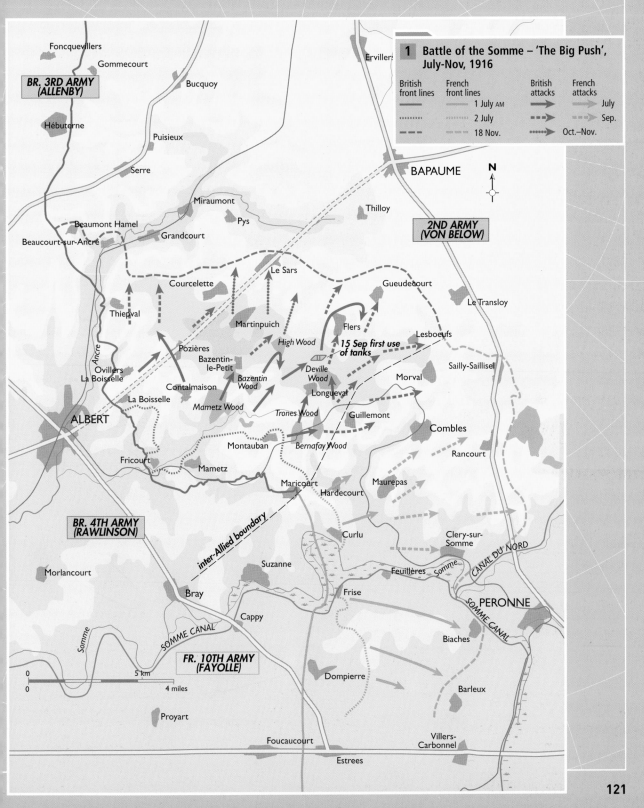

2 Popular British attitudes to the First World War remain dominated by the first day of the Somme offensive, when 57,000 casualties were suffered for negligible gains. Yet the battle went on for another 141 days and German generals described it as the 'muddy grave of the German army'. A night attack two weeks later captured several key positions, British tactics improved and tanks spearheaded the final battles in September.

1 Battle of the Somme – 'The Big Push', July–Nov, 1916

British front lines
French front lines
British attacks
French attacks

1 July AM
2 July
18 Nov.

July
Sep.
Oct.–Nov.

Foncquevillers
Gommecourt
Bucquoy
Ervillers

BR. 3RD ARMY (ALLENBY)

Hébuterne
Puisieux
Serre
Miraumont
Pys
Thilloy

BAPAUME

2ND ARMY (VON BELOW)

N

Beaumont Hamel
Grandcourt
Beaucourt-sur-Ancre
Thiepval
Courcelette
Le Sars
Gueudecourt
Le Transloy

Martinpuich
Flers
Lesboeufs

Pozières
High Wood
15 Sep first use of tanks
Sailly-Saillisel

Ancre
Bazentin-le-Petit
Deville Wood
Morval

Ovillers
La Boisselle
Contalmaison
Bazentin Wood
Longueval

La Boisselle
Mametz Wood
Trones Wood
Guillemont
Combles

ALBERT
Montauban
Bernafay Wood
Rancourt

Fricourt
Mametz
Maurepas

Maricourt
Hardecourt
Clery-sur-Somme

Curlu
CANAL DU NORD

BR. 4TH ARMY (RAWLINSON)

inter-Allied boundary

Suzanne
Feuillères   Somme

Morlancourt
Frise

Bray
PERONNE

Cappy
Biaches

Somme
SOMME CANAL
SOMME CANAL

FR. 10TH ARMY (FAYOLLE)

0   5 km
0   4 miles

Dompierre
Barleux

Proyart

Villers-Carbonnel
Foucaucourt
Estrées

9 April–16 May 1917
Battles of Arras and Vimy Ridge

31 July–18 November
Third Battle of Ypres
(Passchendaele)

20 August 1917
Battle of Hill 304 and Hill 295
Mort-Homme

20 November–3 December 1917
Battle of Cambrai. Massed tanks used for first time

2 Cambrai saw the British Army first coming to grips with the need for tanks and infantry to fight as a combined arms team (map below). This has been, in practice, one of the hardest elements of modern operations and tactics to get right, and was to be responsible for many British defeats in 1941–42.

The Third Battle of Ypres – the British Army's offensive in Belgium in the summer and autumn of 1917 – was in many ways the epitome of 20th-century land combat. Third Ypres was the battle of the mud sea, where heavy rains running down slopes denuded of vegetation turned much of the low-lying areas into quagmire. It is important because it has since defined what people thought about the Great War and, in the years since, the myths have been used to legitimize political, cultural and societal changes.

The offensive arose from a desire to capture the German submarine bases on the Belgian coast, to cover for the weakened and mutinous French army, and to crack a German army that was thought to be reeling from its losses. The bombardment opened on 18 July and continued until zero hour on 31 July. Strong German defences and incessant counter-attacks limited British gains in a series of attacks through September. After regrouping and a change in battlefield command, the British resumed the offensive on 20 September with a series of systematic, limited blows. By October, the new attacks inflicted heavy losses on the Germans, but torrential rains and the need to rush reserves to the Italian Front prevented any lasting success. With Passchendaele Ridge finally taken by the Canadian Corps in November, Third Ypres petered out.

An earlier British plan for a raid with massed tanks through German defences to the railhead town of Cambrai was revived as Third Ypres failed to yield a breakthrough. The massing of tanks and troops was carried out while still retaining some element of surprise. On the morning of 20 November, the artillery fired a short but intense barrage and the tanks went forward, with seven infantry divisions. The German defences were blown wide open. The cavalry divisions even came forward, seeing their long-awaited chance to exploit the breakthrough.

Rapidly arriving German reserves, heavy combat losses and mechanical breakdowns to the tanks, combined with a lack of reserve infantry divisions to follow up, meant that the British never made it to Cambrai, the objective that was so close on 20 November. After bitter fighting for Bourlon Wood, the Germans were able to bring up reserves.

On 30 November, the German counter-attack hit the British flanks after a brief, intense artillery barrage, mainly with gas shells. The infantry advanced. They included what the Germans styled *stosstruppen*, specialist assault troops used to infiltrate and bypass enemy strongpoints. The Germans soon took back most of their losses and even penetrated the British front line in a demonstration of their offensive power.

Cambrai was to shape debates on the use of tanks for decades thereafter. The lessons were read very differently then, but as 1917 closed and more German troops arrived in the west from the Eastern Front, the Germans believed they had managed to forge a solution to the modern battlefield. The British did as well and unlike the Germans, they had the matériel to make it yield victory.

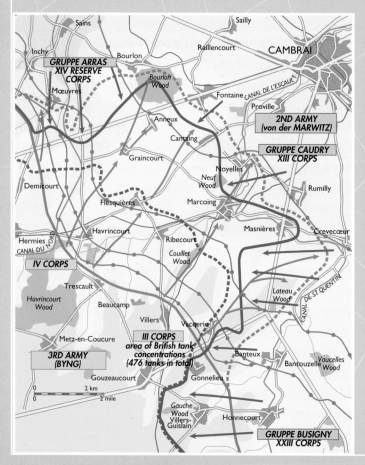

2 Cambrai, nov. – dec. 1917

―――	front line before British attack, Nov. 20
―•―•―	German defence lines
←	British advances
┄┄┄┄	front line, Nov. 29
◄━━	German counter-attacks
―――	front line after German counter-attacks, Dec. 3
▪▪▪▪	front line after British withdrawal, Dec. 5

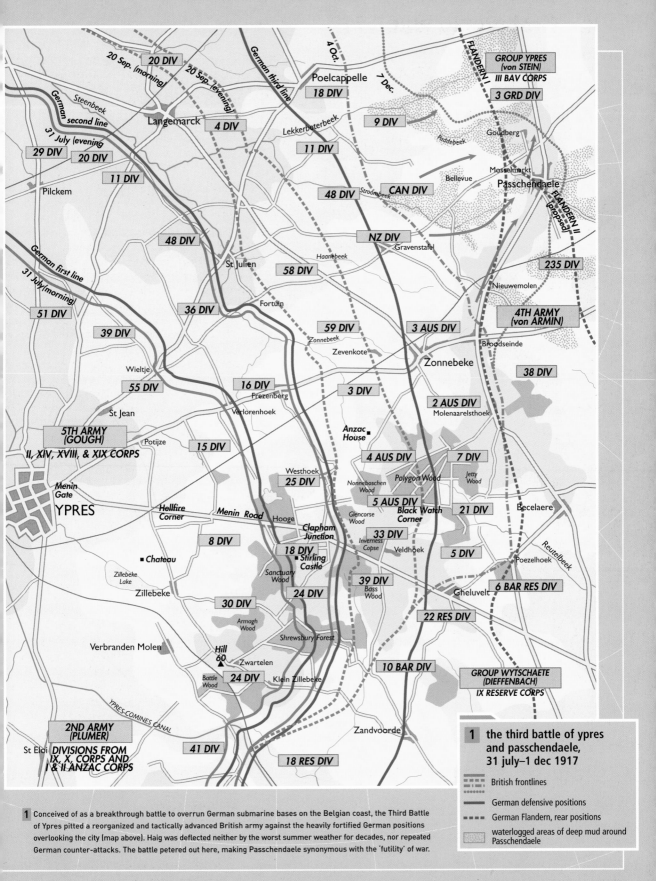

20 Sep. (morning)

20 Sep. (evening)

20 DIV

German third line

4 Oct.

FLANDERN I

7 Dec.

GROUP YPRES
(von STEIN)
III BAV CORPS

Poelcappelle

18 DIV

3 GRD DIV

Steenbeek

German
second line

Langemarck

4 DIV

Lekkerboterbeek

9 DIV

Paddebeek

Goudberg

31 July (evening)

11 DIV

Mosselmarkt

29 DIV

20 DIV

Bellevue

Passchendaele

FLANDERN II
(proposed)

11 DIV

Pilckem

48 DIV

Stroombeek

CAN DIV

235 DIV

German first line

St Julien

Haanebeek

NZ DIV

Gravenstafel

Nieuwemolen

31 July (morning)

58 DIV

51 DIV

36 DIV

Fortuin

59 DIV

Zonnebeek

3 AUS DIV

Zevenkote

4TH ARMY
(von ARMIN)

39 DIV

Broodseinde

Zonnebeke

Wieltje

16 DIV

Frezenberg

3 DIV

38 DIV

55 DIV

St Jean

Verlorenhoek

2 AUS DIV

Molenaarelsthoek

5TH ARMY
(GOUGH)
II, XIV, XVIII, & XIX CORPS

Potijze

15 DIV

Anzac
House

4 AUS DIV

7 DIV

Jetty
Wood

Menin
Gate

YPRES

Westhoek

25 DIV

Nonneboschen
Wood

Polygon Wood

Hellfire
Corner

Menin Road

Hooge

5 AUS DIV

Black Watch
Corner

21 DIV

Becelaere

Glencorse
Wood

Clapham
Junction

33 DIV

5 DIV

Poezelhoek

8 DIV

18 DIV

Stirling
Castle

Inverness
Copse

Veldhoek

Reutelbeek

Chateau

Sanctuary
Wood

24 DIV

39 DIV

Bass
Wood

Gheluvelt

6 BAR RES DIV

Zillebeke
Lake

30 DIV

Armagh
Wood

22 RES DIV

Zillebeke

Shrewsbury Forest

Verbranden Molen

Hill
60

Zwartelen

10 BAR DIV

GROUP WYTSCHAETE
(DIEFFENBACH)
IX RESERVE CORPS

Battle
Wood

24 DIV

Klein Zillebeke

YPRES-COMINES CANAL

2ND ARMY
(PLUMER)

St Eloi   DIVISIONS FROM
IX, X, CORPS AND
I & II ANZAC CORPS

41 DIV

Zandvoorde

18 RES DIV

1 **the third battle of ypres
and passchendaele,
31 july–1 dec 1917**

British frontlines

German defensive positions

German Flandern, rear positions

waterlogged areas of deep mud around
Passchendaele

1 Conceived of as a breakthrough battle to overrun German submarine bases on the Belgian coast, the Third Battle
of Ypres pitted a reorganized and tactically advanced British army against the heavily fortified German positions
overlooking the city (map above). Haig was deflected neither by the worst summer weather for decades, nor repeated
German counter-attacks. The battle petered out here, making Passchendaele synonymous with the 'futility' of war.

21 March 1918
Ludendorff's first offensive to pushed back the Allied frontline at Ypres

9 April and 27 May 1918
Two further Geman offensives were less successful

July 1918
French and American troops attack Germans in the Marne

8 August 1918
British troops crack the German front near Amiens with 400 tanks. German troops surrender in droves

11 November 1918
Germans retreat following mutiny of navy and political collapse

For Germany, there was no option but to launch one final blow at the western allies before the United States Army could make its weight felt on the Western Front.

Ludendorff planned five successive but basically uncoordinated offensives. The first and largest opened on 21 March, hitting the southernmost part of the British line. The Germans made tremendous gains in the first day and followed this up by a week of advance towards Amiens that brought the Germans forward over much of the ground given up after the Somme in 1916. But after a week, heavy casualties, diminishing supplies and the inability to bring the heavy artillery forward brought the offensive to a halt. An attempt to resume the drive, against Arras, was stopped in its tracks.

Ludendorff then launched his second offensive on 9 April, aimed at cutting off the southern flank of the Ypres salient that the British had expanded at such cost in 1917. By the end of April, this offensive had also sputtered out, having failed to achieve its goals.

1 The USA declared war in 1917 but the US Army would take at least 18 months to expand and re-equip for operations in Europe. Germany had one final chance to win the war before the correlation of forces became impossible. In March 1918, reinforced by divisions released from Russia, General Ludendorff began a series of offensives that drove back the British and French, but cost the German army nearly a million casualties (map right). New weapons and tactics were restoring mobility, but the new warfare would be no less deadly.

2 allied offensives

Allied frontlines
- 18 July
- 25 August
- 15 October
- 6 November
- Armistice line (11 November)
- German defences
- supply railways

BELGIAN ARMY (ALBERT)

BRITISH EXPEDITIONARY FORCE (HAIG)

FREN. 1ST ARMY (DEBENEY)

FREN. 3RD ARMY (HUMBERT)

FREN. 5TH ARMY (MICHELER)

FRENCH ARMY (PETAIN)

FREN. 10TH ARMY (MAISTRE)

FREN. 4TH ARMY (GOURAUD)

US 1ST ARMY (LIGGET)

AMERICAN EXPEDITIONARY FORCE (PERSHING)

US 2ND ARMY (BULLARD)

The third offensive hit the French lines in the Chemin Des Dames along the Aisne on 27 May. This was the fastest and deepest drive of all: 13 miles gained the first day, then Soissons taken and German spearheads were back on the Marne. The next offensive, opening 9 June on the Noyon-Montdidier sector of the French line to the north, soon ground to a halt. The last offensive, an attempt to push over the Marne on 15 July, gained a sizeable bridgehead across the river but soon hit strong American resistance and, as reserves arrived, was halted within days.

Germany's offensives failed because they lacked the resources of their opponents and because, in the absence of strong planning and coordination, the Germans' tactical strengths could not be translated to operational strengths. They also lacked the logistics to bring supplies or reserves forward to exploit their successes.

Unlike the German plan, the Allied solution worked, in large part because they had more resources but also because they had worked out a system that was better able to translate tactical victories into operational success that could open up the enemy defences. Despite the terrible losses inflicted by the German offensives, the Allied divisions of 1918 were far from the hapless infantry of 1914–16. Tanks, heavy guns, aircraft, combined arms, through planning and logistics support all made the success possible.

The French and Americans attacked the German penetrations in the Marne in July, within days of the German offensive starting, while the main British blow, on 8 August, with over 400 tanks, cracked the German front near Amiens. After that, Foch ordered "*tout le monde à bataille*" and there followed a repeated series of blows on a broad front. There was nothing left for the Germans but retreat when, on 11 November, the political collapse at home that had followed the mutiny of the German Navy, joined by troops and workers, led to the Armistice.

2 As the German Spring offensives petered out, the Allies counter-attacked with equal tactical skill but greater resources (map above). The German army was never able to stabilize its front as in previous years: successive Allied attacks ruptured its defences and systematically drove the invader from French and Belgian territory. The German high command accepted defeat and demanded Germany's politicians make peace before the Allied armies crossed the Rhine.

the **russian revolution**

February 1917
Tsar Nicholas abdicates

October 1917
Lenin and Bolsheviks seize power

1918
Treaty of Brest-Litovsk: Russia withdraws from First World War

May 1918
Georgia, Armenia and Azerbaijan become independent republics

1918–20
Russian Civil War

1921
Lenin introduces NEP

1922
Stalin appointed General Secretary

The Great War's legacy of the fall of the empires of central and eastern Europe and the rise of ideological states, first the Soviet Union, followed by Fascist Italy and Nazi Germany, had a direct impact on the evolution of war-fighting. Ideology would, in the Second World War, help bring about a return to savagery not seen in Europe since the Thirty Years' War.

Ideologically oriented countries also had as one of their characteristics the mobilization of all potential resources within the state, much as Ludendorff had tried to do with wartime Germany.

Revolutions present their own form of military requirements which, like everything else in war-fighting, had changed with the Industrial Revolution. The dynamics of Petrograd in 1917 differed from Paris in 1789 – the model so many expected it to follow – because of the impact of the railway and the telegraph. The Leninist concept of the élite mobilizing revolutionary vanguard could be realized in military terms because modern weaponry allowed such a group to implement its policies by force of arms. The organizational development of the modern state allowed the secret police of the Soviet Union broader and deeper reach than that of Napoleonic France.

Militarily, the wars in the East did not offer the preview of future operations and tactics that the Western Front of 1918 did. But they were tremendously important for what they led to. The Soviet Union emerged, with both a supranational communist ideology and the potential for superpower status that had been Russia's for decades. The events also shaped the Soviet way of war – the need for mobile combat, for operations over widely dispersed fronts – in ways that would endure as long as that country. The multinational intervention by the Allies along the periphery of the Russian empire, first to continue the war, then to support those fighting the Bolsheviks, was militarily limited. There were few resources available while the Germans were still fighting and, after the Armistice, little spirit for a new conflict.

The end of great wars, like the end of great empires, creates more wars. Once the issue of who would control centralized state power in the former Russian empire was established the next effort was to bring back under its control those peripheral, non-Russian areas that had exerted independence. Poland, with support from France, was able to prevent its re-absorption and check the spread of Bolshevism via the Red Army in its victory in the Russo–Polish War. Elsewhere, the process of military exertion of central authority led to fighting in central Asia during the 1920s and paved the way for its consolidation through the Stalinist terror of the 1930s.

2 the transcaucasus, 1918–23

frontiers, 1914

to the Ottoman empire under Treaty of Brest-Litovsk, Mar 1918

Transcaucasian SSR at declaration of independence, Apr. 1918

to the Ottoman empire under Treaty of Batum, June 1918

Batum-Baku railway; under British control, Nov. 1918–Aug. 1919

controlled by Armenia, Azerbaijan, Georgia and British forces, May 1919

disputed between Armenia and Azerbaijan, July 1919–Aug. 1920

northern frontier of Turkey under Treaty of Kars, Oct. 1921

Transcaucasian SSR, Mar. 1922

Ottoman advances, with dates

Red Army advances, with dates

RUSSIAN EMPIRE

Black Sea

Feb. 1921

Feb. 1921

Feb. 1921

Batum last British-held post; evacuated July 1920

Mar. 192

Feb. 1918

LAZISTAN

GEORGIA (independent May 1918, Bolshevik Mar 1921) • Tiflis

Feb. 192

June 1918

Caspian Sea

Apr. 1920

Aleksandropol (Leninakan) • Yelizavetpol (Kirovabad) •

Sep. 1918

ARMENIA Lake Sevan

AZERBAIJAN (independent May 1918, Bolshevik Apr. 1920)

Baku •

Feb. 1918

Nov. 1920

KARABAGH

occupied by Red Army Apr. 1920

OTTOMAN EMPIRE (independent May 1918, Bolshevik Mar. 1921)

NAKHICHEVAN

July 1920

Lake Van

PERSIA

2 After the fall of the Tsar, a Transcaucasian Federal Republic was set up independent of Russia (map left). It was invaded and occupied by the Turks until May 1918, when Georgia, Armenia and Azerbaijan set up separate independent states under British and French protection. When the British left in December 1919, the Bolshevik armies began the slow reconquest of the region.

1 russia in war and revolution

- ━━━ boundary of Russian empire, 1914
- ▲ towns occupied by Entente forces, Aug. 1918–19
- - - - area controlled by Bolsheviks, Aug. 1918
- ········ eastern boundary of area controlled by Bolsheviks, Apr. 1919
- ▨ controlled by Bolsheviks, Oct. 1919
- ━━━ boundary of areas controlled by anti-Bolshevik forces, Apr. 1920
- ───── deepest advance of Red Army into Poland, Aug. 1920
- - - - - final anti-Bolshevik advance, Oct. 1920
- ───── boundary of Soviet territory, Mar. 1921
- ⟵ movement of White Russian armies
- ⟵ movement of non-Russian anti-Bolshevik forces
- ⟵ anarchist military activities
- ⊙ centres of Confederation of Anarchist Organizations
- ○ Makhno's headquarters, 1918–20
- ───── frontiers, 1923

Entente fleet · Barents Sea
Murmansk
British French Canadians Italians Serbs
White Sea
Canadians Americans · Archangel
British French
FINLAND independence of Finland recognized Dec. 1917
SWEDEN
Finns
Petrozavodsk · Lake Onega
Lake Ladoga
Helsinki
Revel (Tallinn) · **ESTONIA** · Yudenich
Narva
Petrograd (Leningrad)
Novgorod
Vologda
Kornilov's attack on Petrograd Sep. 1917
British/French naval assistance
Riga · Letts · **LATVIA** · Baltic Germans
Pskov
Kostroma
Yaroslavl
Ivanovo
Nizhniy Novgorod (Gorkiy)
Izhevsk
Yekaterinburg (Sverdlovsk)
LITHUANIA
GERMANY (E. PRUSSIA)
Vitebsk
Tver (Kalinin)
B O L S H E V I K **R U S S I A**
Moscow
Kazan
Kolchak 1918–1
Smolensk · Kaluga
Minsk
Trans-Siberian Railway
Czechs
Ufa
Samara (Kuybyshev)
Nicholas II and family shot by Bolsheviks July 1918
Mogilev
Tula
Penza
POLAND
Warsaw
Brest-Litovsk
Poles
Gomel
Orel
Tambov
Orenburg (Chkalov)
CZECHOSLOVAKIA
HUN.
Zhitomir
Kiev
Voronezh
Saratov
Denikin 1919
Kharkov
Poltava
Lozovaya
Don Cossacks 1917–19
Ural Cossack Army 1918–20
Peregonovka
Dibrivki
Yekaterinoslav (Dnepropetrovsk)
Gulyay-Pole
Tsaritsyn (Stalingrad)
Romanians
BESSARABIA
Kishinev
Nikopol
Mariupol
Novocherkassk
Rostov-on-Don
Astrakhan
ROMANIA
Odessa
Berdiansk
Cossacks
Wrangel 1920
Caspian Sea
Sevastopol · Simferopol
Novorossiysk
BULGARIA
French
British
Georgians 1919–20
Mensheviks
Black Sea
Entente fleet
Istanbul
Batum
Tiflis (Tbilisi)
Baku
Krasnovodsk
Kars
Tabriz
British 1918–19
PERSIA

1 Under the pressure of total war the Russian monarchy collapsed in February 1917. The Provisional Government failed either to halt the Germans at the front or the tide of radical revolution at home. In October the Bolsheviks seized power and a bloody three-year civil war followed (map above). This was waged by comparatively small armies over vast swathes of territory, coordinated (or not) by telegraph and supported by armoured trains, aircraft, tanks and armoured cars. The strategic mobility and ideological commitment of the Red cavalry played a major part in the Bolshevik victory, creating an inner circle of military and political leaders that would dominate the USSR under Stalin.

the **sino–japanese** wars

1931
Mukden Incident (18 September); Japanese occupy Manchuria

1932
Shanghai Riots (28 January); Japanese take control of city

1933
Japanese occupy China north of Great Wall; puppet state of Manchukuo established by Japanese

1937
Japanese begin invasion of rest of China (July); Japanese seize Peking (28 July); the 'Rape of Nanking' (December)

1938
Japanese install puppet government in Nanking; capture of Canton (October)

1944
Operation *Ichi-go* – last major Japanese offensive in China

1945
Japanese surrender in China signed (9 September)

1 Japan's occupation of Manchuria in 1931 shattered the cosy belief that the League of Nations could prevent the use of war as an instrument of state policy (map right). No amount of international condemnation stopped the Japanese army in its subsequent invasion of China. Its military operations were conducted with bestial savagery epitomized by the mass slaughter of civilians at Nanking.

By 1914, it had already become apparent that the military history of the world was no longer equivalent to that of just Europe, even though European wars had been fought out on a global stage over the two preceding centuries. Now came Japan's industrialization and entry on the world stage as a military power as a result of the Sino–Japanese and Russo–Japanese Wars.

By 1931, Japan was looking for a solution to its problems and thought it lay in the use of armed force. Japan felt itself a have-not power, with a combination of Western imperialism, closed markets and racist exclusion preventing it from the type of imperial expansion that the West had carried out in the preceding century and which was now

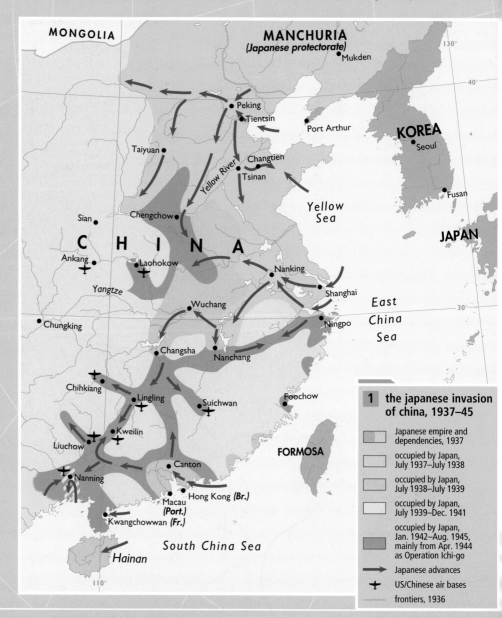

1 the japanese invasion of china, 1937–45

Japanese empire and dependencies, 1937

occupied by Japan, July 1937–July 1938

occupied by Japan, July 1938–July 1939

occupied by Japan, July 1939–Dec. 1941

occupied by Japan, Jan. 1942–Aug. 1945, mainly from Apr. 1944 as Operation Ichi-go

→ Japanese advances

✈ US/Chinese air bases

—— frontiers, 1936

proving increasingly difficult to sustain. The lessons of the Great War had shown that national power was affected by natural resources, and Japan remained resource-poor. Compounding this was the rise of the political power of the Japanese military and an ethos of militarization of society.

This armed force was first applied in the occupation of Manchuria in 1931 (dealing a body blow to another potential 'solution' to the problems of modern statecraft, the League of Nations). It was followed by a war against the rest of China, starting in 1937, in which Japan used its superior sea power to occupy ports and coastal areas. Moving inland from these and from Manchuria, the Japanese soon defeated the Chinese armed forces, weak from decades of internal instability. Militarily, perhaps the most significant threat to the Japanese came from guerrilla warfare, most notably practised by the Communist Eighth Route Army.

The Western powers had long opposed the Japanese expansion in China. This led to increasing US support for China in the years before Pearl Harbor. But despite reinforcements of US air power, the Japanese were still able to launch successful offensives in China well into 1944, reflecting in part the Chinese emphasis on preparing for their upcoming civil war rather than devoting resources to defeating Japan.

2 japan's oil sources, 1936–41

- Japanese empire, 1936
- oilfields
- oil shale
- principal refineries
- Japanese oil routes
- frontiers, 1936

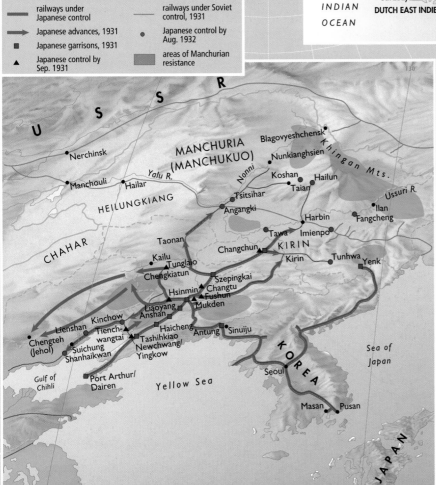

3 the manchurian campaign, 1931–2

- railways under Japanese control
- Japanese advances, 1931
- Japanese garrisons, 1931
- Japanese control by Sep. 1931
- railways under Soviet control, 1931
- Japanese control by Aug. 1932
- areas of Manchurian resistance

2 Entirely dependent on imported fuel, Japan determined to secure the oilfields of the Dutch East Indies (map above). Curiously, Japan made no plans for the security of its supplies if a prolonged war resulted: she had sufficient oil tankers, but few naval escorts and no operational plans for convoying them. The oilfields would be overrun in 1941–42, but US submarines would send her tanker fleet to the bottom by 1944.

3 On 18 September 1931 Japanese soldiers of the Manchurian Kwantung army blew up a short stretch on the South Manchurian railway near Mukden, run by Japan. The 'incident' was taken as the opportunity to extend Japanese control over an area rich in mineral resources. Japan struck north into Manchuria, establishing a puppet government and eventually a new land border with Russia (map left).

the **spanish civil war**

1936
Popular Front wins national elections in Spain (February); military uprisings in Spanish Morocco (July); Franco takes command of army in Morocco 19 July); first International Brigade volunteers arrive in Spain (August)

1937
Nationalist start major offensive against Madrid (February); battle of Guadalajara (March); Guernica bombed (April); Bilbao taken by Nationalists (June)

1938
Republican offensive splits Nationalist territory in two (April); battle of Ebro (July) leads to collapse of Republican army

1939
Barcelona falls to Republicans (January); Madrid surrenders (March)

The Spanish Civil War was, first and foremost, the result of currents in Spanish politics, history and culture that had endured since the French invasion of 1808. Since then, Spain had been seen as increasingly peripheral to the European power system. The loss of most of its colonial empire and its late and limited industrialization compounded this perception.

When, in 1936, Spaniard once again started to fight Spaniard, the place of armed conflict in the European power system ensured that this would have wider ramifications. The Nationalist rebels were identified ideologically with the Fascist states in Italy and Germany, while the Republican government had the Soviet Union as its prime external patron. The weakness of the non-ideological powers and the League of Nations underlined that, at the highest level, ideology was part of the solution of the end of the old order in the Great War.

At the operational and tactical levels other solutions, more developed versions of those seen in 1918, were brought into play. In most cases, this was the result of technological intervention by outside powers, while the bulk of the fighting was Spaniard against Spaniard using older technologies and tactics. Tanks were used in significant numbers but, where not supported by combined arms tactics, they often failed against anti-tank guns or even stalwart infantry, as in 1917–18. Bombers – including the accurate German Stukas – proved important and strategic bombing advocates stressed their efficacy. Anti-aircraft guns – including the German 88mm – were as important in countering the bomber threat. Submarines were able to prey on merchant ships much as in the Great War. Overall, the lessons of Spain were distorted and mythologized, not only by ideologists but also by advocates for military change.

1 In 1936 the Spanish army under Franco rebelled against the Republic established in 1931. The result was a bitter and sanguinary civil war between the nationalist right and the liberal and socialist left, which came to symbolize the wider struggle between fascism and communism (map right). It began with the first strategic airlift in history: German transport aircraft shuttling Franco's Army of Africa to the mainland where it spearheaded the Nationalist revolt. Although aircraft and tanks were employed by both sides, the fighting was reminiscent of the First World War and many pundits, not least Liddell-Hart, published articles basing their prognosis for the future on the persistence of static warfare, a view that would be overturned by the advent of Blitzkrieg in 1939.

with Nationalists:
75,000 Italian,
20,000 Portuguese and
17,000 German soldiers

with Republicans:
500 Russian soldiers,
40,000 foreign volunteers

Gijón

Santander

Guernica

San Sebastián

F R A N C E

BASQUE PROVINCES

frontier closed by France to Republican refugees, 1938

ANDORRA

Bilbao

León

Pamplona

N A V A R R E

Ebro

Burgos
Nationalist Government H.Q.

A R A G O N

Saragossa

C A T A L O N I A

Barcelona

Valladolid

Douro

Belchete

Tarragona

amanca

Guadalajara
besieged by Nationalists; occupied on 28 Mar. 1939

Teruel

from Odessa

Madrid

Brunete

Jarama

Minorca

Mahón

Toledo

Castellón de la Plana

Guadiana

P   A   I   N

Valencia

Palma

Majorca

Albacete
International Brigade base

M U R C I A

Ibiza

Formentera

Lopera

Alicante

Córdoba

adalquivir

Cartagena

le

Granada

Almería

from Genoa

Málaga

S e a

Gibraltar
(Br.)

M e d i t e r r a n e a n

Ceuta
gier

A L G E R I A

0°

SPANISH   MOROCCO

1 the spanish civil war, 1936–39

➔ Nationalist supply routes

➔ Republican supply routes

○ "International Brigade" operations

➔ main Nationalist attacks

➔ main Republican attacks

▢ Nationalist, July 1936

▢ Nationalist, Oct. 1937

▢ Nationalist, July 1938

▢ Nationalist, Feb. 1939

▢ Republican, Mar. 1939

✕ areas of most intense fighting

blitzkrieg – outbreak of the **second world war**

The years between the two world wars saw the greatest transformation of the modern era in society and war over the shortest period of time. The internal combustion engine and the wireless could now take their role at the centre of the enabling technologies of war-fighting. The wireless's offspring, radar, ensured that the pre-war belief that 'the bomber will always get through' was misplaced. Its undersea acoustic counterpart, sonar, did much the same for war at sea. By the end of the Second World War, technologies not even anticipated before its outbreak were introduced: the jet aircraft, the ballistic missile and the atomic bomb.

The Second World War was politically, in many ways, a continuation of the First. The failure of the international system to put in place a stable replacement for the old order that had perished by 1917 became apparent as the transition from a post-war to a pre-war world unfolded. The German campaigns in Europe from September 1939 to June 1941 represented the most complete use of military power to reshape the world since Napoleon.

Those victories demonstrated the quality of the new German armed forces, built for a short, victorious war rather than the massive battles of the previous war. The key element was combined arms panzer divisions. While the quality of German tanks (and their ground weapons in general) was not greatly superior to their enemies, (and most of the German Army still relied on the railroad and horse transport as in 1914), they had mastered the new technologies and the operational level of war far better than any of their opponents.

The Germans were also fortunate in their opponents. Poland was in a strategically indefensible position even before the Hitler–Stalin pact of 1939. The only militarily significant opponents were the French and the British. In 1940, they had, in most areas, numerical superiority over the Germans. Where they failed was in two decisive areas. The first was air power. The Luftwaffe was able to

1 German plans for an invasion of England were improvised in the wake of the French victory. They depended on winning air supremacy, but the integrated air defence of the UK proved impossible to overcome before autumn weather ruled out a sea crossing.

2 Thanks to the skills of her armed forces rather than numerical superiority, between 1939 and 1941 Germany conquered much of continental Europe (map right). Its mastery of what opponents dubbed 'blitzkrieg' (lightning war) allowed it to defeat Poland in two weeks, and to overcome Belgium, Luxembourg, Holland, France, Denmark and Norway in six weeks. The invasion of the USSR in 1941 seemed set to presage Hitler's greatest triumph as German forces swept aside a feeble Red Army.

1 the battle of britain, 1940

- HQ Fighter Command headquarters
- G group headquarters
- --- group boundaries
- ⊤ sector command post
- ▲ fighter bases
- high-level radar station
- low-level radar station
- ✴ observer centres
- ▪ Luftflotte HQ
- ● Luftwaffe bomber base

The Blitz
- ✳ 1–5 major raids (100 tons+)
- ✴ 6–10 major raids
- ✴ more than 10 major raids

seize air superiority and serve as a powerful force multiplier for the ground forces. The second was in the type of combined arms mechanized formations represented by the panzer divisions. The French and British lacked the tanks, tactics and organization to be as effective as the Germans. Even though the British Expeditionary Force had its infantry divisions motorized, the lack of reliable armoured formations limited its operational manoeuvrability.

But the German war machine's limitations became apparent in the months after its greatest triumph, the fall of France. Then, in the Battle of Britain, the Luftwaffe found itself unable to defeat the Royal Air Force. The RAF demonstrated that it was more than equal to the Luftwaffe in the use of technology, using aircraft on a par with any in the world as part of an integrated air defence system, a new British creation, made possible by a British invention, radar. The first decisive campaign fought between air forces ensured that Germany's successes would not solve its fundamental strategic problems.

2 The axis advance, 1939–41

- Axis territory, 1 Sep. 1939
- Axis co-belligerents
- occupied by Axis after Sep. 1939
- Vichy France and territories
- Soviet annexed territory, 1939–41
- neutral powers
- frontiers, 1 Sep. 1939
- Axis advances, 1939
- Axis advances, 1940
- Axis advances, 1941
- Axis airborne landings
- Allied forces
- Soviet advances, 1939–40
- Allied retreat and withdrawal
- major cities severely damaged by bombing

1940
Italians invade Egypt (September); British capture Sidi Barrani (11 December)

1941
Tobruk falls to British (22 January); Germans capture Benghazi (4 April); siege of Tobruk raised (10-11 December); British retake Benghazi (25 December)

1942
Germans take Tobruk (20–21 June); second battle of El Alamein (23–20 October); Operation *Torch*, US invasion of North Africa begins (November)

1943
British capture Tripoli (28 January); Allies enter Tunisia (February); German surrender in North Africa (12 May)

The war in North Africa and, indeed, the Mediterranean as a whole started off as a sideshow to the ill-fated Italian offensives in 1940. It ended up as the major campaign in the West in 1940–43, attracting Britain's strategic reserve.

The initial 1940–41 campaign saw the defeat of non-mechanized Italian forces, which had invaded Egypt from the Italian colony of Libya. They were defeated by a mechanized British force, permanently reducing Italy to the status of a dependent partner on its German ally and leading to the commitment of German land, sea and air forces, although their numbers remained relatively small until just before their final defeat in Tunisia in 1943.

The war in North Africa was part of a larger Mediterranean campaign which, previewed in the Norwegian campaign of 1940, integrated naval, air and ground forces in a new type of warfare. It included Malta-based British air, sea and submarine forces interdicting the Axis supply routes to North Africa while, in

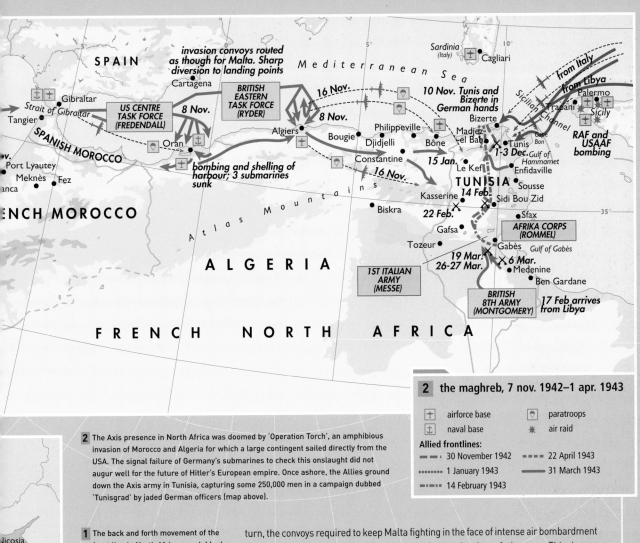

The following text appears within the map:

SPAIN

Mediterranean Sea

invasion convoys routed as though for Malta. Sharp diversion to landing points

Cartagena

BRITISH EASTERN TASK FORCE (RYDER)

Sardinia (Italy) — Cagliari

16 Nov.

10 Nov. Tunis and Bizerte in German hands

from Italy

from Libya

Palermo

Strait of Gibraltar — Gibraltar

US CENTRE TASK FORCE (FREDENDALL)

8 Nov.

8 Nov.

Algiers

Bizerte

Sicilian Channel

Trapani — Sicily

Tangier

SPANISH MOROCCO

Oran

Bougie

Philippeville

Djidjelli

Bône

Madjez el Bab

Cape Bon

Tunis

RAF and USAAF bombing

Port Lyautey

bombing and shelling of harbour; 3 submarines sunk

Constantine

15 Jan.

Gulf of Hammamet

1–3 Dec.

Meknès — Fez

16 Nov.

Le Kef

Enfidaville

FRENCH MOROCCO

Atlas Mountains

Biskra

Kasserine

22 Feb.

TUNISIA

14 Feb.

Sousse

Sidi Bou Zid

Sfax

ALGERIA

Gafsa

Tozeur

Gabès

Gulf of Gabès

AFRIKA CORPS (ROMMEL)

1ST ITALIAN ARMY (MESSE)

19 Mar.

26–27 Mar.

6 Mar.

Medenine

Ben Gardane

BRITISH 8TH ARMY (MONTGOMERY)

17 Feb arrives from Libya

FRENCH   NORTH   AFRICA

2   the maghreb, 7 nov. 1942–1 apr. 1943

| airforce base | paratroops |
| naval base | air raid |

Allied frontlines:

– – – 30 November 1942   – – – – 22 April 1943

·········· 1 January 1943   ———— 31 March 1943

–·–·– 14 February 1943

2 The Axis presence in North Africa was doomed by 'Operation Torch', an amphibious invasion of Morocco and Algeria for which a large contingent sailed directly from the USA. The signal failure of Germany's submarines to check this onslaught did not augur well for the future of Hitler's European empire. Once ashore, the Allies ground down the Axis army in Tunisia, capturing some 250,000 men in a campaign dubbed 'Tunisgrad' by jaded German officers (map above).

1 The back and forth movement of the front line in North Africa was dubbed the 'Benghazi handicap' by Eighth Army cynics, the war raging across Libya and into Egypt as the inspired leadership of General Erwin Rommel compensated for superior British resources (map left). German forces were superbly coordinated, and their commander an indisputable master of modern war.

turn, the convoys required to keep Malta fighting in the face of intense air bombardment resulted in some of the most intense air–sea battles of the war. This larger Mediterranean dimension was critical to the war, shaping it at its start by the diversion of British forces to Greece and, at its end, presenting the Allies with the problem of how to use their hard-won conquest of the North littoral as a trans-Mediterranean springboard against Axis-occupied Europe.

The campaign in North Africa in 1941–43 was dominated by the skill of Erwin Rommel, commander of the German Afrika Korps. But his charisma only compounded the superiority in combined arms mechanized operations and tactics that the Germans had over the British. Once the initial force that had defeated the Italians was dispersed, the British had to learn the business of combined arms mechanized combat – the model for future operations – in action. By their victory at the Second Battle of El Alamein in 1942, they had learned well enough.

The outcome in North Africa was shaped by two factors that did not easily show up in the orders of battle: logistics and intelligence. Logistics decided the outcome on the battlefield to a greater extent than the most brilliant tactical manoeuvres. British Ultra decrypts of German secure communications, when available, provided excellent intelligence but could often not be made available to the war-fighters in time to be of decisive value.

1   the war in north africa, 1940–43

Axis control, Oct. 1941 (including Vichy France)

British control, Oct. 1941

→ Axis advances in the desert war, with details

→ Allied advances in the desert war, with details

→ Allied landings, with date

— southern limit of actual area of operations of the desert war

— limit of Axis control, 23 Nov. 1942

— frontiers, 1942

June 1941
German invades USSR (22nd);
Germans capture Minsk (28th)

July 1941
Germans capture Riga (1st);
Capture of Smolensk (15th)

August 1941
Germans surround Leningrad
(19th)

September 1941
Germans occupy Estonai (5th);
first snows slow German
advance (12th); Germans take
Kiev (19th)

October 1941
Odessa falls to Germans (16th);
Germans take Kharkov (24th)

November 1941
Germans capture Kursk (3rd);
Kerch (16th); German attack on
Moscow, panzers within 20
miles of city (25th)

December 1941
Germans abandon attack on
Moscow (5th)

The War in the East represented the largest-scale combat operations of the Second World War and many of the most intense. The Soviets long distinguished it as a separate conflict the Great Patriotic War from the Second World War of which it was a part. While for decades after 1945 Western historians tended to focus on their countries' own combat actions, the German Army suffered some 80 per cent of its total casualties in the East.

The German 1941 invasion of the Soviet Union again reflected the increased importance on strategic surprise that resulted from techno-logical change. Aircraft and mechanized forces could inflict lasting damage swiftly, before the shock effect had worn off. It also showed that the increasing significance and sophistication of intelligence as a counter to surprise – the rise of the wireless meant that signals intelligence and cryptology were now a crucial element of war-fighting – meant nothing if the decision-makers chose to believe their own preconceptions. Hitler was the only man Stalin ever trusted.

The initial months of the invasion saw tremendous advances and volumes of prisoners but, as the summer came to an end, increasingly savage if disorganized Soviet resistance and Hitler's shifting of objectives prevented the rapier thrust to Moscow that was thought necessary to bring down the Soviet Union. The blitzkrieg forces intended to win a quick, limited-liability conflict now found themselves faced by a conflict for which Germany's lack of thorough industrial mobilization had not prepared them. The Soviets were able to evacuate much of their industrial base to the Urals, assuring that future forces could be supported even while those in the field in 1941 were destroyed.

The destruction of the pre-war Soviet forces in the western military districts did not win the campaign. Military improvization, the arrival of the Soviet strategic reserve from Siberia and the Far East, and the over-stretch of the few German motorized units when the Russian autumn and then winter arrived, brought the advance to a halt.

At the end, the German spearheads actually could see the spires of the Kremlin. But it was too late. In December, the Soviets launched their first major counter-attack. Their losses were heavy, but in the end the Germans were forced to give ground in front of Moscow. They would never come as close to the prize again.

1 **the german assault on the ussr, june–sep. 1941**

	Germany and her allies, 22 June 1939
⊓⌐⌐	Stalin line
➝	German attacks
	occupied by Germany and her allies by 9 June 1941
– – –	frontline, 1 Sep. 1941
	occupied by Germany and her allies by 30 Sep. 1941
	under Soviet control on 30 Sep. 1941
◯	trapped Soviet pockets
	frontiers, early 1941
NORTH-WEST FRONT (VOROSHILOV)	Soviet army groups

1 On 22 June 1941 Germany launched an attack against the Soviet Union on a front of almost 1,000 miles with three million troops (map right). In three months German armies, supported by troops from Romania, Finland, Hungary and Italy, almost reached Moscow and Leningrad. By December the advance was halted and the Red Army began the counter-offensive which saved the Soviet capital.

FINLAND

Lake Ladoga

Turku

Helsinki

Hangö

Stockholm

Vyborg

Leningrad

NORTH-WEST FRONT (VOROSHILOV)

Baltic Sea

Tallinn

Pskov

Ríga

ARMY GROUP NORTH (LEEB)

Daugaupils

Vitebsk

Smolensk

Moscow

USSR

Tula

Königsberg

Vilnius

WEST FRONT (TIMOSHENKO)

Don

Danzig

Minsk

ARMY GROUP CENTRE (BOCK)

Brest

Pripet Marshes

Kursk

Vistula

Warsaw

GERMAN

Lodz

EMPIRE

GENERAL GOVERNMENT

Kiev

SOUTH-WEST FRONT (BUDENNY)

Kharkov

Dnieper

Craców

L'vov

Vinnitsa

Dnepropetrovsk

Dniester

SLOVAKIA

Kassa

ARMY GROUP SOUTH (RUNSTEDT)

Budapest

Debrecen

HUNGARY

Kolozsvár

Jassy

Kishinev

Odessa

Pécs

Szeged

Timiĭoara

Braìov

Novi Sad

ROMANIA

Belgrade

Sebastopol

YUGOSLAVIA
under Axis occupation

Bucharest

Black Sea

Sarajevo

Danube

Ruse

the **eastern front**

January–August 1942
Russians recapture Kiev (13 January); Russian offensive in Crimea (March); Germans recapture Kerch peninsula (20 May); Germans take Sebastopol (3 July); Germans cross River Don (31 July); Germans capture Krasnodar and Maikop (9 August)

September 1942
Fierce fighting around Stalingrad (1st); 'Final' German offensive at Stalingrad (13th)

October 1942
Second 'Final' offensive at Stalingrad (14th)

November 1942
Russian counter-attack at Stalingrad begins (19th); German 6th Army surrounded (23rd); Russian offensive on Central Front (28th)

January 1943
Germans begin withdrawal from Caucasus (3rd); siege of Leningrad raised (18th); Russians capture airfield supplying Stalingrad (21st); General Paulus surrenders 6th Army at Stalingrad (31st)

The Germans did not put their weight into renewing the drive on Moscow that had come so close to success the year before, although in many ways the 1942 campaign opened as a continuation of the year before. The Germans were still able to use their superior capability at combined arms mechanized operations to defeat numerically superior Soviet forces. Increasing German industrial mobilization provided more resources.

The Soviet spring 1942 offensives largely failed, especially at Kharkov, and the Germans were able to follow this up with a planned thrust to Rostov and into the oil-rich Caucasus, an improvised switch to attempting a resource-based strategy. This would require blocking the river Volga's north–south communications at the city of Stalingrad. As in 1941, operational skill and mobility led to many victories and large numbers of prisoners. But even as the Germans swept down the north shore of the Black Sea to the northern slopes of the Caucasus, they lacked the forces and resources to consolidate these gains against increasing Soviet strength.

2 In Stalingrad German armies drove the Soviet defenders to the very edge of the river Volga in the factory district and the city centre. In November 1942, German forces were encircled and two months later capitulated with a total loss of 200,000 men.

2 the siege of stalingrad, sep.–nov. 1942

➤ German advances
━━ German frontline, 13 Sep.
Soviet frontlines
──── 13 Sep.   ─ ─ ─ 3 Oct.
─ ─ ─ 27 Sep.   ─ ─ ─ 12 Nov.

The battle for Stalingrad negated the German advantages as dogged Soviet resistance created a massive house-to-house battle of attrition. While the Germans fed more forces into Stalingrad, without achieving ultimate success, the Soviets began to plan a counter-attack that would cut off both the forces in Stalingrad and those in the Caucasus.

The value of surprise was again demonstrated. Despite excellent reconnaissance and intelligence capabilities, aircraft and signal intercepts, the power of self-delusion was too strong. The Germans were convinced there was no threat to the vulnerable flanks of the forces committed to Stalingrad. The Soviets put in place an effective deception plan – the first of many – to make sure they remained undisturbed until, on 19 November, the blow fell on weakened forces holding the flanks, many from Germany's poorly equipped client states. Stalingrad was encircled. The forces in the Caucasus escaped the same fate through withdrawal.

Thanks to German indecision and the inability to sustain Stalingrad by airlift, the Soviets were able to defeat attempts to relieve the besieged German forces. The 1942 campaign ended on 31 January 1943 with the surrender of the German headquarters in the Stalingrad pocket.

1 No longer strong enough to attack across the width of the Russian front, the German strategy for 1942 was to drive across the south, its target the oil wells of the Caucasus (map below). Stalingrad was a subsidiary objective; its occupation would block Soviet use of the river Volga, a vital strategic artery.

1 stalingrad area
june–sep. 1942

- - -▶ German armoured movement
——▶ German army movement
▲▲▲ Russian defence line
——▶ Russian army movement
▦▦▦ Russian fronts

ARMY

1ST ARMY

3RD ARMY **6TH ARMY**

4TH ARMY (TANK) **1ST ARMY (TANK)**

Voronezh
60TH ARMY

Balashov

Saratov

VORONEZH FRONT ARMY GROUP (VATUTIN)

40TH ARMY

6TH ARMY

6TH ARMY
Soviet Reserve armies advance to stem German advance

21ST ARMY

5TH ARMY

STALINGRAD FRONT ARMY GROUP (TIMOSHENKO)

28 Sep. re-named Don Front

from Sep. Soviet reserves built up on north side of salient. Limited troops deployed to hold Stalingrad

63RD ARMY

German advance creates Stalingrad salient

Don

11 July

Bokovskaya

SOUTH EAST FRONT ARMY GROUP (YEREMENKO)

28 Sep. re-named Stalingrad Front

62ND ARMY

7TH ARMY

Kalach

Stalingrad

Raigorod

57TH ARMY

1ST ARMY

Volga

38TH ARMY

Donets

64TH ARMY

23 July

4 Pz Army switched from drive on Caucasus to Stalingrad

Don

ARMY

Nizhne-Chirskaya

Sal

37TH ARMY

Rostov-na-Donu

12TH ARMY

SOUTH FRONT ARMY GROUP (MALINOVSKI)

18TH ARMY

56TH ARMY

NORTH CAUCASUS FRONT ARMY GROUP (BUDENNI)

1939
Graf Spee sinks first ship (30 September); Battle of River Plate (13 December)

1940
Allied shipping losses reach 585,000 tons in a month (June); Convoy SC-7 loses 21 of 30 ships to U-boats (17-19 October); Sunderland flying boat detects U-boat by using radar for first time (November)

1941
US navy begins to patrol West Atlantic; *Bismarck* sunk (27 May)

1942
Beginning of US convoy system (1 April); Allied shipping losses 834,200 tons in June;

1943
Biggest convoy battle of war, 22 Allied ships sunk (5-20 March); Battle of Convoy ONS-5, 7 U-boats sunk (28 April); Dönitz suspends U-boat operations in North Atlantic (22 May); Wolf pack raids resume in North Atlantic (September); Germans abandon U-boat operations in Atlantic (15 November)

Germany's strategic warfare relied primarily on its submarine force, the U-boats. In 1939, the Royal Navy believed that between the use of the convoy system and the introduction of ASDIC (now known as sonar), the U-boats would not prove the menace they had been in 1917.

The Germans had devised what they believed a counter to both the convoy and ASDIC. The U-boats were to operate not singly, like their Great War predecessors, but in a coordinated wolf pack. U-boats would be called in by others or by aircraft. This put a premium on radio communication. Thus, the British ability to decrypt these signals for much of the war was instrumental to eventual success. Still, the Germans also had success with decrypts and on a number of occasions throughout 1940-43 were able to inflict painful losses on merchant shipping, but they were never able to sever the Atlantic lifelines.

As in the First World War, the German surface navy was unable to defeat the Royal Navy in a major surface engagement. After its role in the invasion of Norway in 1940, its primary mission became commerce raiding. But while the Germans had originally emphasized surface ships rather than U-boats, they proved a less effective investment despite a number of victories, notably the sinking of HMS *Hood* by the *Bismarck* and the scattering of Convoy PQ 17 by the threat of the *Tirpitz*.

The tide turned in the Battle of the Atlantic in 1943. The Allied victory resulted from many of the same elements as their ultimate victory in the war: a coalition effort, the superior numbers made possible by industrial and material strength, superior technology, adaptive tactics employed by increasingly effective forces, all enabled by intelligence.

2 the battle of the atlantic

· areas of merchant ship sinkings

--- maximum extent of air cover

sep. 1939–dec 1941

jan. 1942–july 1942

2 Until the USA entered the war, the bulk of U-boat sinkings occurred in the North Atlantic, although long-range Type IX U-boats had some success off West Africa (maps right). Insufficient aircraft were allotted to anti-submarine patrol by the British, and even if they found a U-boat, only a single attack resulted in a kill during this period. From summer 1942 to spring 1943 the U-boats were defeated in the Atlantic. Allied airpower covered progressively wider areas and aerial attacks became lethally effective. There were sufficient escort vessels to spare some for dedicated 'hunter-killer' groups and the Allies had won the electronic battle with better radar and sonar.

24 May Hood sunk, Prince of Wales damaged

23 May 1922 ICELAND

Hood, Prince of Wales and 6 destroyers

King George V, Victorious and 2 cruiser sqdns

Faeroe Is.

24-5 May Victorious attacks Bismarck

24 May

23 May Rodney and Britannic

Shetland Is.

Bergen

Oslo

Orkney Is.

22 May home fleet sails

North Sea

18 May 1941 Bismarck and Prinz Eugen set sail

Trondheim

Narvik

NORWAY

SWEDEN

Stockholm

FINLAND

Baltic Sea

1800 25 May *Atlantic Ocean*

Glasgow

Edinburgh

Dublin

GREAT BRITAIN

Manchester

DENMARK

Copenhagen

Danzig

Berlin

NETHS.

GERMANY

25 May King George V turns north east in error

25 May

0800 hrs, 27 May battleships attack the Bismarck

London

BEL.

Prague

26 May Bismarck sighted by RAF Catalina

1036 hrs, 27 May Bismarck sunk

Paris

Brest

Munich

Vienna

AUSTRIA

26 May torpedo strike from Ark Royal cripples Bismarck

FRANCE

SWITZERLAND

Lyons

Milan

ITALY

Bay of Biscay

Prinz Eugen to Brest, arrives 1 June

Marseilles

Corsica

Rome

Naples

Madrid

PORTUGAL

SPAIN

Sardinia

Mediterranian Sea

Palermo

26 May Force H Renown, Ark Royal, Sheffield sail from Gibraltar

Lisbon

Gibraltar (Br.)

ALGERIA

TUNISIA

1 German hopes that surface raiders could disrupt the convoys were ended in May 1941 when the *Bismarck* was brought to action and sunk by the Royal Navy (map left). The tragic loss of the battlecruiser *Hood* marred an otherwise successful operation, but the German battle squadron in Brest would never risk itself in the Atlantic after this. Hitler withdrew his heavy units back to Germany and Norway the following winter.

1 the pursuit of the bismarck, may 1941

Battleship routes
— Bismarck
--- Prinz Eugen
--- Hood
-·-· Victorious
--- King George V
-·-· Rodney and Britannic
— Task Force H
🕊 sinkings

USSR

CANADA

UK

GERMANY

UNITED STATES OF AMERICA

North Atlantic

AFRICA

SOUTH AMERICA

South Atlantic

USSR

CANADA

UK

GERMANY

UNITED STATES OF AMERICA

Azores

North Atlantic

AFRICA

SOUTH AMERICA

South Atlantic

aug. 1942–may 1943

june 1943–may 1945

the **war** in **italy**

1943 to 1945

1943

Operation Husky, main Allied landings on Sicily (10 July); Americans capture Palermo (23 July); Mussolini resigns (25 July); Allies take Messina (17 August); Armistice signed with Italy, Allies land in Calabria (3 September); Allies land at Salerno (9 September); Allied landings at Bari (14 September); 8th Army takes Ortona (28 December)

1944

Allied landing at Anzio (21 January); attack on Monte Cassino begins (15 March); Poles capture Monastery Hill at Cassino (18 May); Allies enter Rome (4 June); Perugia falls to Allies (20 June); 8th Army enters Florence (4 August); 8th Army attacks Gothic line (31 August); Gothic line breached (8 September); Allies reach Forlì (10 November)

1945

Allied offensive in Po Valley (14 April); German armies in Italy surrender (2 May)

The Mediterranean Theatre of 1943–45 was the direct result of the Allied victory in North Africa. The invasion of Sicily – bigger than D-Day the following year – was the next step and was seen as required to open the Mediterranean to shipping.

Churchill advocated the invasion of Italy as providing a way into the 'soft underbelly' of occupied Europe. This was opposed by the US, which saw it as a diversion of resources away from the coming climactic invasion of France. In the end, the Italian campaign emerged as a strategic compromise. The way it was treated reflected greatly on decision-making within democracies and between democracies, issues in modern-era strategy that Clausewitz never foresaw.

The Italian campaign proved highly frustrating. It was marked by the hard-fought Salerno invasion and repeated attacks on fortified German positions, most notably that of Monte Cassino. The largest attempt to use Allied amphibious mobility capabilities, the Anzio invasion, failed due to Allied tactical deficiencies. The skilled German defensive tactics and the Italian terrain and weather made sure that the Allies had great difficulty applying the advantages of their superiority in numbers, material and air power. Indeed, the secondary status of the Italian front made sure this superiority would be limited. It demonstrated how a low-investment strategy, such as that waged by the Germans through most of the campaign, can use operational and tactical skills to negate a stronger opponent.

British interest in the 'soft underbelly' applied also to the Balkans. There, the Yugoslav partisan movement represented the largest national rising of the conflict. However, its lack of equipment and preoccupation with establishing post-war political control meant that the Germans were able to keep the lid on the Balkans with a minimum-force, minimum-cost approach. It was the advance of the Soviet Army in 1944 that finally forced the German withdrawal, allowing Greece and Yugoslavia to get on with internal conflicts.

2 The Italian navy (chart right) was thrown into the scales against the Allies in June 1940. It suffered a damaging air attack at Taranto in November 1940 and was constantly harassed by British submarines and naval aircraft. By 1943 two thirds of Italian shipping had been sunk.

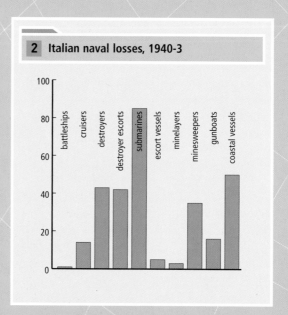

2 Italian naval losses, 1940-3

(Bar chart showing Italian naval losses by vessel type: battleships, cruisers, destroyers, destroyer escorts, submarines, escort vessels, minelayers, minesweepers, gunboats, coastal vessels. Vertical axis 0 to 100.)

ARMY GROUP C
(KESSELRING/
VIETINGHOFF)

Alpine Line

advance to cut
Brenner Pass road

14TH ARMY
(LEMELSEN)

Venice

10TH ARMY

Verona

e to clear
nd Turin

Milan

crossed using Fantails
and Duplex drive tanks

Adige (Venetian) Line

Po

g. 8 extra divisions (4 from Russian front)
designated for defence of Gothic Line

76TH PANZER
CORPS

1ST AIRBORNE
CORPS

in

NA ARMY
ZZIANI)

ARMY GROUP
SOUTHWEST
(KESSELRING)

Modena

crossed by marine boat
squadron 9 Apr. 1945

Genoa

Genghis Khan Line

14TH PANZER
CORPS

51ST AIRBORNE
CORPS

Gothic Line

27 Oct. 1944

Jan.– Mar. 1945 front line

5TH, 10TH &
13TH CORPS

8TH ARMY
(McCREERY)

L I G U R I A N   S E A   25 Aug.

2ND & 4TH
CORPS

2ND
CORPS

Pisa

Florence

15TH ARMY
GROUP (CLARK)

Ancona

19 July 1944

19 July

Arno

5TH ARMY
(TRUSCOTT)

51ST MTN
CORPS

21 June 1944

10TH ARMY

ug. German forces blow up all
but one bridge in Florence and
withdraw to N. bank of Arno

14TH PANZER
CORPS

76TH
CORPS

10TH CORPS

13TH CORPS

1ST AIRBORNE
CORPS

13TH CORPS

2ND CORPS

1ST CORPS

20 June 1944

FRENCH EXP.
CORPS

Ortona   20–28 Dec. 1943

4TH CORPS

Trasimene Line

Tiber

R. Sangro
27 Nov.–2 Dec. 1943

Viterbo Line

5 June 1944

13TH CORPS

5 June 1944

5TH CORPS

5 June 1944

Rome

4 June 1944

76TH CORPS

13TH CORPS

1ST AIRBORNE
CORPS

14TH PANZER
CORPS

Monte Cassino 24 Jan.–18 May 1944

Anzio

8TH ARMY
(MONTGOMERY)

21 Jan. 1944

Gustav Line

6TH CORPS

1 The 'soft underbelly' of the Axis proved nothing of
the sort once the Germans occupied Italy. Allied
amphibious assaults at Salerno and Anzio failed
to break the deadlock as fierce German counter-
attacks and lacklustre Allied leadership confined
the invasion forces to their beachheads. Both
sides believed they were forcing the enemy to
devote disproportionate resources to the Italian
campaign.

15 Jan. 1944

10TH CORPS

2ND CORPS

25 Sep.
1943

Bari

14 Sep. 1943

Napoli
(Naples)

US 5TH ARMY
(CLARK)

6TH CORPS
(LUCAS)

Salerno
9–16 Sep. 1943

Taranto

9 Sep. 1943

10TH CORPS
(McCREERY)

US 5TH ARMY
(CLARK)

15 Sep.
1943

6TH CORPS
(DAWLEY)

13 Sep. 1943

T Y R R H E N I A N

8 Sep. 1943

10 Sep. 1943

S E A

San Stefano Line
23 July 1943

San Frantello Line

Messina
13 July
1943

14TH
PANZER CORPS
(HUBE)

I O N I A N

Palermo

16 Aug.

S E A

14TH PANZER CORPS
(HUBE)

6TH ARMY
(GUZZONI)

10 Sep. 1943

11 July 1943

10 July 1943

8TH ARMY
(MONTGOMERY)

10 Sep. 1943

7TH ARMY
(PATTON)

15TH ARMY GROUP
(ALEXANDER)

Legend:

1 italy, 1943–45

→ Allied advance
— Allied fronts
— Axis fronts
✕ battle
U.S.
British
Canadian
Polish
German
Italian

the **german retreat** in **russia**

1943 to 1944

February 1943
Russians take Kursk (8th),
Rostov (14th), Kharkov (16th)

March 1943
Germans retake Kharkov (15th)

July 1943
largest tank battle in history at
Kursk (12th)

August 1943
Russians take Orel (5th),
Kharkov (23rd)

September 1943
Germans begin evacuation of
Ukraine (7th); Russians take
Smolensk (25th)

November 1943
Russians take Kiev

Despite Stalingrad, as 1943 opened the Germans could point to a number of battlefield successes that could suggest – especially to Hitler but also to senior military commanders – that Germany could regain the offensive initiative. These successes included the halting of a number of Soviet offensives in front of Moscow. One major offensive, Operation Mars, went so poorly that it was retrospectively downgraded to a diversion for Stalingrad. More important was General von Manstein's halting of the Soviet advance that threatened to capitalize on their victory at Stalingrad, one of the best-executed manoeuvre defences of the war. In the battles in the Donetz basin and around Kharkov in January–February, von Manstein restored stability to the front.

The Germans decided in the summer of 1943 that they would restart the blitzkrieg by cutting off the Soviet-held salient near Kursk. This time, there was no operational surprise. The Germans delayed the opening of the offensive until July, bringing up new Tiger and Panther tanks, but this gave the Soviets time to dig in their defensive forces – with improved tactics learned over the past two years – and carefully plan the commitment of armoured reserves.

In the resulting week-long climax of the Battle of Kursk, the blitzkrieg, for the first time, was stopped. It was unable to penetrate into the depths of the Soviet forces as it had in previous years. Where the Germans bludgeoned their way through defensive belts, Soviet tank counter-attacks – most notably at Prokhorovka – stopped them.

The Soviets immediately went over to the offensive, which they continued through the summer and autumn. Kiev was liberated and, as winter set in, bridgeheads were pushed over the Dnieper. Von Manstein tried to recreate his successes of the previous winter but failed; his forces were much weaker, the Soviets stronger and more adept. The Soviet war machine was no longer a struggling giant.

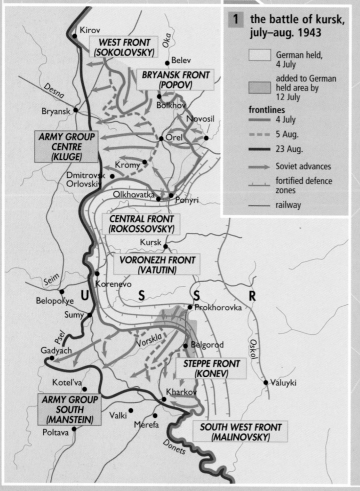

1 **the battle of kursk, july–aug. 1943**

German held, 4 July

added to German held area by 12 July

frontlines
— 4 July
--- 5 Aug.
— 23 Aug.
→ Soviet advances
fortified defence zones
— railway

1 The Red Army had never yet succeeded in stopping a full-scale German summer attack short of the strategic depths. With good intelligence of German intentions, the Russians fortified the Kursk salient and, optimistically, prepared offensives of their own to take place once they had absorbed the German blow (map left). The blunting of the German offensive was duly followed by a Soviet onslaught that liberated Orel and ultimately most of the Ukraine.

2 The collapse of German ambitions in the Caucasus and the loss of the Sixth Army at Stalingrad was followed by a Soviet offensive that briefly recaptured Kharkov (map right). By spring 1943 the Germans had recovered and the army high command urged a third summer offensive in Russia, this time aimed at the Kursk salient.

Map labels: Kirov, WEST FRONT (SOKOLOVSKY), Oka, Belev, BRYANSK FRONT (POPOV), Desna, Bolkhov, Bryansk, Novosil, ARMY GROUP CENTRE (KLUGE), Orel, Kromy, Dmitrovsk Orlovskiy, Olkhovatka, Ponyri, CENTRAL FRONT (ROKOSSOVSKY), Kursk, VORONEZH FRONT (VATUTIN), Seim, Korenevo, U S S R, Belopol'ye, Sumy, Prokhorovka, Psel, Vorskla, Gadyach, Belgorod, Oskol, Kotel'va, Kharkov, STEPPE FRONT (KONEV), Valuyki, ARMY GROUP SOUTH (MANSTEIN), Valki, Merefa, Poltava, SOUTH WEST FRONT (MALINOVSKY), Donets

FINLAND

Viipuri

Gulf of Finland

Leningrad

Lake Ladoga

12-30 Jan. Leningrad blockade broken.

Velsk

Vozhega

Byelosersk

LENINGRAD FRONT (GOVOROV)

VOLKHOV FRONT (MERETSKOV)

Vologda

Pskov

Bologoye

Rybinsk

NORTH-WEST FRONT (TIMOSHENKO)

Yaroslavl

Demyansk

KALININ FRONT (SOKOLOVSKI)

Kotelnich

NORTH (KUECHLER)

Velikiye Luki

Rzhev

5 Feb.-30 Mar. German withdrawal from Vyazma and Demyansk salients.

Gorki

Kazan

Polotsk

56°

Moscow

Vladimir

U S S R

Orsha

Mogilev

Smolensk

CENTRE (KLUGE)

Dnieper

Kaluga

Serpukhov

Ryazan

WEST FRONT (KONIEV)

Vlianorsk

Bobruisk

Rogachev

Tula

BRIANSK FRONT (POPOV)

Pripet Marshes

Mozyr

Gomel

Briansk

Orel

VORONEZH FRONT (GOLIKOV)

Tambov

Syzran

52°

Yelets

Volga

Korosten

Chernigov

Desna

Konotop

Kursk

Voronezh

Saratov

Kiev

Prihiki

Sumy

Voron

SOUTHWEST FRONT (VATUTIN)

Vasilkov

Lebedin

Bielgorod

Kalach

Uman

B (WEICHS)

Poltava

Kharkov

Donets

Kupyansk

Boguchar

Starobelsk

UKRAINE

Krovo

Millerovo

Stalingrad

Dnepropetrovsk

Voroshilovgrad

19-30 Nov. Stalingrad counter-offensive.

48°

Balta

Stalino

Don

DON FRONT (YEREMENKO)

DON (MANSTEIN)

Taganrog

Novocherkassk

Nikolayev

Mariupol

Rostov-na-Don

Odessa

Azov

Yeisk

NORTH CAUCASUS FRONT (MASLENNIKOV)

Perekop

Sea of Azov

CRIMEA

Kerch

Voroshilov

1 Jan.-4 Feb. N. Caucasus Operation

Sevastopol

Novorossiisk

A (KLEIST)

B l a c k

S e a

Mozdok

Sochi

Caucasus Mts

Grozny

32°

36°

40°

44°

Ordzhonikidze

2 eastern front nov. 1942–may 1943

Russian frontline Nov. 1942

Russian operations

19–30 Nov. 1942

1–31 Dec. 1942

1–31 Jan. 1943

2–18 Feb. 1943

18 Feb.–31 Mar. 1943

German counter-attacks

1–4 Jan. 1943

18 Feb.–31 Mar. 1943

June 1944
D-Day landings (6th); all Normandy landing zones linked up (12th); Americans capture Cherbourg (27th)

July 1944
Caen falls to Allies (9th); Operation Goodwood begun by Allies (18th)

August 1944
Nantes falls to Allies (6th); Operation *Anvil/Dragoon* begins, Allied 7th Army invades southern France; Canadians surround Falaise (16th); Allies liberate Paris (25th); Marseilles and Toulon fall to Allies (28th); British 1st Army reaches Amiens (31st)

September 1944
Dieppe and Rouen fall to Allies (1st); Antwerp and Brussels liberated (3rd–4th); US 1st Army enters Germany (12th); Operation *Market Garden* ends in destruction of Allied airborne forces (17–21st); Calais surrenders (28th)

October 1944
Germans surrender Aachen (21st)

November 1944
US 3rd Army crosses Moselle (9th); French take Strasbourg (24th)

December 1944
Battle of the Bulge (16th–25th); US 3rd Army relieves Bastogne (26th)

The D-Day landings were a triumph of planning and organization, with follow-up support including a harbour to be towed across the Channel and an underwater pipeline. Air superiority was assured; only two German fighters made it over the beachhead on D-Day.

The execution was less than smooth. On Omaha, one of the US beaches, reinforced German defences threatened to halt the invasion until resolute US infantry action took them inland. Opposition on the other beaches, while strong, was less and yet despite the dropping of three divisions of paratroops, the invasion force was unable to seize its first day's objectives, most significantly the city of Caen. Taking it would now require many weeks of hard fighting.

The subsequent Normandy campaign ashore was bitter and frustrating, with the German Army demonstrating its defensive tactics, honed in the east, among the hedgerows. The Allies had planned the invasion itself splendidly, but had left the key operational issue of how to win the battle of Normandy to improvisation.

When the breakout from Normandy finally came, the Allies missed the chance of encircling the German forces opposing them. The manpower, if not their equipment, escaped through the Falaise Gap. As the Allies pursued, liberating much of France, logistics now became the great determinant. Seizing ports such as Antwerp (through a long campaign for the Schelde estuary) and Marseilles (through the invasion of southern France), lines of communication became seriously stretched and it was a great tribute to Allied logistics capability that they did not break.

A last grab at victory in the west in 1944 came in September, with Operation Market Garden. Three airborne divisions, seizing key bridges, would open a highway across the Rhine for a British armoured corps. Hastily improvised, the plan failed as the Germans defeated the British airborne bridgehead at Arnhem.

Bitter fighting on the German frontier at Aachen, the Huertgen Forest, in Lorraine and Alsace showed that the logistical limitations of the rapid advance and stiffening of German resistance meant there was still much hard fighting ahead.

1 The greatest amphibious invasion in history, the Normandy landings were preceded by a successful deception campaign that diverted major German forces to the defence of the Calais area. The initial beachhead was not as deep as anticipated, but German counter-attacks were too little and too late to drive the invaders into the sea. The ensuing battle of attrition in the Normandy boscage could only have one ending (map right).

30 June: end of German resistance in Cotentin Peninsula

27 June: US troops take Cherbourg

Auderville

Beaumont

Cherbourg

St Pierre-Eglise

9th Div.

4th Div.

Les Pieux

Valognes

Montebou

9th Div.

C O T E N T I N

Merderet

Douvre

79th Div.

P E N I N S U L A

Ste Mère-

Barneville

St Sauveur-le-Vicomte

US 7TH C

Portbail

9th Div.

La Haye-du-Puits

90th Div.

Lessay

Périers

Coutances

2 the allied advance through france, july–dec. 1944

→ Allied advances
- - → Allied frontlines and date
planned Allied frontlines
⊢⊤⊢ West Wall

BRITAIN

North Sea

London
Portsmouth

English Channel

50

The Hague
Amsterdam

15 Dec.
15 Sep.
NETHERLANDS
Arnhem
Rhine

CANADIAN 1ST ARMY
Antwerp
Eindhoven
Cologne

Cherbourg
16 Aug.
25 Aug.
BRITISH 2ND ARMY
Brussels
Mons
BELGIUM
GERMANY

24 July
Caen
Vire
Coutances
Avranches
Elbeuf
Somme
US 1ST ARMY
Ardennes
Mainz

Brest
Argentan
Seine
Aisne
Meuse

Brittany
Mortain
Paris
Marne
Verdun
Metz
Karlsruhe

D-Day +25
Chartres
US 3RD ARMY
Strassburg

Lorient
Le Mans
16 Aug.
25 Aug.
15 Dec.

D-Day +60
Orléans
Voges Mts
Colmar

D-Day +90
Loire
15 Sep.

F R A N C E
US 7TH ARMY
Mulhouse
Belfort
SWITZ.
Dijon

1 the normandy campaign, june–july 1944

🪂 airborne landings

🚩GOLD🚩 beach heads

→ Allied advances

✝ airfields

⚓ mulberry harbours

➡ German advance

⬛ built-up areas

⬜ flooded areas

⬛ woodland

front lines
   midnight 6 June
   10 June
   18 June
   1 July

2 On 25 July 1944 the American forces in Normandy launched 'Operation Cobra' to force a breakout (map above). American air power and armour made remarkable strides. General Patton's Third Army pushed into Brittany and then wheeled east towards Paris as the Germans retreated. By September the Allies had crossed France, but the attempt to drive into Germany was defeated.

21ST ARMY GROUP (MONTGOMERY)

US FIRST ARMY (BRADLEY)

UTAH

Pointe du Hoe

Grandcamp les-Bains
Vierville-sur-Mer
O M A H A

BRITISH SECOND ARMY (DEMPSEY)

29th Div.
US 5TH CORPS
Colleville-sur-Mer
Port-en-Bessin
G O L D
J U N O
S W O R D

10 June: US troops link
Aure
2nd Div.
1st Div.
Arromanches

Carentan
Isigny
Trévières
Colombières
1st Div.
Bayeux Seulles
7 June
Creuilly
Courseulles-sur-Mer
Lion-sur-Mer
Ouistreham

30th Div.
St Jean-de-Daye
5th Div.
US 19TH CORPS
BRITISH 30TH CORPS
BRITISH 1ST CORPS
Ranville

Vire
35th Div.
Forêt de Cérisy
Drôme
1st Div.
BRITISH 12TH CORPS
BRITISH 8TH CORPS
CANADIAN 2ND CORPS

Balleroy
Tilly-sur-Seulles
Caen

29th Div.
Gaumont
26–9 June: Operation Epsom
Tourmauville
Bourguébus

St Lô
Villers-Bocage

18–2
Oper

the **german defeat** in the **east**

January 1944
Leningrad relieved after 900-day siege

May 1944
Russians capture Sebastopol

June 1944
Russian offensive in Byelorussia. Dnieper crossed (27 June)

August 1944
Russians take Bucharest

January 1945
Russians take Warsaw (17th), liberate Auschwitz (26th)

April 1945
Russians take Vienna (7th-13th), enter Berlin (23rd). US 1st army and Russian patrols meet at Torgau (26th)

May 1945
Battle for Berlin ends (2nd). Russians occupy Prague (9th)

The 1944 fighting in the East saw the Germans driven from the banks of the Dnieper to the Oder River in front of Berlin.

Winter and spring offensives by the Soviets liberated the Ukraine and raised the three-year siege of Leningrad. The most significant of the many Soviet offensives which rippled from north to south in June–August was Operation Bagration, which effectively destroyed the German Army Group Centre in the salient it was holding at Hitler's insistence, pushing the Germans out of Byelorussia and to the banks of the Vistula.

The Soviets next looked to clear their flanks, attacking to clear the Ukraine and then, as Romania and Bulgaria changed sides, into the Balkans. In the north, the surviving German forces were pushed into the Courland peninsula as the Soviets advanced into East Prussia. Finland switched sides: only Hungary would be made to fight to the end. Repeated offensives against the German centre then followed; the hammer blows of the Vistula–Oder operation; and the assault on East Prussia. By February 1945, the Soviets were on the Oder.

The Soviets were now short of manpower due to massive losses, but their industrial production – with Western aid – increased while that of their opponents weakened. Never as tactically adept as the Germans, the Soviets were able to prevail by mastering the operational level of war. The great breakthroughs of 1944 were made possible not by overwhelming numbers but by massing force at the decisive spot, an approach made possible by intelligence and deception.

The War in the East was on a massive scale. Battles in which the Soviets suffered hundreds of thousands of casualties were simply never discussed, lost in the 'noise' of the clash not only of armies but also of ideologies. The Soviets had realized since 1941 that the Germans' racial ideology meant that defeat would lead to utter collapse, preventing Germany from using the national and political fissures in the Soviet Union against Moscow. Now, the Soviets made sure of the political consolidation of the areas they occupied.

Germany's ability to shift and reorganize troops, along with the breathing space provided by the failure of Market Garden and the need to clear ports and build up supplies, gave Hitler the chance for a last counter-attack in the West. This, along with the V1 and V2 missile attacks, was seen as having given Germany a chance for successes that might divide the Allies.

The resulting offensive, the Battle of the Bulge, achieved some early success, but was soon halted and forced back. Allied offensive operations continued and, with the weather and logistics situations improving, they resumed the offensive. In the spring, a final drive over the Rhine led to resistance crumbling. By 1945, the Western Allies and the Soviet Union had widely differing military forces that represented widely different solutions to the problem of waging modern industrial war. These forces not only gained the final victory in the Second World War but shaped those that followed over subsequent decades.

The Soviets continued to attack, in Hungary (site of the last German counter-offensive at Lake Balaton in March), East Prussia, Silesia, Yugoslavia, Czechoslovakia, driving to Vienna by March. But the main Soviet goal was planning and bringing up supplies for the final drive across the Oder to Berlin. This opened in April and, after strong early resistance, the German defences gave way. Berlin was encircled and then reduced, Hitler committing suicide. Soviet spearheads moved West.

The Soviets met US forces on the Elbe, but already the political landscape was being set for another conflict of a different type. Civil wars were in progress in Poland, Greece and Yugoslavia. Germany was divided into what would, in the following decade, emerge as the western Federal Republic and eastern Democratic Republic.

PORTUGAL   SPA

40°

Nov. 1942

30°

1 Hitler's failure to defeat Britain by bombing and the Atlantic submarine campaign, coupled with the reverse of German fortunes at Stalingrad, left Germany fighting a two-front war (map right). While the German army in the east was worn down by Soviet forces in a series of gigantic battles, Anglo–American armies invaded North Africa in 1942, Italy in 1943 and France in 1944. Western air forces undermined the German war effort through bombing, while partisans and resistance movements challenged German occupation. The Allies' insistence on unconditional surrender was never to be tested by a credible peace offer from Germany. The minority of military officers opposed to Hitler fantasized that they could make a separate peace with the Western powers, but none of their assassination plans worked. In consequence, the German army resisted to the end, fighting with diabolical efficiency until 1945.

1 the defeat of germany

- ▭ Grossdeutches Reich, 1942
- ← Axis attacks
- ◄-- Axis withdrawals
- ← Allied attacks
- 🏭 major cities under heavy air attack
- ✶ major battle with date
- ✊ partisan/resistance movements
- ● commando raids
- ⬈ V1 launching sites
- ⬈ V2 launching sites
- —— frontiers, 1942

UNION OF SOVIET SOCIALIST REPUBLICS

Shetland Is
Orkney Is

GREAT BRITAIN

North Sea

London
Calais
Dieppe
St. Lô
Caen
Paris 1944
1942–4

FRANCE

Lyon

VICHY FRANCE

Marseilles 1943–5
Toulon
Aug. 1944

Kirkenes
Petsamo
1944
Murmansk
1944
1944
1944
1944
1944

Archangel

NORWAY 1940–5
Oslo

SWEDEN

Stockholm

FINLAND

Lake Ladoga
1944
Helsinki
Leningrad
Narva
1941–2
1944
Novgorod

Baltic Sea

Copenhagen
Flensburg 1940–4
Lübeck
Hamburg
Bremen
HOLLAND *Sep. 1944*
Rotterdam
Arnhem
Antwerp
BEL. Brussels
Hanover
Berlin
Düsseldorf
Cologne Torgau
Dec. 1944
Rheims
Metz Frankfurt
Mannheim
Stuttgart
Munich

Memel
LITHUANIA
Feb.–Apr. 1945
Kaunas
Königsberg
E. PRUSSIA
1944
Białystok
1944–5
Warsaw *Jan. 1945*
1941–4
POLAND
May 1945
Dresden
Prague
May 1945

Riga
LATVIA
Velikiye Luki
1944

Estonia

GERMANY
Oder
Stettin
Vistula
June–Aug. 1944
1943–4

Smolensk
Mogilev
Minsk
Gomel
July–Aug. 1943

Rzhev *Dec. 1941*
Moscow
1942–3
Tula 1941–2
Bryansk
Orel
Kursk

Gorkiy Volga
Saratov
Voronezh
Don Volga

Stalingrad
Nov. 1942–Feb. 1943

Kharkov

Kiev *Nov.–Dec. 1943*
Dnieper
1942–3 **UKRAINE**
Krivoy Rog
Stalino
Rostov 1942–3
1942–3
1942–3

SWITZERLAND
Milan
Po
Genoa 1944–5
Livorno
Rome *taken June 1944*
July 1943
Anzio
Naples
Salerno *Sep. 1943*
Jan.–March 1944
Corsica
Sardinia

Linz
Vienna
AUSTRIA *Apr. 1945*
1945
Budapest 1944–5
Zagreb 1945
Trieste
CROATIA
Rimini
Florence
Zara
Sarajevo
1941–4
MONTENEGRO
Kotor
ITALY

Danube
SLOVAKIA 1944
Debrecen
HUNGARY
Carpathians
Belgrade
SERBIA 1941–4
Danube
ALBANIA 1944
1941–4
Sofia
BULGARIA 1944

Jassy
Odessa
ROMANIA
Ploesti
Bucharest

Dniester
Transnistria

Crimea
Sebastopol
Kerch
Yalta
Caucasus

Black Sea
Batum

Balearic Is
Algiers
Bougie
Nov. 1942
Bizerta
Tunis
TUNISIA
April–May 1943
Feb.–May 1943
Tripoli
Nov 1942
Messina
Sicily *July 1943*
Pantelleria
Malta
Sep. 1943
Bari
Taranto
Crete 1941–5

Salonika
GREECE
Athens
Oct. 1944
Aegean Sea
Leros
Kos
Rhodes
Cyprus

TURKEY
Ankara

SYRIA

Mediterranean Sea

LIBYA
Benghazi
El Agheila
Cyrenaica
EGYPT
Jan.–June 1942
Tobruk
Bardia
23 Oct. 1942 British offensive
Oct.–Nov. 1942
Alexandria
El Alamein
Cairo

PALESTINE
TRANSJORDAN
LEBANON

ALGERIA

war in the pacific

— December 1941
Japanese bomb Pearl Harbor (7th); Japanese land in Siam and Malaysia; Japanese land on Juzon (10th), in North Borneo (17th); Hong Kong falls to Japanese (25th)

— 1942
Japanese occupy Manila (2 January); Japanese take Kuala Lumpur (11 January); Japanese land in Solomon Is. (26 January); British surrender Singapore (15 February); Japanese invade Bali (19 February); Battle of Java Sea (27 February); Japanese land on Mindanao (2 March); Japanese land on Dutch New Guinea (1 April); Battle of the Coral Sea (4–8 May); Battle of Midway (4 June), 4 Japanese carriers sunk; US Marines land on Guadalcanal (7 August)

The opening stages of the Second World War in the Pacific demonstrated many of the themes seen throughout the era: resource war, anti-imperialism, surprise, intelligence, transoceanic warfare (largely unique to this theatre on such a massive scale, and the rise of air warfare.

The origins of the conflict included the demands of industrial-age material war. Japan needed the resources of Southeast Asia to generate and sustain the forces needed to prevail in its war against China, let alone implement its larger expansionist goals. Japan's shortage of currency, Allied action and US embargoes had cut off access to these resources.

Despite its own repressive occupations of Korea and China, Japan sought to legitimize its actions in anti-imperialist terms and indeed it proved that Western rule in Asia never recovered from the military defeats Japan inflicted on it in the first six months of the war in the Pacific. The late modern-era 'barbarization of warfare' was also apparent in Japanese treatment of Asians and Allied prisoners of war alike.

The importance of surprise in late modern warfare was seldom better demonstrated than in the Japanese attack on Pearl Harbor: 'the day that will live in infamy', 7 December 1941. Japan had counted on the initial, surprise-generated success to provide six months of victory, and then they would dig in and hold their defensive perimeter, the Greater East Asia Co-Prosperity Sphere. Only when the 'victory disease' led them to attack outside the perimeter was their advance decisively halted at the battles of the Coral Sea and Midway. US intelligence failure made possible the Japanese success at Pearl Harbor as much as intelligence success was responsible for the later victories.

The geography of the Pacific meant that navies would be the primary war-fighting assets, but the opening months of the war soon reinforced that aircraft, land- or, more importantly, carrier-based, made naval movement possible. Coral Sea and Midway were the first fleet actions in which opposing surface warships never sighted each other, relying on aircraft to attack and for much of their defence as well.

2 battle of the midway, 04.00–08.30 hours 4 June 1942

✈— US air and naval forces

✈— Japanese air and naval forces

2 Japan's run of victories came to an abrupt halt in June 1942 when all four fleet carriers escorting the Midway Island invasion force were sunk in action with the US Navy (maps below). US signals intelligence provided timely warning, while Japanese over-confidence led them to disperse their superior forces.

1 The Japanese military leadership calculated that it could carve out an empire then defend it so aggressively that the western powers would concede rather than run up an endless casualty bill (map below). However, the Pearl Harbor raid was politically disastrous; Admiral Halsey echoed the general mood when he swore 'by the time we're done, the only place they'll still speak Japanese will be Hell'.

- – – – Japanese empire, 1941
- ⟶ Japanese advance or strike
- ● Japanese base
- ■ Allied base
- ✕ battle

U S S R

Bering Sea

Sea of Okhotsk

Komandorski Is.

Aleutian Is.

Attu Kiska

Kurile Is.

MANCHURIA (MANCHUKUO)

INNER MONGOLIA

Sea of Japan

JAPAN

Tokyo

Japanese perimeter July 1942

Japanese forces repulsed 3–6 June 1942
✕
Midway

KOREA

Tsingtao

East China Sea

Yangtze

Nanking
Shanghai

CHINA

Changsha

Volcano Is.

Bonin Is.

Hawaiian Is.

Oahu

attack on Pearl Harbor, 7 Dec. 1941
Pearl Harbor

Kunming

Laokai

Hanoi

Japanese take Hainan Rangoon 8 Mar. 1942

FRENCH INDO-CHINA

Formosa

Hong Kong captured 1941

Japanese attack on Philippines 8 Dec. 1941

Pacific Ocean

Wake I.

SIAM

Phnom Penh

Gulf of Siam

Saigon

Manila
Corregidor surrenders 6 May 1942

Philippine Is.

Saipan

Guam

Caroline Is.

Truk

Kwajalein

MALAY STATES

Japanese land on Malay coast 8 Dec. 1941

Mindanao

Zamboanga

Palau

Makin

Gilbert Is.

Kuala Lumpur

Singapore

Japanese take Singapore 15 Feb. 1942

Borneo

Halmahera

Admiralty Is.

Manus

Abemama

Bismarck Arch.

New Ireland
Green Is.
Bougainville

Ellice Is.

of the Java 7 Feb. 1942; cessful attempt Japanese on of Java
✕

Sumatra

DUTCH EAST INDIES

Celebes

Ceram

New Guinea

Rabaul

Solomon Is.

Batavia

Java

Surabaya

Macassar

Banda Sea

Tanimbar Is.

Aru Is.

Buna

Guadalcanal

Santa Cruz Is.

Lombok

Flores

Sumba

Timor

Port Moresby

✕
Battle of the Coral Sea May 1942: Japanese forces repulsed

Espiritu Santo

New Hebrides

Fiji Is.

Cape York

Coral Sea

US forces land 9 Feb. 1942

New Caledonia
■
US forces land 12 Mar. 1942

A U S T R A L I A
US commit ground forces to defence of Australia from Feb. 1942

Sydney

Melbourne

110° 130° 150° 170°

burma and malaysia

1942
Japanese enter Rangoon (8 March); Japanese cut Burma Road (29 April); British and Indian forces advance into Burma (21 December)

1943
First Chindit raids (8 February); Japanese occupy Maungdaw (14 May); Burma-Siam 'Death Railway' completed (25 October)

1944
British recapture Maungdaw (9 January); Japanese offensive in Arakan drives Allies back into India (4 February); Battle of Imphal (8–14 March); siege of Imphal begins (29 March); siege of Imphal lifted (22 June); last Japanese resistance in India ends (16 August); Allies take Kaduma (30 December)

1945
Burma Road reopened (22 January); Japanese evacuate Mandalay (19 March); Allies capture Rangoon (3 May); Japanese surrender in Burma signed (13 September)

2 The British 14th Army absorbed the Japanese 1944 offensive at Imphal and Kohima, then launched the most brilliantly conducted offensive conducted by Commonwealth forces in the war (map far right). The Japanese were wrong-footed by the British advance, and the long overdue employment of substantial air and armoured forces in Burma. The race was on to take Rangoon before the monsoon rains turned the roads to liquid mud.

1 The Burma campaign followed the Japanese occupation of French Indochina (despite the authorities' loyalty to the Vichy regime) and their entry into Thailand (map right). The Japanese leadership toyed with an invasion of India, and formed a nationalist Indian army, but by the time the Imphal-Kohima offensive began, Japan was losing the war in the Pacific.

The Japanese advance into Burma in 1942 represented, like the advance into New Guinea at the other end of their would-be empire, a continuation of the offensive tidal wave. The Japanese were able to overcome the initial British resistance of the 1942 campaign.

Their victory was assured, despite British reinforcement and even in the absence of strategic surprise, given Japanese air superiority and the tactical superiority of an army experienced in China and in hard training against second-line garrison forces. A major naval raid into the Indian Ocean made an invasion of India appear imminent.

But the mountains and jungles of the Northeast Frontier of India proved an effective barrier, along with Japanese logistics limitations. The Burma front was a low priority for resource allocation on both sides. The British rebuilt their forces and attempted several limited offensives, with varying degrees of success. The Japanese tactical superiority was only slowly countered, through a combination of training a new, predominantly Indian army for the liberation of Burma and the capabilities provided by new technologies, most notably air resupply. This made possible the Chindit operations behind Japanese lines.

These operations led to the Japanese allocating resources – brought forward over the infamous Burma Railway, built across Thailand by prisoners – to a 1944 offensive into India. This was stopped at Imphal and Kohima and, going over to the offensive, the British then liberated Burma in a lengthy campaign which, in its use of both operational manoeuvre and logistics, was one of the most astutely conducted of the conflict. Just as early modern conflict could be waged in remote areas that had acquired strategic value, late modern conflict in these areas was made possible, but only by substantial investments in logistics and adaptation of forces and tactics developed for Europe. The need to adapt to land warfare in Asia would confront all the world's major powers in the years after 1945. Few, if any, would do so as well as the forces that liberated Burma.

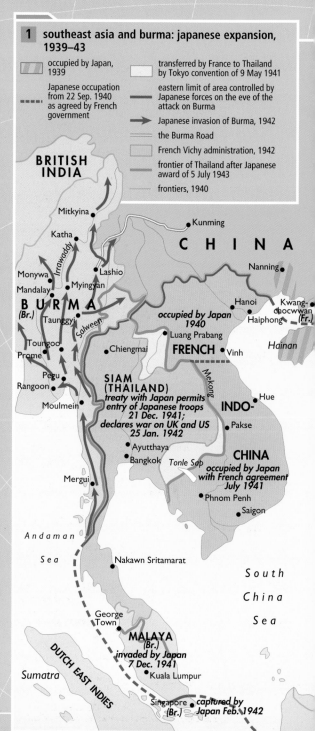

1 southeast asia and burma: japanese expansion, 1939–43

occupied by Japan, 1939

Japanese occupation from 22 Sep. 1940 as agreed by French government

transferred by France to Thailand by Tokyo convention of 9 May 1941

eastern limit of area controlled by Japanese forces on the eve of the attack on Burma

Japanese invasion of Burma, 1942

the Burma Road

French Vichy administration, 1942

frontier of Thailand after Japanese award of 5 July 1943

frontiers, 1940

BRITISH INDIA

Mitkyina

Katha

Kunming

CHINA

Monywa

Mandalay

Myingyan

Lashio

Nanning

BURMA (Br.)

Taunggyi

Hanoi

Kwang-chocwwan (Fr.)

Haiphong

Toungoo

Prome

Chiengmai

occupied by Japan 1940

Luang Prabang

FRENCH

Vinh

Hainan

Pegu

Rangoon

Moulmein

SIAM (THAILAND)
treaty with Japan permits entry of Japanese troops 21 Dec. 1941; declares war on UK and US 25 Jan. 1942

INDO-

Hue

Pakse

Ayutthaya

Bangkok

Tonle Sap

CHINA
occupied by Japan with French agreement July 1941

Mergui

Phnom Penh

Saigon

Andaman Sea

Nakawn Sritamarat

South China Sea

George Town

MALAYA (Br.)
invaded by Japan 7 Dec. 1941

Sumatra

DUTCH EAST INDIES

Kuala Lumpur

Singapore (Br.)

captured by Japan Feb. 1942

INDIA

Dimapur
Kohima
Naga Hills

Imphal

14TH ARMY (SLIM)

19 DIV
Sittaung
4 Dec.

Kabaw Valley

33 CORPS

4TH CORPS (MESSERVY)
Kalewa
24 Dec.

Myitmoka

Chindwin

Gangaw

Monywa
Myinmu
21 Feb.
Ngazun

2 Jan.
Thabeikkyin
Shwebo

Tilin   Tuin
Pauk
Pakokku
26 Jan.
Myitche   21 Feb.
Seikpyu   Nyaungu
21 Feb.   7 DIV
Chauk

27TH ARMY (SAKURAI)

BURMA AREA ARMY GROUP (KIMURA)
Yenangyaung

82 DIV (W. AFRICAN)

Buthidaung
Kyauwtaw
Myohaung

Minbya
Minbu
Foul Point
25 DIV   16 Feb.
Akyab   Myingun
Myebon   19 Apr.
Ru-ywa   20 DIV

16 Feb.

Kyaukpyu   13 Mar.
Ramree I. secured 28 Feb.   Thayetmyo
26 DIV   28 Apr.
Cheduba I.   Taungup

Sandoway   9 May

Inbin   Minhla
Letpadan
Gwa   13 May
Henzada

Bay of Bengal

Myanmyo
Bassein
Myaungmyo

Cape Negrais

Mouths of the Irrawaddy
amphibious landing supported by Eastern Fleet

INDIA ARMY GROUP (STILLWELL)
36 DIV   Namti   5 Aug.
Myitkyina
Samaw   Mogaung   Kazu
6 Aug.   **1ST ARMY**
Pinbaw   **6TH ARMY**
19 Oct.   Nalong
1 Nov.   26 Oct.
Mawlu   22 DIV   Myothit
6 Nov.   38 DIV   30 DIV
Katha   Bhamo   Momauk
11 Dec.   Mosit
Kunchaung   Namhkam
Tigyaing   6 Dec.
11 Feb.   Hsenwi
Myitson
24 Jan.   9 Mar.   Bawdwin
Twinnge   Mong Mit   Namtu
19 Mar   50 DIV   Namhaan   7 Mar.
Magok   Lashio
16 Mar.
Kyaukme   Hsipaw

5–24 Dec. 14 Division despatched to China

CHINA

16 Dec. 1944– Jan. 1945 22nd Division despatched to China

Mar. 1945 Mars brigade to China

SHAN STATES

BURMA

Zawgyi

Myingyan
33RD ARMY (HONDA)   **15TH ARMY (KATAMURA)**
Thazi
Meiktila   17 DIV
10 Apr.
Pyawbwe
11 Apr.
Yamethin

13 Apr.   16 Apr.

Pyinmana
21 Apr.

28 Apr.
Kyaukpadaung

Toungoo   22 Apr.   **KAREN STATES**
Prome   Oktwin
2 May
Shwedaung   25 Apr.

Salween

SIAM

Nyaunglebin   Shwegyin
Daik-U   26 Apr.

Pegu   Waw
Zayatkwin   29 Apr.
Mingaladon   Hlegu
Rangoon
secured 3 May   Dala   Thongwa
Thakutpin   Kyauktan   Thaton

Gulf of Martaban

Pyapon   26 DIV (IND.)

Andaman Sea

2	burma, july 1944–may 1945

- Allied armies
- Stillwell's Chinese divisions
- Merrill's Marauders
- Chindit landing ground
- Japanese armies
- ✠ Japanese airforce base
- Ledo Road

victory in the pacific

1942
Japanese driven back on Guadalcanal (21 August); Battle of Cape Esperance off Guadalcanal (11–12 October); Kokoda taken by Australians (2 November)

1943
Allies take Buna (2 January); Japanese evacuate Guadalcanal (1–19 February); Battle of Bismarck Sea (2–5 March); end of Japanese resistance in New Guinea (28 August); US Marines land on Bougainville (1 November)

1944
US Marines land on Saipan (15 June); Japanese wiped out on Saipan (7 July); Allies land on Guam (21 July); US troops land in Leyte Gulf (17 October); First B29 raid on Tokyo (24 November); Japanese resistance on Leyte ends (22 December)

1945
Battle for Iwo Jima (19 February–16 March) Corregidor captured (28 February); US lands on Okinawa (1 April); Japanese resistance on Mindanao ends (18 June); end of resistance on Okinawa (22 June); Japanese agree to unconditional surrender terms (14 August)

2 Many armies talk about fighting to the last man and last cartridge, but only the Japanese army has done so consistently. Island garrisons often resorted to bayonet charges in the face of overwhelming US firepower, survivors preferring suicide to surrender. On Iwo Jima they dug extensive tunnel networks, holding out inside Mount Suribachi long after the US flag was famously planted on the summit (map right).

The US counter-offensive against Japan started with the invasion of Guadalcanal in August 1942. It came to its conclusion with the end of resistance on Okinawa almost three years later. The bitter fighting of the island-to-island advance, bypassing many major centres of resistance such as Truk and Rabaul, was made possible by massive naval battles: those of the Guadalcanal campaign, the Philippine Sea and Leyte Gulf. The Japanese capability to wage war was directly attacked by the US submarine offensive and, starting in late 1944, strategic bombing.

1 iwo jima, 19 feb.–26 mar., 1945

Jungle

Green 1 beach codename

The US offensive required mastering modern amphibious operations, a type of warfare seen as obsolete after Gallipoli. It required unprecedented investment in logistics, to be able to sustain forces at sea or in distant jungles. All this was made possible by the US's industrial potential and the adaptability of its military and war-fighting institutions. The US was able to overwhelm Japan with only a fraction of its total capability. From the carrier task forces to the base-building bulldozers, it was all an immense triumph of organization, and the levels of strategy, operations and tactics were high enough to make sure it was effectively applied.

Savage resistance and the introduction of large-scale kamikaze suicide plane attacks marked the last battle of the Pacific War on Okinawa. It became obvious that despite US control of the air and sea, an invasion of Japan would require many months of intense close-quarters combat. The Soviet invasion of Manchuria and the US use of the atomic bomb finally led to the Japanese surrender.

The Bomb was certainly the most dramatic example of the technology and industrial strength that gained the victory in the Pacific. The fact that it had to be used at all also underlined the limits of that sort of strength even against less well-equipped and supplied but highly resolute enemies. War termination also was shown to be a key element of effective war-fighting. It is no longer enough to win, but to do so without paying the cost associated with total victory.

The US forces had a choice of routes to Japan. General MacArthur wished to liberate the Philippines, advancing via the Solomons and New Guinea; the US Navy preferred an 'island-hopping' strategy aimed directly across the Pacific. In the event, the US had the resources to do both (map below). While these plans unfolded, Japan maintained a substantial field army in Manchuria. Some 750,000 troops remained there until 1945 when the Soviet army demolished the Japanese defences in a week.

U S S R

Bering Sea

Sea of Okhotsk

Kamchatka

Komandorski Is.

Attu Aleutian Is.
Kiska   Amchitka

17 Aug. 1945

May–Aug. 1943

Soviet army attacks 9 Aug. 1945

Khabarovsk

MANCHURIA (MANCHUKUO)

Kurile Is.

INNER MONGOLIA
Peking

Hakkaido

Tientsin Dairen

KOREA Seoul

Sea of Japan

JAPAN

Tokyo

10 Oct. 1943

Japanese perimeter Mar. 1944

Japanese perimeter Oct. 1944

East China Sea Fusan

Hiroshima
6 Aug. 1945

Nagasaki
9 Aug. 1945

Shikoku

Kyushu

fighters sweep over Japan from May 1945

Pacific Ocean

e advance into
after Oct. 1943
se offensive into
ia Feb.–June 1944
offensive into
r Nov. 1944
retaken May 1945

C H I N A

Nanking
Shanghai

1944 Japanese
Ichi-Go Offensive

bombing raids
from June 1944

Bonin Is.

Volcano Is.

Midway

Chinese counter-
offensive
Apr.– June 1945

Kunming

Amoy

Okinawa

direct air attack on
Japan from Okinawa
from May 1945

Iwo Jima
Feb.–Mar. 1945

20th Air Force begins
direct air attack on Japan
from 24 Nov. 1944–14 Aug. 1945

Hawaii Is.

Laokai
Hanoi

Canton

Farmosa

Wake I.

Oahu
Pearl Harbor

FRENCH INDO-CHINA

Gulf of Tongking

Hong Kong

Hainan

Luzon
landings Jan.
1945

Battle of Philippine Sea.
Japanese carrier
aviation annihilated
June 1944

Marianas
Saipan
June 1944

Tinian

Pacific Ocean
area forces

SIAM
on

Bangkok

Philippine Is.

Manila

25 Oct. 1944
Battle of Leyte Gulf.
Heavy Japanese naval losses

Guam
July 1944

Eniwetok
Feb. 1944

M a r s h a l l   I s.

m Penh

Gulf of
Siam

Saigon

Leyte

Leyte landing 20 Oct. 1944

Ulithi
Sep. 1944

Caroline Is.

Truk

Kwajalein
Feb. 1944

Majuro
Jan. 1944

ALAY
ATES

Kuala Lumpur

Mindanao
May 1945

Zamboanga

Sulu
Sea

Palau
Sep. 1944

Makin

Gilbert Is.
Tarawa Nov. 1943

Abemama

BRUNEI
June 1945

SARAWAK

Singapore

Tarakan
May 1945

Borneo

Morotai
Sep. 1944

Halmahera

Noemfoor
July 1944

Sansapur
July 1944

Sorong

Biak
May 1944

Manus
Feb. 1944

Admiralty
Is.

Bismarck Arch.

New Ireland

Ellice Is.

D U T C H   E A S T   I N D I E S
July 1945

Sumatra

Palembang

Bandjarmasin

Celebes

Amboina
Ceram

Hollandia

Wewak
New Guinea
Saidor
Jan. 1944

Rabaul

Bougainville
Nov. 1943

Solomon Is.

Battle of Santa Cruz Oct. 1942
Eastern Solomons Aug. 1942
Japanese forces repulsed

Macassar

Banda Sea

Aru Is.

Tulagi

Batavia
Java Surabaya

Lombok

Sumba

Timor

Flores

Tanimbar
Is.

Buna
Port Moresby

Guadalcanal
7 Aug. 1942–
Feb. 1943

South Pacific
area forces

Espiritu
Santo

New
Hebrides

Fiji Is.

Japanese perimeter Aug. 1945

Timor
Sea

Darwin

Cape York

17–25 Sep. 1942
Japanese ground
forces repulsed

Coral Sea

New Caledonia

A U S T R A L I A

1 the allied counter-offensive

Allied advance   Japanese base   Japanese perimeters

Allied air attack   Japanese base   ······· March 1944
                              bypassed or   —·—·— October 1944
Allied base   neutralized   — — — August 1945

atomic bomb   battle
target

Sydney

Melbourne

the **chinese civil war**

1947 to 1949

1927
Purge of communists in Shanghai and other cities

1934
'The Long March' of the Communists to Shansi; Mao Zedong emerges as communist leader

1947
Civil War between Communists and nationalist erupts; Nationalists capture Yenan (1947); Communist offensive in Manchuria (summer)

1948
Communists capture Chinchow (October), thereby controlling most of Manchuria; Huai-Huai battle in central China, 500,000 Nationalist troops defeated (November–December)

1949
Beijing falls to Communists (January); Shanghai falls to Communists (May); Communists capture Canton (October); People's Republic of China proclaimed (October); Chiang flees to Taiwan (December)

How wars are fought in a world with nuclear weapons was demonstrated in two Asian conflicts within five years of Hiroshima. Insurgencies (as exemplified by the Chinese Civil War) and limited wars (exemplified by Korea, see page 162) set a pattern repeated many times – though seldom with such intensity – up to 1991.

The Chinese Civil War which erupted in the 1940s had its roots in the overthrow of the Manchu emperors in 1911. period of turmoil ensued in which Chinese political forces struggled to found a post-imperial state which could com mand widespread allegiance. The task was almost impossible and China fragmented into a number of military dicta torships. Between 1925 and 1937 Chiang Kai-shek and his Kuomintang movement suppressed most of the warlord power bases and brought the majority of China under one central control. In the early phases of this process th Kuomintang worked hand-in-hand with the fledgling Chinese Communist party, but in 1927 the communist cells the major cities were destroyed. Mao Zedong kept resistance alive in the province of Kiangsi, and when Chiang's force attacked there in 1934, the fragments of the Chinese Communist party trekked 6,000 miles to the northern province Shensi.

Following the Japanese establishment of the puppet state of Manchukuo in the north in 1935, the priority becam resistance to the Japanese, whilst still consolidating local power-bases. But after the war with Japan ended in 194! a full-scale civil war broke out between the Communists and Nationalists. Initially successful, Chiang thought h could smash Mao's cadres. But the Communists could rely on a powerful reservoir of support amongst the peasantr and their army swelled in number. Communist tactics relied on holding off attacks by the larger Nationalist armies i the south, whilst picking off Kuomintang units in Manchuria and the north. Once this northern flank had fallen, by autumn 1948, the Communists pushed southwards, winning battle after battle and taking Beijing itself in January 1949.

By September 1949 the Nationalist cause had all but collapsed. The loss of Canton in October 1949 left only south-west China in Nationalist hands. The hopelessness of the situation precipitated the flight of Chiang to Taiwan, which the Nationalists succeeded in holding, and from where the Kuomintang continued to claim to be the legitimate government of China.

The Chinese Civil War represented the implementation of the Maoist paradigm of insurgency. Starting with a Leninist cadre in arms, it culminated (after 1945) with conventional warfare. It presented a way to challenge the West where it was weakest, where its colonial empires were either receding or struggling to hang on. Against insurgency, neither nuclear weapons, nor air power nor the technological warfare evolved from the two world wars could present an effective barrier.

1 After the defeat of Japan, the Chinese nationalists and the Chinese communists competed for the administration of the liberated areas. The communists dominated Manchuria and the north. In 1947 full-scale civil war broke out betwee the two sides. Nationalist armies were defeated in Manchuria in 1948, and at Suchow from November 1948 to January 1949. In October 1949 a communist republic was proclaimed and in May 1950 the nationalist remnants fled to Taiwan. The Maoist prescription for revolutionary warfare began with small-scale guerrilla action and culminated in full-scale conventional warfare. Communist movements would try to put this model int operation all over the world, but few woulc be as successful as Mao Zedong.

1 communist victory in the civil war, 1946–50

- occupied by Communist armies at outbreak of civil war
- occupied July 1946–June 1948
- occupied July 1948–June 1949
- occupied by 1950
- Communist guerrilla operations 1945–9
- → Communist forces advance
- *Apr. 1946* date of capture by Communists
- ★ battles, with date

place names in brackets are 'Pinyin' forms adopted after 1949

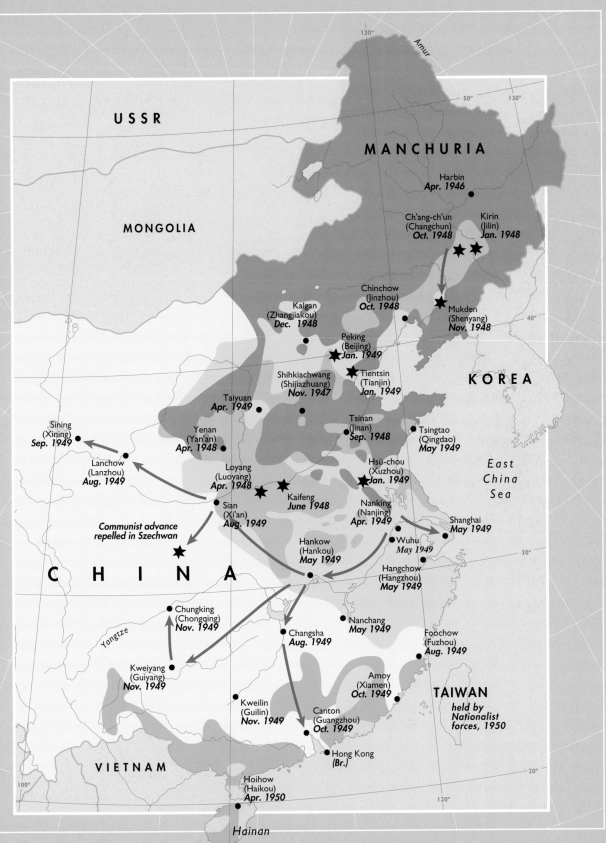

USSR

MONGOLIA

MANCHURIA

Amur

Harbin
Apr. 1946

Ch'ang-ch'un
(Changchun)
Oct. 1948

Kirin
(Jilin)
Jan. 1948

Mukden
(Shenyang)
Nov. 1948

Chinchow
(Jinzhou)
Oct. 1948

Kalgan
(Zhangjiakou)
Dec. 1948

Peking
(Beijing)
Jan. 1949

Tientsin
(Tianjin)
Jan. 1949

KOREA

Shihkiachwang
(Shijiazhuang)
Nov. 1947

Taiyuan
Apr. 1949

Tsinan
(Jinan)
Sep. 1948

Tsingtao
(Qingdao)
May 1949

Sining
(Xining)
Sep. 1949

Yenan
(Yan'an)
Apr. 1948

Lanchow
(Lanzhou)
Aug. 1949

Loyang
(Luoyang)
Apr. 1948

Kaifeng
June 1948

Hsü-chou
(Xuzhou)
Jan. 1949

East
China
Sea

Sian
(Xi'an)
Aug. 1949

Nanking
(Nanjing)
Apr. 1949

Shanghai
May 1949

**Communist advance
repelled in Szechwan**

Hankow
(Hankou)
May 1949

Wuhu
May 1949

CHINA

Hangchow
(Hangzhou)
May 1949

Chungking
(Chongqing)
Nov. 1949

Yangtze

Changsha
Aug. 1949

Nanchang
May 1949

Foochow
(Fuzhou)
Aug. 1949

Kweiyang
(Guiyang)
Nov. 1949

Kweilin
(Guilin)
Nov. 1949

Canton
(Guangzhou)
Oct. 1949

Amoy
(Xiamen)
Oct. 1949

TAIWAN
*held by
Nationalist
forces, 1950*

Hong Kong
(Br.)

VIETNAM

Hoihow
(Haikou)
Apr. 1950

Hainan

161

1945
Korea divided into US and Soviet occupation zones, split along 38th parallel

1950
North Korean army invades South Korea (28 June); North Koreans capture Seoul (29 June); US ground forces ordered into Korea (30 June); Battle of Taejon forces US retreat (22 July); Pusan perimeter established (4 August); UN counterattack fails (13 August); UN forces land at Inchon (15 September); UN forces attack and capture Seoul (19–29 September); UN forces cross 38th parallel (7 October); Chinese forces cross into Korea (14 October); UN forces capture Pyongyang (20 October); Chinese attacks at Chosin force UN retreat (11 December)

1951
Chinese capture Seoul (4 January); renewed UN offensive (25 January); UN reaches point between 37th and 38th parallels (1 March); UN retakes Seoul (14 March); British 1st Battalion Gloucester Regiment annihalated at 'Gloucester Hill'; UN forces take Heartbreak Ridge following 18-day battle (23 September); truce talks begin at Panmunjom (27 November)

1953
Battle of Pork Chop Hill (18 April); peace talks resume (26 April); renewed Communist offensive (14 June); ceasefire signed (27 July)

The war in Korea was made possible by the Communist victory in the Chinese Civil War. While its roots were in long-suppressed Korean nationalism, the lasting impact of the Korean War was to define the Communist threat to the West primarily in military terms, of tanks rolling across borders, rather than the internal penetration that had threatened Europe (and claimed Czechoslovakia) in 1945–48. Korea led to the emergence of NATO as a military alliance.

Korea was also a proxy war. It was how the two nuclear-armed superpowers fought. In addition to providing the majority of Communist air power, the Soviet Union provided the material support that allowed the Chinese and the North Koreans to be sustained on the battlefield.

Militarily, the initial North Korean invasion conquered most of the peninsula. Forced back to the Pusan perimeter US and UN reinforcements were able to counter-attack. They were aided by the Inchon landings, deep behind Communist lines, one of the few brilliant operational strokes of the war. The over-optimistic UN offensive had, within a few months, overrun most of North Korea until it too was defeated in a massive Chinese intervention. The Chinese pushed south until they, like the North Koreans before them, outran their logistics and were pushed back. Then, by mid-1951, static warfare and truce talks dominated the remainder of the conflict.

Militarily, Korea led to the United States emphasizing nuclear deterrence rather than conventional war-fighting capability. Most pronounced in the late 1950s, it still had not been undone when the next US land war in Asia, in Vietnam, started in the 1960s.

1 the inchon landings, korea 1950
beachead, evening 15 September
→ US attacks
---- US positions

1 US naval supremacy enabled General MacArthur to outflank the communist forces by an amphibious landing at Inchon. The following month, airborne and amphibious assaults seized new bridgeheads in the north, compelling the enemy to withdraw towards the Chinese border (map above).

2 The Korean War carried the Cold War to the Far East. Occupied in 1945 by Soviet and American forces, the country was already divided *de facto* by 1948 (map right). In 1950, after the withdrawal of the occupying armies, the North Koreans attacked the South. The United States and United Nations immediately intervened. After initial North Korean successes, the Americans under General MacArthur counter-attacked and advanced to the Chinese frontier. This resulted in Chinese intervention and stalemate, ended only by the armistice of Panmunjom and the partition of the country along the 38th parallel.

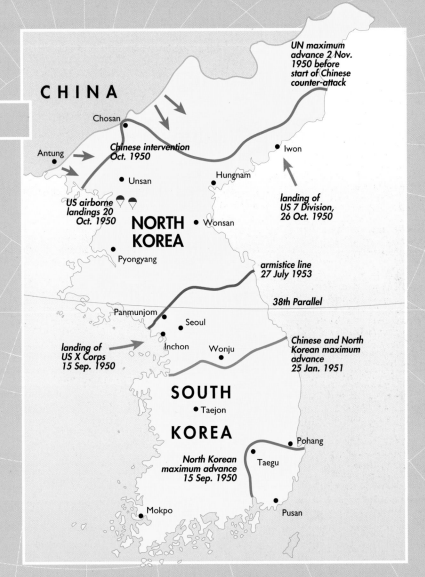

CHINA

UN maximum advance 2 Nov. 1950 before start of Chinese counter-attack

Chosan

Chinese intervention Oct. 1950

Antung

Iwon

Unsan

Hungnam

US airborne landings 20 Oct. 1950

NORTH KOREA

Wonsan

landing of US 7 Division, 26 Oct. 1950

Pyongyang

armistice line 27 July 1953

Panmunjom

38th Parallel

Seoul

landing of US X Corps 15 Sep. 1950

Inchon

Wonju

Chinese and North Korean maximum advance 25 Jan. 1951

SOUTH

Taejon

KOREA

Pohang

North Korean maximum advance 15 Sep. 1950

Taegu

Mokpo

Pusan

the first **indochina wars**

1948
Malayan Emergency begins with insurrection by Malayan Communist Party (MCP)

1949
France grants limited independence to Vietnam, Laos and Cambodia

1950
China and USSR recognise Ho Chi Minh's Communists as legitimate government of Vietnam; Viet Minh launch offensive against French (September); in Malaya 'Briggs Plan' resettles villagers away from Communist controlled areas

1952
French operation near Nghia Lo fails to draw Viet Minh into full-scale battle

1954
The Viet Minh decisively defeat the French at Battle of Dien Bien Phu; French surrender 6 May; Geneva accords dividing Vietnam into North and South (July); last French troops leave Hanoi (October)

1957
Malaya become independent (31 August)

1960
Malayan government declares Emergency over

Just as the end of wars causes new wars, so does the end of empires. The British gave up India without a conflict, but the Netherlands' colonial empire ended only after a lengthy war of independence.

The course of post-imperial Asia was shown in the outcome of two insurgencies. In French Indochina, from 1945–54, the Viet Minh, with the benefits of extensive Chinese aid, were eventually able to implement the Maoist example, starting as guerrillas linking nationalism with Leninism. In 1953–54, they were able decisively to defeat the French in a conventional battle at Dien Bien Phu. In Malaya, from 1948–60, the British defeated an insurgency aiming at the same result.

1 France clung to her colonial empire, but with Chinese military aid, the communist revolutionaries dominated the north of the country and much of the Mekong Delta (map right). The French government shrank from sending conscripts to Indochina, relying mainly on her colonial regiments and the Foreign Legion.

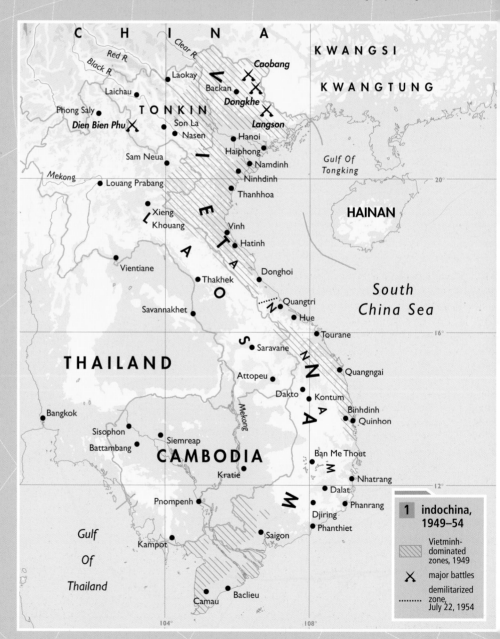

1 indochina, 1949–54

Vietminh-dominated zones, 1949

✕ major battles

········· demilitarized zone, July 22, 1954

2 battle of dien bien phu, 1954

Viet Minh attacks
→ Mar. 13–29
→ Mar. 30–Apr. 9
→ April 10–May 7

◟ Encirclement after first attack

▫ Viet Minh artillery

▦ French defensive zones

→ French counter-attacks

Gabrielle

Ban Keo

Anne-Marie

Beatrice

Dominique

Main Airstrip

Huguette

Ban Ban

Elaine

Ban Ong Pet

Claudine

Dien Bien Phu

French command H.Q.

Ban Hong Lech Cang

Ban Pa Pe

Ban Na Loi

Ban Ten

Ban Palech

Ban Bom La

Ban Nhong Nhai

Ban Kho Lai

emergency airstrip

Ban Hong Cum

N

Isabelle

The British implemented what became the paradigm of effective counter-insurgency, a slow, primarily political process, with military action aimed principally at permitting the evolution of legitimate indigenous institutions. They were able to help defend these against a later, more conventional military challenge in the confrontation with Indonesia in the early 1960s.

In Malaya, the guerrillas could claim neither foreign arms nor the banner of nationalism. Two communist insurgencies in the Philippines were also defeated despite that country's political weakness.

The component countries of the British Indian empire opened their independence with mass slaughter and 'transfer of populations'. India and Pakistan have clashed in three limited, conventional wars: 1948 and 1965, over the disputed state of Kashmir; and in 1971, which led to the creation of Bangladesh. India lost a brief border conflict with China in 1962. India has also, in recent years, been involved in substantial internal security operations including, in the 1980s, one in the island nation of Sri Lanka which, as in Burma, has ongoing ethnic insurgencies. Now, with India and Pakistan both nuclear-armed and the Kashmir issue unresolved, the future of conflict in Asia is likely to make all that has occurred since 1945 seem tame and safe.

2 Overestimating the power of their air force and underestimating the quantity of artillery available to the Viet Minh, the French decision to challenge the enemy to a stand-up battle at Dien Bien Phu backfired hideously (map above). Surrounded by vastly superior forces, the élite of the colonial army was wiped out.

civil wars in africa

1945 to 2004

1954–62
War of Algerian Independence

1967–70
Civil war in Nigeria against Biafran secession

1975–
Civil war in Mozambique

1975–91, 1993–9
Angolan civil wars

1977–78
Ethiopian-Somali war in Ogaden

1989
Civil war begins in Liberia

1991
Ethiopian regime of Mengistu overthrown; civil war begins in Sierra Leone

1994
Rwandan genocide

1996–2002
Civil War in Congo-Zaire draws in forces from Rwanda, Uganda, Zimbabwe and Namibia

Conflict in Africa after 1945 was, at first, aimed at the apparently weakened French empire, leading to risings in Madagascar and Algeria. The French ability to suppress these, plus the counter-insurgency lessons from Indochina, gave the French confidence that they could retain Algeria as a possession as well as a position of influence with other colonies and protectorates that achieved independence. The resulting war in Algeria, eclipsing the previous French colonial conflicts, led to Algerian independence. The French military was never defeated and was winning on the battlefield until the day it lost the war. Politically, the war brought down the Fourth Republic.

1 Savage civil wars have been fought throughout the Horn of Africa since the 1970s (map right). Military rule came to Somalia in 1970, to Ethiopia in 1974 and to the Sudan in 1969. In Ethiopia the Marxist–Leninist regime of Mengistu Haile Mariam fought a long war against the Eritrean and Tigrean independence movements until his overthrow in 1991, as well as a war with Somalia over the Ogaden region. In 1998–99 Ethiopia fought a war against the newly independent state of Eritrea for control of disputed border areas. By 1999 the central Somali state had effectively ceased to exist, with the north-west breaking away as 'Somaliland' and the south divided between competing warlords. Civil war between the Islamic north and Christian south has been endemic in the Sudan since independence.

The British war in Kenya in the 1950s was much smaller and lacked the political costs of Algeria. The British successfully applied their counter-insurgency tactics developed in Malaya, helped by the insurgents being a tribal minority and lacking external support. But the war still brought home the need for colonial possessions to achieve independence to prevent future conflicts.

Portuguese efforts to hold on to their three colonies of Guinea, Angola and Mozambique, starting in the late 1950s, lasted until after the government in Lisbon fell in a left-wing revolution in 1974. The Portuguese had also militarily kept the upper hand, fighting effectively despite their limited resources. The end of these conflicts led to civil wars

In 1954, disappointed at failing to win independence for Algeria after the war, Algerian nationalists set up the Front de Libération Nationale (FLN) and launched a guerrilla war which lasted until 1962 (map right). The French settler community fought back through their own organization, the OAS, which perpetrated atrocities against both Algerians and the French administration. High losses and high costs forced the French hand and independence came on 5 July 1962. The French army and Algerian rebels had drawn different lessons from the war in Indochina. Militarily the French succeeded in containing the rebels and even clearing out their urban strongholds, but the political cost was prohibitive.

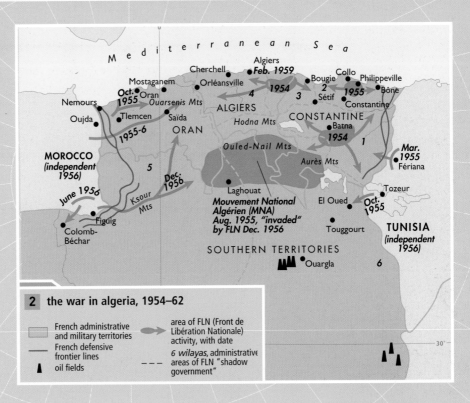

2 **the war in algeria, 1954–62**

	French administrative and military territories		area of FLN (Front de Libération Nationale) activity, with date
	French defensive frontier lines		*6 wilayas,* administrative areas of FLN "shadow government"
	oil fields		

1 **ethiopia, somalia and sudan 1985–2003 (left)**

Ethiopia

provinces claimed by Somalia, 1977-88

held by Eritrean People's Liberation Front, 1986

captured by EPLF by Mar. 1988

secured by Tigre People's Liberation Front, Apr. 1988

government counter-attacks, June 1988

captured by TPLF, early 1989

captured by EPLF, Feb. 1990

advance of anti-government forces, Apr. 1991

de facto independent Apr. 1991, independence declared May 1993

Somalia

controlled by competing tribes, clans and factions from 1989

Siad Barre's base, Feb. 1991-Apr. 1992

de facto independent, Mar. 1991

Siad Barre's last attempt to regain power, Apr. 1992

controlled by Aidid, June 1992

areas of most intense fighting

Sudan

southern Sudan (non-Muslim, non-Arab), limited autonomy from 1972

non-Arab populations in northern Sudan

main areas of operation of South Sudan People's Liberation Army from 1984

under SPLA attacks, Aug. 1986

SPLA attacks, Nov. 1987 and May 1989

areas of intense fighting, 1990

frontier claimed by Egypt

others

Eritrean war, 1998-2000

refugees and refugee movements

between the participants in the liberation struggle (that in Angola still ongoing in 1999; that in Mozambique halted in the late 1980s). They also increased the pressure on Rhodesia and South Africa.

Rhodesia and South Africa, with tactically excellent armed forces, were militarily undefeated but succumbed to inter national pressure which led them to hand over their countries to representatives of the insurgents they were fighting.

In the 1990s, Africans have largely been fighting Africans in much of the continent. These conflicts include the civil conflicts in the former Belgian Congo (leading to an early UN intervention) and Nigeria in the 1960s. Other civil conflicts have been long-running and bloody, often with foreign intervention: Chad, Sierra Leone, Rwanda, Burundi and Sudan among many others. More recently, there has been an increasing tendency towards inter-state and well as intrastate conflict in Africa. This is not a new development, but the end of Cold War has led to an increasing willingness on the part of neighbouring states to intervene in intrastate conflicts.

1948
establishment of State of Israel; first Arab-Israeli war

1956
the Suez Crisis: Britain, French and Israeli forces attack Egypt (29 October)

1964
establishment of the PLO

1967
the Six Day War (5-10 June)

1973
the Yom Kippur War (6-24 October)

Arab–Israeli conflict started with the waning of the British mandate in Palestine. The Israeli War of Independence that followed demonstrated that the improvised Israeli Defence Forces (IDF) were capable of overcoming the post-imperial armies of its Arab opponents in a low-technology conflict.

The Cold War inevitably invested the Arab–Israeli conflict with a proxy war element. Soviet involvement increased after the 1955 arms deal with Egypt. Israel's pro-western orientation was sealed by its covert alliance with France and Britain to invade Egypt in the 1956 Suez crisis. After the 1967 war, Israel turned increasingly to the US for arms, economic aid and diplomatic support.

By 1967, the IDF was no longer a third-world military force, and US arms increased its already high level of technology. The Israelis seriously studied operations and tactics, resulting in original approaches to low-cost, high-technology warfare.

Starting with the 1967 war, Arab–Israeli confrontations brought about increasing interest in how emerging technologies performed in combat. In 1967, it was the conventional pre-emptive strike, stressing air attacks and armoured forces, by Israel that influenced both Soviet and NATO military thinking. In the 1967–71 War of Attrition, it was the evolution of an integrated air defence system (IADS) by Egypt and Syria to counter Israeli air power, a trend also seen in the 1976 war. At that time, the emergence of the anti-tank guided missile seemed to threaten the superiority of Israel's tanks.

2 the yom kippur war, 1973: the golan heights and the suez canal

Golan Heights
— de facto frontiers before the war
— occupied by Israel at the end of the Six Day War, 1967
→ Arab advances
→ furthest Arab advance into Israeli territory
→ Israeli counter-offensives
— Syrian territory held by Israel at ceasefire, 24 October

Suez Canal
occupied by Israel at the end of the Six Day War, 1967
— de facto frontier before the war
→ Egyptian advances
→ furthest Egyptian advance into Israeli-held territory
→ Israeli counter-offensives

Israeli territory held by Egypt at ceasefire, 24 Oct.

Egyptian territory held by Israel at ceasefire, 24 Oct.

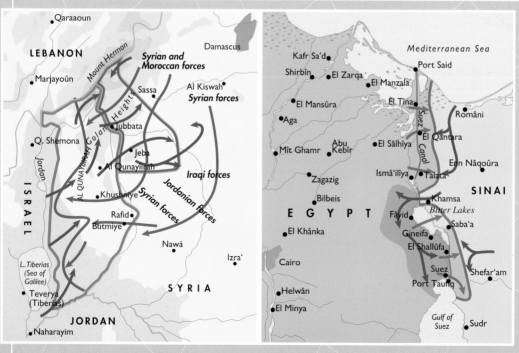

2 In October 1973 Egypt and Syria launched on surprise attack on Israeli-held territory. After initial success, Egyptian forces were surrounded by an Israeli counter-attack. Syria's attempt to recapture the Golan Heights ended in bloody defeat, its masses of Soviet tanks proving no substitute for the better-trained and more determined Israeli mechanized units (maps left).

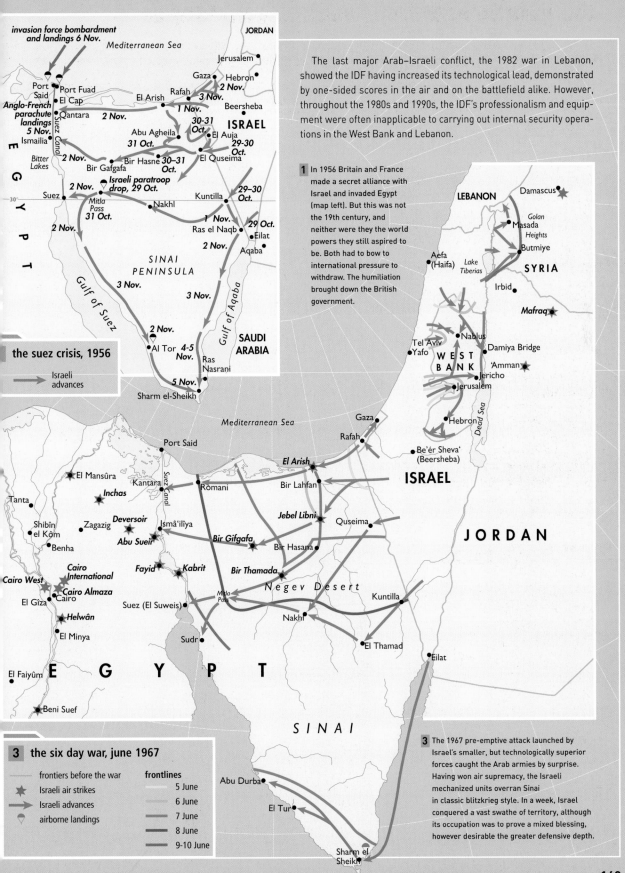

the suez crisis, 1956

invasion force bombardment and landings 6 Nov.

Mediterranean Sea

JORDAN

Jerusalem

Gaza · Hebron
2 Nov.

Port Said · Port Fuad
El Cap
Anglo-French parachute landings 5 Nov.
Qantara
Ismailia
Bitter Lakes

Rafah
3 Nov.
El Arish
1 Nov.
Beersheba
2 Nov.
30-31 Oct.
ISRAEL
Abu Agheila
31 Oct.
El Auja
29-30 Oct.
Bir Hasne 30-31 Oct.
El Quseima
Bir Gafgafa
2 Nov.
Israeli paratroop drop, 29 Oct.
Kuntilla
29-30 Oct.
Suez
30 —
Mitla Pass 31 Oct.
Nakhl
1 Nov.
Ras el Naqb
29 Oct.
2 Nov.
Eilat
Aqaba
2 Nov.

E
G
Y
P
T

Gulf of Suez

3 Nov.

3 Nov.

SINAI PENINSULA

Gulf of Aqaba

SAUDI ARABIA

2 Nov.
Al Tor 4-5 Nov.
Ras Nasrani
5 Nov.
Sharm el-Sheikh

→ Israeli advances

The last major Arab–Israeli conflict, the 1982 war in Lebanon, showed the IDF having increased its technological lead, demonstrated by one-sided scores in the air and on the battlefield alike. However, throughout the 1980s and 1990s, the IDF's professionalism and equipment were often inapplicable to carrying out internal security operations in the West Bank and Lebanon.

1 In 1956 Britain and France made a secret alliance with Israel and invaded Egypt (map left). But this was not the 19th century, and neither were they the world powers they still aspired to be. Both had to bow to international pressure to withdraw. The humiliation brought down the British government.

LEBANON
Damascus ★
Golan Masada
Heights Butmiye
Aefa (Haifa)
Lake Tiberias
SYRIA
Irbid
Mafraq ★
Tel Aviv
Yafo
Nablus
Damiya Bridge
WEST BANK
'Amman ★
Jericho
Jerusalem
Hebron
Dead Sea

Gaza
Rafah
El Arish
Bir Lahfan
Romani
Jebel Libni
Quseima
Be'ér Sheva' (Beersheba)
ISRAEL

Port Said
Kantara
Suez Canal
El Mansûra ★
Inchas ★
Tanta
Zagazig
Deversoir ★
Ismâ'ilîya
Bir Gifgafa
Bir Hasana
JORDAN
Shibîn el Kôm
Benha
Fayid ★ Kabrit ★
Abu Sueir ★
Bir Thamada
Negev Desert
Kuntilla
Cairo International ★
Cairo West ★
Cairo Almaza ★ Cairo
El Gîza
Mitla Pass
Suez (El Suweis)
Nakhl
El Thamad
Helwân ★
El Minya
Eilat
El Faiyûm
E G Y P T
Sudr
Beni Suef ★

S I N A I

Mediterranean Sea

3 **the six day war, june 1967**

— frontiers before the war
★ Israeli air strikes
→ Israeli advances
⬇ airborne landings

frontlines
— 5 June
— 6 June
— 7 June
— 8 June
— 9-10 June

Abu Durba
El Tur

Sharm el Sheikh

3 The 1967 pre-emptive attack launched by Israel's smaller, but technologically superior forces caught the Arab armies by surprise. Having won air supremacy, the Israeli mechanized units overran Sinai in classic blitzkrieg style. In a week, Israel conquered a vast swathe of territory, although its occupation was to prove a mixed blessing, however desirable the greater defensive depth.

the **cold war**

The way the Cold War was waged – without direct military confrontation but always in readiness – put a great emphasis on the balance of forces between the opposing sides. While competition in peacetime between military forces was hardly a new thing, the Cold War placed an unprecedented emphasis on the balance sheet of overall capability of the two principal powers.

The strategic nuclear balance compared the number of nuclear weapons systems that the United States and the Soviet Union could deliver against each other. The US nuclear monopoly ended in 1948, but despite fears first of a 'bomber gap', then a 'missile gap', the Soviets were outnumbered in both categories well into the 1960s. The emergence of Soviet nuclear parity and then a potential first-strike capability in the SS-18 ICBM force in the 1970s was one of the reasons the Soviets then thought the 'correlation of forces' had shifted in their favour, only to see it swing back in the 1980s.

Crises and confrontations were what marked the course of the Cold War. Events gained importance because of the role of the opposing sides in them. The fears were that 'backing down' would cost prestige and position both internationally and domestically, while the danger was, if both sides escalated, some spark could initiate a conflict.

The Berlin airlift of 1948 (when the US and Britain supplied Berlin by air after the Soviets imposed a ground blockade) set the pattern. The willingness of the Western Allies to take risks to support the Germans, their enemies of a few years before, paved the way for the integration of West Germany into western Europe in the following decade and, as the Cold War ended, for German unification.

The Greek Civil War evolved from an internal Greek conflict to a Cold War proxy conflict, the other form for the use of military force in an era of nuclear weapons. First Britain, then, after the 1947 Truman declaration, the US, supported the Greek government against Communist guerrillas. The war ended only when Tito's

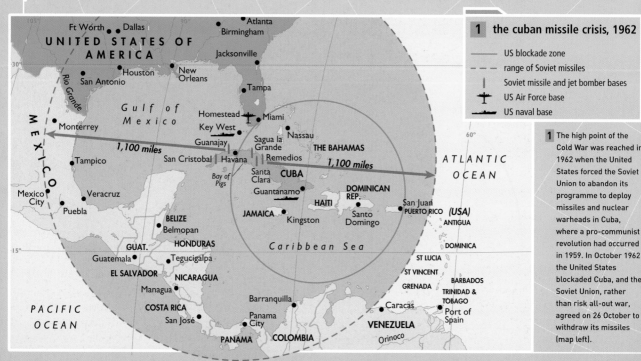

1   the cuban missile crisis, 1962

— US blockade zone
- - - range of Soviet missiles
⬩ Soviet missile and jet bomber bases
✈ US Air Force base
⚓ US naval base

1 The high point of the Cold War was reached in 1962 when the United States forced the Soviet Union to abandon its programme to deploy missiles and nuclear warheads in Cuba, where a pro-communist revolution had occurred in 1959. In October 1962 the United States blockaded Cuba, and the Soviet Union, rather than risk all-out war, agreed on 26 October to withdraw its missiles (map left).

150°   **180°**   **150°**

UNITED STATES

CANADA

ALASKA

GREENLAND

ICELAND

JAPAN

S. KOREA

Okinawa

N. KOREA

TAIWAN

PHILIPPINES

MALAYSIA
SEATO 1954–76

VIETNAM

THAILAND

U S S R

MONGOLIA

Warsaw Pact from 1955

CHINA
split from Soviet camp, 196

BANGLADESH

INDIA

90°

FINLAND

NORWAY

SWEDEN

W. GERMANY

E. GERMANY

UNITED KINGDOM

POLAND

CZECH. HUNGARY

1955

RUMANIA

YUGO. BULGARIA

GREECE TURKEY
1952   *1952*

SYRIA

IRAQ
1958

AFGHAN-ISTAN

PAKISTAN

IRAN

*Baghdad Pact
(from 1959 CENTO)
1955–79*

FRANCE

ITALY

SPAIN
1983

*defected from
Soviet camp, 1948,*

*left Warsaw
pact, 1968*

MOROCCO

ALGERIA

LIBYA

EGYPT

SAUDI ARABIA

N. YEMEN

S. YEMEN

60°

Atlantic Ocean

MAURITANIA

MALI

CHAD

SUDAN

ETHIOPIA

Indian Ocean

60°

LIBERIA

NIGERIA

CONGO

ZAIRE

ANGOLA

TANZANIA

30°

0°

2 the cold war

- members of Rio Pact, 1948
- founding members of NATO, 1949
- later NATO members (with date)
- dependencies occupied by NATO members, 1954
- non-NATO members of Baghdad Pact and/or SEATO, 1955
- ■ principal overseas US military bases, (1962)
- ● principal overseas Soviet military bases
- states and dependencies with defence treaties with, and/or offering military facilities to, NATO, 1962
- Soviet led communist camp, 1954
- Warsaw Pact members and allies, 1985
- members of the conference of non-aligned states, 1987
- frontiers, 1987

2 In the decade following the Second World War, much of the world was divided into two armed camps, one based around the Soviet Union and China, as the leading communist states, the other centred around the United States, the most powerful and economically successful of the Western democracies (map above). Both sides built up military alliance blocs and engaged in a long-term arms race.

Yugoslavia split from Moscow and stopped aiding the guerrillas. Other post-1945 civil wars in Europe, such as that in Poland, were not supported as proxy conflicts.

The Cuban missile crisis of 1962 was generally considered the closest the Cold War came to open hostilities. A Soviet move to deploy intermediate range missiles to Cuba was reversed when the US imposed a naval 'quarantine' and threatened an invasion.

The 1973 crisis was less serious, stemming from the heightened alert status of first the Soviet Union and then, in response, the United States arising from fears of Soviet intervention on behalf of Egypt in the closing stages of the 1973 Arab–Israeli War. Compounding the situation was the US political weakness as the Nixon administration was engulfed in the Watergate scandal, and there was concern that a weak government could not afford to be seen to be 'backing down'.

1954
Geneva Conference: Laos, Cambodia and Vietnam become independent states

1957
Communist insurgency in South Vietnam begins

1959–75
War between North and South Vietnam

1964
Gulf of Tonkin incident

1965
Operation 'Rolling Thunder'; first US ground forces arrive in Vietnam

1968
The 'Tet 'Offensive

China was not the only area to come under communist control following the collapse of the Japanese empire in 1945. In South East Asia, Vietnam became the focus of communist activity.

In 1946 Vietnamese communists under Ho Chi Minh (the Viet Minh) declared a Democratic Republic of Vietnam, but the French were determined to re-impose colonial control. In November 1946 French forces bombarded Ho's capital at Hanoi, killing 6,000 people. The Viet Minh launched a guerrilla war against the French, which ended in May 1954 in a spectacular French defeat at Dien Bien Phu. Under agreements reached at Geneva in July 1954, a communist state was established north of the 17th parallel, and a pro-American regime under Ngo Dinh Diem set up in the south with its capital at Saigon. Diem ignored the Geneva agreement and refused to hold elections in 1956. The north then launched a guerrilla war in 1957, and in 1960, in reaction to the excesses of the Diem dictatorship, the NLF (or Viet Cong) was established to work for his overthrow. The Vietcong came to control most of the countryside, and were supplied with arms from the north.

Direct US involvement to shore up the south came in 1964 after North Vietnamese gunboats fired at US destroyers in the Gulf of Tonkin. The US Congress then passed a resolution which virtually amounted to a declaration of war. The Vietnam War, in which the United States now found itself embroiled, was not the 'classic' counter-insurgency of Malaya. Once US land and air forces started to deploy as combat units in 1964, rather than as 'advisors' as in the previous decade, their opponents always included the Peoples' Army of Vietnam (PAVN) regulars and the Viet Cong main force.

North Vietnam could put and sustain large forces in the field because, as this was a proxy conflict, they were being supported by the Soviet Union and, especially prior to 1970, China. It takes nothing away from the North Vietnamese achievement in providing a logistics system that was able to translate this support into combat power on the ground to see that the North Vietnamese 'war economy' was located in the Soviet Union and China. The US bombing campaigns against North Vietnam represented a large percentage of the total US war effort, but it was far from hitting the enemy's Clausewitzian 'centre of gravity'.

The US was able to defeat every North Vietnamese challenge to the pro-Western Republic of Vietnam government in Saigon. The most serious challenge to the southern regime in the early days of US involvement came with the large-scale Tet offensive at the 1968 lunar new year. Whilst the offensive was crushed and the Viet Cong suffered severe losses that left its ranks ever more dependent on reinforcements from North Vietnam, the southern government's internal stability and legitimacy was shown to remain limited and, in its turn dependent, if not on US troops, then on air support and aid.

1 indo-china, 1966–68

areas of control, early 1966:

controlled by the Vietcong	controlled by the Government
under Vietcong influence	under Government influence
heavily contested area	'Tet' offensive, 1968

Vinh

Dong Hoi

NORTH VIETNAM

Vinh Linh

Hue
Phu Bai

Da Nang

L A O S

Ho Chi Minh trail

Chu Lai

Qui Nhon

C A M B O D I A

S O U T H

V I E T N A M

Saigon

7th US fleet 1964

Mekong

1 The Viet Cong was the indigenous guerrilla movement that threatened to storm South Vietnam before the US Army intervened (map left). It sustained fearsome losses in conventional battles with the US forces and was all but destroyed in the 1968 Tet offensive. After that, most Viet Cong formations were filled out with North Vietnamese soldiers.

2 US intervention in South Vietnam prevented a communist take-over in the early 1960s, but the guerrilla war that followed remains controversial (map right). The US forces never lost a major battle, but vocal internal opposition to the war persuaded successive presidents to end US involvement. The impact of daily TV coverage, often graphic images not seen in World War II, had a profound influence on public opinion.

CHINA

Nanning

Lao Cai

6A (USAF)

NORTH VIETNAM

Yen Bai
5 (USAF)
Lang Son
Kep
NORTH
Dien Bien Phu
Phuc Yen
6B (USN)
Na San
Hoa Loc
Gia Lam
Hon Gai
Bac Mai
Hanoi
Haiphong
Na Khang (LS 36)
Dong Song
LS 85
Kien An
Cat Bi
EAST
4 (USN)
Quang Te
LS 6
LS 32
Bai Thuong
Thanh Hoa Bridge
Gulf of Tonkin
LS 201
Quang Lang
3 (USN)
Thanh Hoa
LS 2
Long Tien (LS 20A)
WEST
Luang Prabang
Mekong
Green AP
Orange AP
Red AP
White AP
STEEL TIGER
Vinh
2 (USN)
Hainan Island

B-52's from Guam and Okinawa

Do Khe
Vientiane
Lemon
White
Peach
Mekong
Chanh Hoa
Khe Phat
Dong Hoi
YANKEE STATION
Coral Sea
Hancock
Ranger
plus escorts
Black
Green
Orange
Red
Cherry
Phu Qui
1 (USAF)
first air strikes February 1965
Udorn (1965–76)
Nakhon Phanom (1965–75)
Demilitarized Zone
Blue
Savannakhet
Hue
STEEL TIGER (after 1969)
TIGER HOUND
Da Nang (1962–72)

THAILAND

Takhli (1964–69)
Korat (1964–76)
Ubon (1965–74)
Amber
Pakse
Yellow
SOUTH
Pleiku (1962–70)
Phu Cat (1967–71)
VIETNAM
Don Muang Airport (1964–70)
Bangkok
Battambang
Tonle Sap
CAMBODIA
Mekong
Tuy Hoa (1966–70)
Nha Trang (1962–9)
Cam Ranh Bay (1965–72)
Phan Rang (1966–72)
U Tapao (1966–76)
Phnom Penh
Bien Hoa (1961–71)
Tan Son Nhut Airport (1961–72)
US Seventh Air Force HQ
Saigon
DIXIE STATION
Vung Tau (1967–70)
Bin Thuy (1965–70)
Mekong Delta
Grey
Mango
South China Sea

2 the vietnam air war, 1965–72

— US 7th Fleet (Task Force 77)
✛ US airbase (jet serviceable)
✛ US airbase (non jet serviceable)
● US air tanker base
⊕ US B-52 base
x—x aerial re-fuelling tracks and anchor points (AP)
WEST air combat zones (route packages)
▬ North Vietnamese airfield
◻ SAM cover
■ major Lima site
- - - Chinese buffer zone (prohibited area)

Operation Rolling Thunder, 2 Mar.–1 Nov. 1968
main targets; airfields, SAM sites, bridges and supply routes
targeting restrictions 1965–68:

Hanoi: prohibited zone: 10 nautical miles
restricted zone: 30 nautical miles
Haiphong: prohibited zone: 4 nautical miles
restricted zone: 10 nautical miles

Operation Linebaker 1, 8 May–23 Oct. 1972
✳ strikes
fewer target restrictions than Rolling Thunder

Operation Linebaker 2, 19–30 Dec. 1972
✳ strikes
unrestricted bombing; all targets of importance in Hanoi and Haiphong hit

1968
Tet offensive (January); battle for Hue (February); Paris Peace talks begin (10 May)

1969
US troop withdrawals from Vietnam begin (25 June); Bombing of Cambodia begins

1970
Prince Sihanouk overthrown in Cambodia; number of US troops in Vietnam falls to 280,000

1971
South Vietnamese troops in failed thrust into Laos

1972
Nixon cuts troop levels by 70,000; B-52s bomb Hanoi (April)

1973
Offensive operations in North Vietnam halt (15 January); cease-fire signed in Paris (27 January); last US troops leave Vietnam (29 March)

1974
Communists capture much of Mekong Delta

1975
Communists capture Phuoc Long; Hue falls to Communists; Saigon falls (30 April)

Following the Tet offensive of 1968, the United States sought to disengage from Vietnam and pursued a policy of 'Vietnamization', handing increasing responsibility to its local allies. As US troop numbers fell, Viet Cong strength increased, leading in 1973 to the inevitable fall of the regime.

The Tet offensive and the subsequent battle for Hue had significantly undermined the political stability of the southern regime. Not long thereafter peace talks began in Paris aimed at finding a peaceful settlement for Vietnam. Yet the war was destined finally to be settled on the battlefield: the United States gradually withdrew more and more of its troops, with numbers falling from over 450,000 in 1969, to 280,000 in 1970 and to barely 25,000 at the time of the final US pullout in 1975. The Vietnamese army, increasingly demoralized by its failure to contain the Viet Cong and significant territorial losses, began to crumble. US domestic political opposition had started to greatly increase after three years hard fighting showed no end in sight and the cut-off of aid to South Vietnam set the stage for the eventual North Vietnamese conquest of the south in 1975. Saigon itself fell on 30 April. The war had cost the lives of over 50,000 American troops, more than 200,000 South Vietnamese soldiers and possibly more than a million on the North Vietnamese side.

Further wars in Indochina followed. For a while it seemed that prophecies of a 'domino' effect whereby pro-Western regimes would fall one-by-one to Communist insurgencies were proving to be accurate. The governments of Cambodia and Laos, with similar profiles to Vietnam of reliance on US military aid, rule by military strongmen and dissolving legitimacy in rural areas, were simply unable to resist the pressure of peasant-based communist uprisings. In Laos, the Pathet Lao seized power in 1975, whilst in Cambodia the Khmer Rouge toppled the regime of Lon Nol. Renaming their country Kampuchea, the Khmer Rouge commenced a revolutionary remaking of society through auto-genocide, with up to a third of the population being slaughtered in three-and-a-half years. Destabilization, ethnic tensions and ideological rivalry with the Vietnamese led to their invasion of Kampuchea in 1978 to over-throw the genocidal Pol Pot regime. The Chinese, allies of the Khmer Rouge, responded by invading Vietnam, but the Sino-Vietnamese War resulted in a costly repulse at the hands of an outnumbered Vietnamese force.

The Vietnamese waged a counter-guerrilla war in Cambodia against the Khmer Rouge and non-communist guerrillas through-out the 1980s, trying to keep a friendly government in power in Phnom Penh, but as the Cold War was ending, the Soviet Union could no longer support these operations. The Vietnamese with-drew and a United Nations force moved in and held elections. Despite this, conflict still continued in Cambodia into the 1990s.

1 Left to its own devices, the military junta in Saigon had neither the political foundations nor military strength to resist the North Vietnamese invasion in 1975. Retreat became rout: within a month the scramble began to escape to the US fleet offshore.

1 vietnam, 1975

Communist controlled areas (approx), mid-Jan 1975

and by 25 March

PAVN advances

frontline, 3 April 1975

Demilitarized Zone

Savannakhet

Khe Sanh

Quang Tri

Huế

26 March 1975
Hué falls to Communist forces

Da Nang
30 Mar.

L A O S

THAILAND

Tam Ky
23 Mar.

Quang Ngai

Pakse

Central
Highlands
Kontum

South

China

Pleiku

Ho Chi Minh trail

SOUTH

Qui Nhon
1 Apr.

Sea

Tuy Hoa
1 Apr.

Battambang

CAMBODIA

Ban Me Thuot

Tonle Sap

Nha Trang

VIETNAM

'Fishhook'

Phuoc Binh

Dalat

Cam Ranh Bay

Phnom Penh
17 Apr.

Mekong

Tay Ninh

An Loc

Kompong
Som

Neak Luong

Bien Hoa

Xuan
Loc

*'Parrot's
Beak'*

Saigon

Phan Thiet

30 April 1975
**Communist forces
enter Saigon**

Vung Tau

Can Tho

*Mekong
Delta*

Mekong

16°

12°

108°

104°

the **soviet war** in **afghanistan**

1978
President Mohammed Daoud overthrown and killed in Marxist coup

1979
USSR invades Afghanistan.

1980
Mujahideen rebels in Pakistan
form alliance. Guerrilla war against
Soviet-backed regime starts

1987
Soviet troop withdrawals start

1988
Geneva agreement for
withdrawal of Soviet troops

1989
last Soviet soldier leaves
Afghanistan (April)

1992
Mujahideen take Kabul

1994
Mullah Omar establishes the
Taliban

1996
Taliban capture Kabul
(September)

The Soviet Union waged the Cold War through a number of invasions –
including those of Hungary in 1956, Czechoslovakia in 1968 and
Afghanistan in 1979 – and the threat of potential ones, most notably that
of Western Europe.

The three actual invasions were all aimed at replacing nominally pro-Soviet governments that were not following
the course set by Moscow. All three invasions demonstrated the Soviet operational thinking that would also have
been seen in an invasion of Europe: pre-empt resistance wherever possible; move to decapitate enemy centres of
resistance; stress speed and shock of advance.

In Hungary (after considerable fighting) and Czechoslovakia, the invasions succeeded, after a fashion, but in the
long run the political damage caused by the military action outweighed this success. When Moscow's East European
empire came apart in 1989, no one was willing to take up arms in its defence. The fall of the Soviet empire itself was
to follow in two years. It was economics rather than the clash of arms that decided the Cold War.

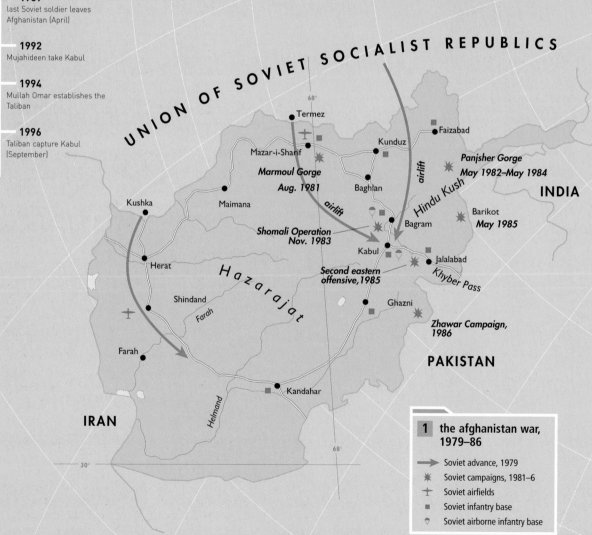

1 the afghanistan war,
1979–86

➤ Soviet advance, 1979
✳ Soviet campaigns, 1981–6
✚ Soviet airfields
■ Soviet infantry base
⬦ Soviet airborne infantry base

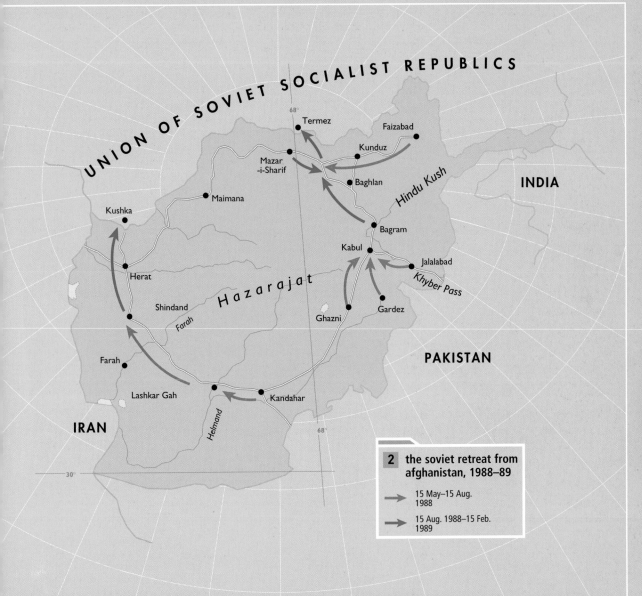

UNION OF SOVIET SOCIALIST REPUBLICS

68°

Termez

Faizabad

Kunduz

Mazar
-i-Sharif

INDIA

Baghlan

Maimana

Hindu Kush

Kushka

Bagram

Kabul

Jalalabad

Herat

Khyber Pass

Hazarajat

Shindand

Ghazni

Gardez

Farah

Farah

PAKISTAN

Lashkar Gah

Kandahar

Helmand

68°

IRAN

30°

| 2 | the soviet retreat from afghanistan, 1988–89 |

→ 15 May–15 Aug. 1988

→ 15 Aug. 1988–15 Feb. 1989

The invasion of Afghanistan in December 1979 was intended as a short, surgical operation to restore a pro-Soviet regime in Kabul. It degenerated into a protracted guerrilla war that the Soviet army was never able to win – map 1 . After the withdrawal of Soviet forces – map 2 , the guerrilla armies fought among themselves for control of the country, until the mujahideen government was overthrown by the Taliban in 1996.

Afghanistan was to the Soviet Union what the Boer War was to the British empire or Vietnam was to the United States. Unlike those, however, the Soviet Union did not survive its frustrating, costly war. Afghanistan has been described as the 'fatal pebble' that finally tripped up the stumbling Soviet colossus. Afghan resistance represented the largest national rising of the century. While the Afghan guerrillas lacked organization and training throughout the war – they did not aim to create their own Dien Bien Phu – they had the advantage of large-scale support from the Soviet Union's Cold War opponents, becoming another proxy war, and strong Islamic faith to provide motivation.

Wars of national liberation have often been followed by civil wars that can prove even more costly and Afghanistan has been no exception. The Soviets invaded in 1979, waged a frustrating firepower-intensive war for many years and started to withdraw in 1987, completing that withdrawal in 1989. Afghan civil wars followed from 1989 to 2001. Then, the US intervened to oust the Taliban regime (holding Kabul since 1996) and their Al-Qaeda terrorist allies, leading to the first (relative) peace since 1978.

1982 to 1989

2 April 1982
Argentine navy lands thousands of troops on Falklands. British Royal Marine detachment surrenders

3 April 1982
Argentines seize South Georgia

25 April 1982
British commando force recaptures South Georgia

2 May 1982
Argentine cruiser *General Belgrano* sunk

25 May 1982
HMS Coventry sunk off the Falklands

28 May 1982
Battle of Goose Green. 200 Argentine soldiers killed.

14 June 1982
Argentine garrison in Port Stanley surrenders (nearly 10,000 troops)

1983
US invasion of Grenada

1989
US intervention in Panama to overthrow General Noriega

Western interventions of the 1980s were not directly connected with conflict with the Soviet Union in the last decade of the Cold War but made a contribution to its outcome. Most notable was the British war to reclaim the Falkland Islands after their invasion by Argentina in 1982.

The Falklands was not the war on the north German plain or the streets of Ulster – for which British forces had trained. As so often throughout history, the war that had to be fought was not the war that had been planned. The result put a premium on improvisation and the logistics capability that, far from being mere 'tail', made victory possible thousands of miles from any base in the South Atlantic. It also underlined the continued importance of quality of military forces, especially when not undercut by technological weakness.

1   the falklands war, 1982

- – – – British maritime exclusion zone
- British ships sunk
- Argentine ship sunk
- → main British advance
- ✱ principal engagement with date

1 'The empire strikes back', as more than one serviceman observed when British forces splashed ashore to liberate the Falklands. The Argentine junta gambled that it would not come to a shooting war, so failed to extend the runway for fast jets, leaving their garrison to rely on air support from the distant mainland. In the naval war, the Argentine fleet withdrew to harbour after the British submarine *Conqueror* sank the cruiser *Belgrano*.

In many ways the Falklands was a low-technology conflict. The British infantry had to fight their way into Port Stanley in a series of hill battles, relying on fine-honed tactics rather than firepower or technological advantage. Infantry patrols carried out reconnaissance that today would be carried out by a UAV. Yet the Argentine Air Force, failed in its attempt to defeat the British invasion force, despite inflicting painful casualties. Brave men in low-technology aircraft lacked the supporting infrastructure of modern air war: the tankers, jamming planes, anti-radiation missiles and the like. Argentina's greatest successes came from the use of Exocet air-launched anti-ship guided missiles.

The US, overcoming the aftermath of its defeat in Vietnam, increased its capability to carry out unilateral actions, including the failed Iranian hostage rescue of 1979, the landing on Grenada in 1983, clashes with Libya in 1981 and 1986 and the intervention in Panama in 1989. There was also the abortive multinational force in Beirut in 1982–83, withdrawn after the US and French contingents suffered heavy losses to suicide terrorist bombings.

2 Across terrain remarkably similar to the training areas in Wales used by the British forces, the British army broke the Argentine defences outside Stanley on the eve of the Antarctic winter. Both sides used similar weapons, but Britain's long service professionals made short work of inexperienced conscripts. The trend since the 1980s has been towards smaller, professional armies instead of the conscript armies once favoured by Western industrialized nations.

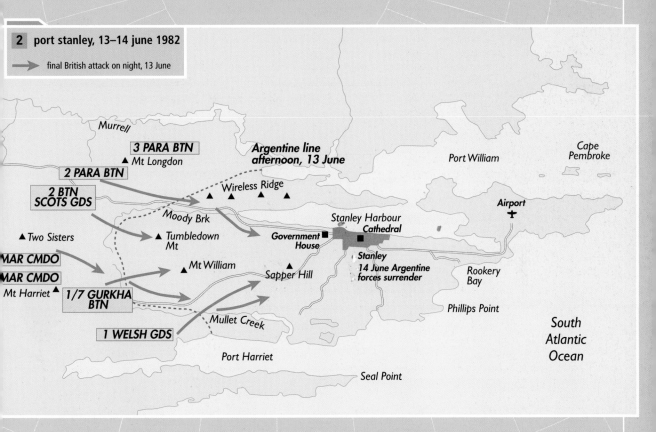

2 port stanley, 13–14 june 1982

final British attack on night, 13 June

These interventions had implications for the course of the Cold War beyond their limited military significance. Along with the policy of supporting those indigenous groups resisting the Soviet Union and its allies – most notably in Afghanistan – these actions demonstrated that the West was not permanently put on the defensive. The Soviets had hoped to achieve this by the shift in the 'correlation of forces' emerging with the attainment of nuclear parity, by Vietnam, and by the potential erosion of support for the military implementation of the strategy of containment the West had tried to implement since the early 1950s. These interventions also showed the way to later 'out of area' actions such as the Gulf War in 1990–91 and Kosovo in 1999.

1980 to 1999

1979
Iranian revolution: brings Khomeini to power

1980
Iraq invades Iran

1982
Iranian counter-offensive pushes Iraqis back to their borders

1988
ceasefire brings end to war

1990
Iraq invades Kuwait (August)

1991
coalition air attacks on Iraq; ground offensive starts (24 Feb.); Iraq accepts ceasefire (3 Apr.)

The regions bordering the Gulf increased in strategic importance with the first oil shortage of 1973–74. Iran, then under the Shah, increased its armed forces, looking to assure its regional dominance, but the Iranian revolution of 1979 brought a revolutionary Islamic government to power. The hostage crisis of 1979–81 brought US forces to the region and, after the war in Afghanistan started in 1978, superpower tensions. The 'Carter Doctrine' and the organization of the Rapid Deployment Force, later Central Command, put then-weakened US credibility on the line for Gulf stability.

With Iran in disorder, the weaker but aggressive regime of Saddam Hussein in Iraq saw a chance for a military victory and, in 1980, invaded, starting the Iran–Iraq War. In years of bitter fighting and battles of attrition, the Iran–Iraq war included the first mutual use of chemical weapons since 1918 and mutual use of ballistic missiles in the 'war of the cities' until Iran, finally exhausted, sued for peace.

Saddam's goal of regional domination was still unrealized when, in August 1990, he invaded and occupied Kuwait, to which Iraq had long-standing claims. Saudi Arabia and the Gulf states, now threatened by their former protector, asked for foreign help. The bulk of the foreign troops were from the US, but support came also from Britain, France, Egypt and Syria. Aircraft arrived from even more allies.

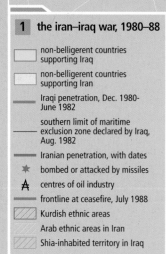

1 the iran–iraq war, 1980–88

- non-belligerent countries supporting Iraq
- non-belligerent countries supporting Iran
- Iraqi penetration, Dec. 1980–June 1982
- southern limit of maritime exclusion zone declared by Iraq, Aug. 1982
- Iranian penetration, with dates
- ✳ bombed or attacked by missiles
- ⚓ centres of oil industry
- frontline at ceasefire, July 1988
- Kurdish ethnic areas
- Arab ethnic areas in Iran
- Shia-inhabited territory in Iraq

1 Saddam Hussein took advantage of the Iranian revolution, invading the oilfields in the hope that the weakened Iranian forces would be no match for his well-equipped army. But Iraqi reluctance to take casualties and the fanaticism of the Iranian Revolutionary Guards led the offensive to break down. A 10-year war of attrition followed, with both sides attacking foreign oil tankers plying the Gulf. The destruction of an Iranian airliner by the USS *Vincennes* inspired a wave of terrorist attacks against the West.

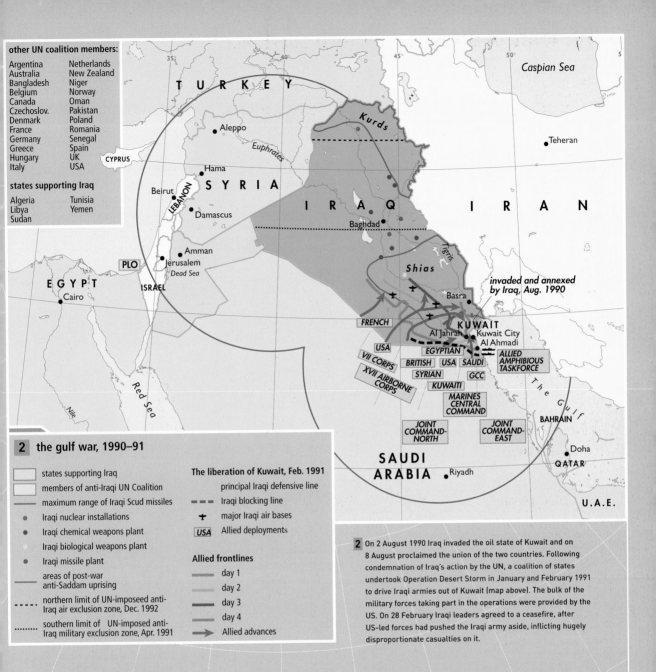

other UN coalition members:

Argentina	Netherlands
Australia	New Zealand
Bangladesh	Niger
Belgium	Norway
Canada	Oman
Czechoslov.	Pakistan
Denmark	Poland
France	Romania
Germany	Senegal
Greece	Spain
Hungary	UK
Italy	USA

states supporting Iraq

Algeria	Tunisia
Libya	Yemen
Sudan	

2 the gulf war, 1990–91

- states supporting Iraq
- members of anti-Iraqi UN Coalition
- maximum range of Iraqi Scud missiles
- ● Iraqi nuclear installations
- ● Iraqi chemical weapons plant
- ○ Iraqi biological weapons plant
- ● Iraqi missile plant
- areas of post-war anti-Saddam uprising
- ‒ ‒ ‒ northern limit of UN-imposeed anti-Iraq air exclusion zone, Dec. 1992
- ········· southern limit of UN-imposed anti-Iraq military exclusion zone, Apr. 1991

The liberation of Kuwait, Feb. 1991
- principal Iraqi defensive line
- ‒ ‒ ‒ Iraqi blocking line
- ✛ major Iraqi air bases
- USA Allied deployments

Allied frontlines
- day 1
- day 2
- day 3
- day 4
- → Allied advances

2 On 2 August 1990 Iraq invaded the oil state of Kuwait and on 8 August proclaimed the union of the two countries. Following condemnation of Iraq's action by the UN, a coalition of states undertook Operation Desert Storm in January and February 1991 to drive Iraqi armies out of Kuwait (map above). The bulk of the military forces taking part in the operations were provided by the US. On 28 February Iraqi leaders agreed to a ceasefire, after US-led forces had pushed the Iraqi army aside, inflicting hugely disproportionate casualties on it.

A lengthy build-up and diplomatic efforts were followed by a 40-day air bombardment and a ground offensive which swiftly evicted Iraq from Kuwait. The Gulf War of 1991 was a unique event. It represented a coalition effort not seen since the Second World War. The movement of large-scale mechanized forces from the US, Europe and the Middle East to the Gulf was possible due to the in-place infrastructure and the six months between the invasion of Kuwait and the opening of the land war. While it featured many elements of the digital revolution incorporated in operational and tactical war-fighting, it probably represented at best a transitional stage, with the armed forces of the Cold War and the modern eras fighting their last large-scale conventional battle.

The military situation became less clear-cut after the cease-fire. Allied forces intervened to support Kurds in the north of Iraq, but not as Saddam slaughtered Shia opponents in the south. No-fly zones were imposed in both the north and the south of Iraq, and the country's skies were patrolled for over a decade by allied air forces. International alarm at Iraq's massive stocks of chemical and biological weapons, the Scud missiles fired during the war, and how close they had come to a nuclear weapon, led to the imposition of an intrusive arms-control verification regime. Limited attacks since 1991, largely by US and British forces, were provoked by continued Iraqi non-compliance with UN resolutions, especially as to their weapons of mass destruction, and action against the Kurds. Saddam's alleged continued efforts at acquiring weapons of mass destruction and links to terrorism were to prompt a US–UK-led coalition to invade Iraq and oust Saddam in 2003.

the **civil wars** in **yugoslavia**

1990 to 1999

1987
Milosevic comes to power in Serbia

25 June 1991
Slovenia and Croatia declare independence

July 1991
War between Croatia and Serbia

April 1992
Bosnia declares independence; civil war breaks out

August 1995
NATO warplanes attack Serb positions in Bosnia. Croats retake the Krajina

1995
Dayton Peace Accords

1998–99
Serb massacres of Albanians in Kosovo prompt international outcry

March 1999
NATO launches air strikes on Yugoslavia

June 1999
Yugoslav forces evacuate Kosovo

Peacekeeping and peacemaking are largely about what comes after failure. When wars themselves fail in their aim of achieving political goals by Clausewitz's 'other means', the underlying conflicts remain.

Peacekeeping was a product of the end of the Cold War. During the Cold War, the realities of the global balance meant that the use of the military in peacekeeping would either be purely domestic (such as in the British commitment of forces to Northern Ireland, starting in 1969) or in peripheral conflicts when neither superpower had heavy investments in one side (the Congo, Cyprus, south Lebanon). In these years, the use of military observers to assure impartial application of disengagement provisions was also used.

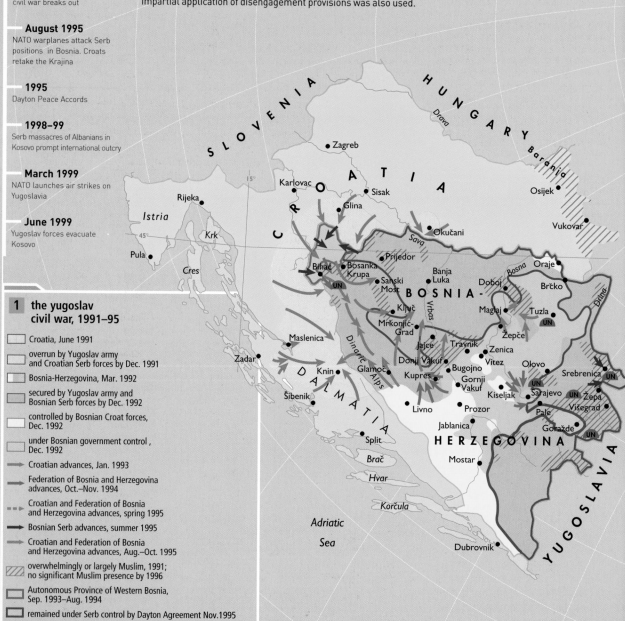

1   the yugoslav civil war, 1991–95

- Croatia, June 1991
- overrun by Yugoslav army and Croatian Serb forces by Dec. 1991
- Bosnia-Herzegovina, Mar. 1992
- secured by Yugoslav army and Bosnian Serb forces by Dec. 1992
- controlled by Bosnian Croat forces, Dec. 1992
- under Bosnian government control, Dec. 1992
- Croatian advances, Jan. 1993
- Federation of Bosnia and Herzegovina advances, Oct.–Nov. 1994
- Croatian and Federation of Bosnia and Herzegovina advances, spring 1995
- Bosnian Serb advances, summer 1995
- Croatian and Federation of Bosnia and Herzegovina advances, Aug.–Oct. 1995
- overwhelmingly or largely Muslim, 1991; no significant Muslim presence by 1996
- Autonomous Province of Western Bosnia, Sep. 1993–Aug. 1994
- remained under Serb control by Dayton Agreement Nov.1995
- returned to Croatian control 1997 under Zagreb Agreement
- UN-designated 'safe areas'

1 The former Yugoslav federal republic of Bosnia and Herzegovina declared its independence in March 1992. There followed three and a half years of civil war between the Muslim, Serb and Croat populations, with interventions from Croatia and Serbia (map below left). In 1992 the United Nations sent peacekeeping forces, and in November 1995 NATO intervened to keep the warring peoples apart and impose a peace settlement.

2 In 1990 the government of Slobodan Milosevic cancelled the autonomy which Kosovo had enjoyed within Serbia. Pressure for its restoration grew. In 1998 a low-level guerrilla war between the Albanian KLA and Serb security forces escalated sharply (map below). At peace talks in France in 1998–99 the Albanian side accepted and the Serbs repudiated peace terms. As massacres of Albanians continued, pressure for NATO action mounted. On 24 March NATO bombers attacked Serbia, beginning an 11-week campaign. Yugoslav security forces responded by forcing Albanians from their homes, looting and killing. In early June Milosevic capitulated: his forces left Kosovo, and 40,000 NATO peacekeeping troops took over.

Post-Cold War peacekeeping and peacemaking covers a broad spectrum. Of the interventions into failed states, the multinational force in Somalia stands out as both an example of the potential for humanitarian relief – preventing imminent starvation when internal fighting interfered with food distribution – and of the inevitability that the peacekeepers would become involved in the local fighting, most notably in a bloody battle in Mogadishu with US Army Rangers that prompted the US withdrawal.

Russia's peacekeeping and peacemaking interventions in the former Soviet Union have never been impartial. In Moldova, Georgia and Tajikistan, however, safeguarding Moscow's interests coincided with reducing the level of violence. In Chechenia, attempted secession from Russia was met with an inept attempt to use massed force and intense firepower to defeat resilient and hard-fighting guerrillas. The Russians were forced to grant the Chechens *de facto* independence, though they have never received international recognition. A resumption of Russia's war in Chechenia remains unresolved.

The most intensive use of international peacekeeping and peacekeeping forces after the Cold War has been in the former Yugoslavia. International forces have operated in Croatia, Bosnia–Herzegovina, Macedonia and Kosovo. In Bosnia, the initial commitment of peacekeepers under UN auspices proved ineffective in halting the conflict; the UN was never set up to be an effective military decision-maker. After the military defeat of Serb forces in Croatia and Bosnia and a NATO bombing campaign led to the Dayton Accords, UN peacekeepers were replaced by a NATO-led stabilization force. In Kosovo, peacemaking, in the form of a 78-day bombing campaign (notable for its lack of aircrew casualties and use of precision weapons), was followed by peacekeeping in the form of a multinational NATO-led force.

2 the crisis in kosovo

- flight of Kosovan Albanian refugees, Mar.–May 1999
- towns bombed by NATO forces, Mar.-June 1999
- ⊕ sites of religious significance to Serbs
- - - - NATO zone of occupation with nationality of Multi-national Brigade, 2003
- KLA strongholds
- major massacres

183

chechenia, afghanistan and iraq

1991
Chechen leader Dzhokar Dudayev declares Chechenia independent.

1994
first Russian invasion of Chechenia

1995
Russian troops take Grozny

1996
Khasavyurt agreement ends first Chechen War

1998
Iraq withdraws co-operation with UN weapons inspectors (January); 'Operation Desert Fox', intensive air strikes on Iraq (16–19 December)

1999
Chechen attack on Dagestan; Russia launches second invasion of Chechenia

2001
terrorist attacks on US (11 September); US air attacks on Afghanistan begin (7 October); Northern Alliance take Mazar-e-Sharif (9 November), Kabul (12th), Herat (12th) and Jalalabad (14th); Kunduz falls to Northern Alliance (25 November); last Taliban stronghold at Kandahar falls (6 December)

2002
UN weapons inspectors arrive back in Baghdad (18 November); US accuses Baghdad of being in 'material breach' of UN resolution on weapons inspections (19 December)

March 2003
US air strikes on Baghdad begin, Coalition ground forces enter Iraq at Faw peninsula (20th); port of Umm Qasr seized by US troops; heavy fighting around Nasiriya and Basra (24th); US forces reach Euphrates at Samarra (27th)

April 2003
US troops surround Karbala (2nd); US troops reach Baghdad airport (3rd); British forces enter Basra (6th); Baghdad falls to US forces (9th); Kirkuk falls to Kurdish fighters (10th); Mosul falls (11th); last major town in control of Iraqi army, Tikrit, falls to US Marines (15th)

The increasingly disparate and diffuse challenges faced by military planners since the Cold War ended is amply demonstrated by the range and scope of the conflicts which have erupted in the early 21st century.

The violent nationalist tensions which had emerged in the wake of the break-up of the Soviet empire continued to engage Russian forces in a bitter guerrilla war in Chechnya. In Afghanistan, following the 11 September 2001 attacks on the US, the American government was forced into a forced into action to oust the Taliban and Al-Qaeda in a mixture of a post-imperialist policing expedition and a very modern intelligence war to exterminate the multi-headed threat of religiously inspired international terrorism. Meanwhile, in 2003, the US fought a more conventional war in Iraq, ostensibly to prevent that country gaining unconventional weapons of mass destruction.

The Chechen conflict had its origins in the collapse of the Soviet Union in 1991. Chechen nationalists under Dzhokar Dudayev declared the Caucasus republic's independence. A stand-off ensued, ended only by a massive Russian invasion in 1994. The assault on the Chechen capital of Grozny underlined the limitations of poorly trained conscripts with little real intelligence and an over-reliance on heavy armour. In the urban landscape of Grozny, the Russian tanks turned in to deathtraps. Eventually the Chechen resistance was pushed out, but continued vigorous resistance in the mountainous south of the republic ultimately forced a ceasefire and Russian withdrawal in 1996. Impatient at cross-border terrorist attacks, Russia again invaded in 1999. Lighter, more manoeuvrable columns and long-range artillery bombardments sapped Chechen resistance in the urban areas but, once more, the Russians failed to subdue the southern mountain regions and guerrilla attacks have caused a constant stream of Russian casualties.

In Afghanistan in 2001, the US seemed to have learnt the lesson of previous foreign forays into south Asia. Unable to rely on the full spectrum of its high-tech weaponry or to bring massive force to bear in difficult terrain, the US relied on local proxies (the Northern Alliance) with knowledge of the battlefield and everything to gain by overthrowing the Taliban regime. Sustained air-strikes against which the Taliban had no defence or reply, and the targeted use of Special Forces to bolster the patchy tactical abilities of their allies, meant that the Taliban regime folded like a pack of cards. Just, however, as past imperial powers have found in the region, victory has not brought stability and Osama bin Laden and other leading lights of the Al-Qaeda terrorist movement against which the assault had been aimed slipped away to menace US interests from even more impenetrable or inscrutable hideouts.

In Iraq, too, in 2003, the US found that, in 21st-century terms, winning the war can potentially mean losing the battle. Saddam Hussein's refusal to co-operate with UN inspectors gave rise to the belief that his regime was hiding weapons of mass destruction, and the Iraqi dictator did nothing to dispel this impression. By March 2003 the momentum for war was unstoppable. This time the coalition was in terms of member countries and number of forces than in

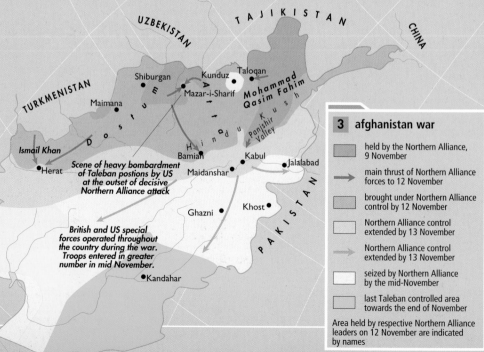

Scene of heavy bombardment of Taleban postions by US at the outset of decisive Northern Alliance attack

British and US special forces operated throughout the country during the war. Troops entered in greater number in mid November.

3 afghanistan war

	held by the Northern Alliance, 9 November
→	main thrust of Northern Alliance forces to 12 November
	brought under Northern Alliance control by 12 November
	Northern Alliance control extended by 13 November
→	Northern Alliance control extended by 13 November
	seized by Northern Alliance by the mid-November
	last Taleban controlled area towards the end of November

Area held by respective Northern Alliance leaders on 12 November are indicated by names

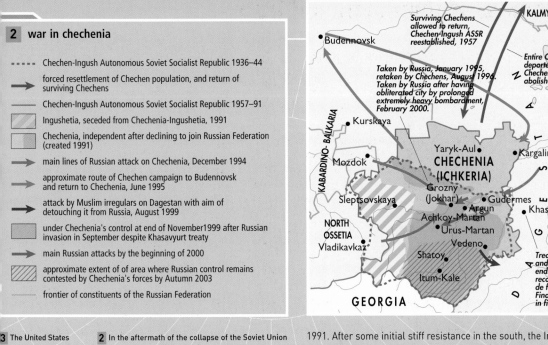

2 war in chechenia

- - - - - Chechen-Ingush Autonomous Soviet Socialist Republic 1936–44

→ forced resettlement of Chechen population, and return of surviving Chechens

──── Chechen-Ingush Autonomous Soviet Socialist Republic 1957–91

▨ Ingushetia, seceded from Chechenia-Ingushetia, 1991

▢ Chechenia, independent after declining to join Russian Federation (created 1991)

➤ main lines of Russian attack on Chechenia, December 1994

➤ approximate route of Chechen campaign to Budennovsk and return to Chechenia, June 1995

➤ attack by Muslim irregulars on Dagestan with aim of detouching it from Russia, August 1999

▨ under Chechenia's control at end of November 1999 after Russian invasion in September despite Khasavyurt treaty

➤ main Russian attacks by the beginning of 2000

▨ approximate extent of of area where Russian control remains contested by Chechenia's forces by Autumn 2003

──── frontier of constituents of the Russian Federation

Map labels (War in Chechenia):

KALMYKIA

Budennovsk

Surviving Chechens allowed to return, Chechen-Ingush ASSR reestablished, 1957

Entire Chechen poulation deported to Central Asia, Chechen-Ingush ASSR abolished, 1944

Taken by Russia, January 1995, retaken by Chechens, August 1996. Taken by Russia after having obliterated city by prolonged extremely heavy bombardment, February 2000.

Kurskaya

Yaryk-Aul   CHECHENIA (ICHKERIA)   Kargalinskaya

KABARDINO-BALKARIA

Mozdok

Grozny (Jokhar)   Gudermes

Sleptsovskaya   Argun   Khasavyurt

Achkoy-Martan

NORTH OSSETIA   Urus-Martan   Makhachkala

Vladikavkaz   Vedeno

Shatoy   Treaty between Chechenia and Russia, August 1996 ends 1st Chechen war by recognizing Chechenia's de facto independence. Final status to be decided in five years time.

Itum-Kale

GEORGIA

---

3 The United States began air attacks on Afghanistan in October 2001. By early November America's Northern Alliance partners had begun advancing in earnest and the Taleban regime crumbled. Within a month its last stronghold at Kandahar had fallen.

2 In the aftermath of the collapse of the Soviet Union in 1991, nationalist leaders in Chechenia took advantage of the chaos to declare independence. A Russian invasion in 1994 to reassert control ended with bitter street fighting for the capital Grozny and the withdrawal of the Russian army. A further invasion in 1999 succeeded in establishing a more lasting Russian presence, but large areas of the republic eluded Moscow's control, while continuing Chechen guerrilla and terrorist campaigns claimed large numbers of Russian lives both inside and outside Chechenia.

1991. After some initial stiff resistance in the south, the Iraqi army's elite formations simply evaporated rather than fight street-by-street for Baghdad. All the US army's smart weaponry, and ruthlessly-effective war-fighting tactics which delivered victory at the cost of little over 100 American losses, could not staunch a growing Iraqi resistance which seemed united in little save its distaste for the foreign occupiers. The US army had become unrivalled in its capacity to fight and to win wars, but its ability to win the battle for hearts and minds was far less developed. The US military machine was left feeling unchallenged but unloved.

1 Saddam Hussein was allowed to survive the 1991 Gulf War, but without international consensus on further action against his regime.

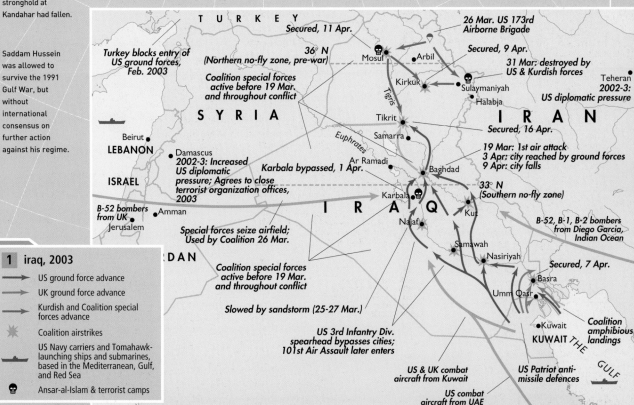

Map labels (Iraq, 2003):

TURKEY

Secured, 11 Apr.

26 Mar. US 173rd Airborne Brigade

36° N (Northern no-fly zone, pre-war)   Mosul   Arbil   Secured, 9 Apr.

Coalition special forces active before 19 Mar. and throughout conflict   Kirkuk   Sulaymaniyah   31 Mar: destroyed by US & Kurdish forces

Teheran   2002-3: US diplomatic pressure

SYRIA   Tigris   Halabja   IRAN

Tikrit   Secured, 16 Apr.

Beirut   Samarra   19 Mar: 1st air attack / 3 Apr: city reached by ground forces / 9 Apr: city falls

LEBANON   Euphrates   Ar Ramadi   Baghdad

Damascus   2002-3: Increased US diplomatic pressure; Agrees to close terrorist organization offices, 2003   Karbala bypassed, 1 Apr.   33° N (Southern no-fly zone)

ISRAEL   Karbala

B-52 bombers from UK   Amman   I R A Q   Kut   B-52, B-1, B-2 bombers from Diego Garcia, Indian Ocean

Jerusalem   Najaf

Special forces seize airfield; Used by Coalition 26 Mar.   Samawah

...DAN   Coalition special forces active before 19 Mar. and throughout conflict   Nasiriyah   Secured, 7 Apr.

Slowed by sandstorm (25-27 Mar.)   Basra

US 3rd Infantry Div. spearhead bypasses cities; 101st Air Assault later enters   Umm Qasr   Coalition amphibious landings

Kuwait

KUWAIT   THE GULF

US Patriot anti-missile defences

US & UK combat aircraft from Kuwait   US combat aircraft from UAE

1 iraq, 2003

➤ US ground force advance

➤ UK ground force advance

➤ Kurdish and Coalition special forces advance

✳ Coalition airstrikes

⚓ US Navy carriers and Tomahawk-launching ships and submarines, based in the Mediterranean, Gulf, and Red Sea

☠ Ansar-al-Islam & terrorist camps

future war

Future war will be shaped by a range of post-modern changes in politics, culture and society as well as by technology. Non-state actors have become as powerful on the world stage today as they were in the pre-industrial age. Transnational threats include international crime, narcotics and even population flow. Organized crime and terrorism have demonstrated their ability to shake even developed governments. They have the capability to affect the quality of life of the citizens of even the most comfortable developed countries. In the developing world, they can bring down governments and fuel insurgencies. A war against terrorism has dominated US policy since the September 2001 attacks.

Subnational threats had been submerged in the larger conflicts of 1914–91, but were seldom resolved by them. The nationalism and violence of Northern Ireland, Serbia and Bosnia–Herzegovina, and elsewhere showed that violence within states was more likely to have an impact on those outside once the damping effects of the Cold War and the firewalls of superpower patronage had been removed.

State threats, however, may well return, more potentially deadly for having access to new weapons technology. The superpowers used the deterrent combination of missiles and weapons of mass destruction to wage a war without mass violence. It is uncertain whether these weapons will have the same effect when interjected in regional rivalries.

Other proliferation is less easy to project. In addition to the widespread information-age technologies now in the world's armed forces – the US Air Force has more computers than personnel – a range of spin-offs is emerging. Intelligence – vital ever since the wireless was introduced – has now grown into 'information warfare', seeking to use these new technologies while denying their benefits to an opponent.

2 Intermediate range ballistic missiles are becoming cheaper and more plentiful and the technology to add a nuclear tip to them is available on the internet. The end of the Cold War has ushered in a new age of anxiety (map below).

2 proliferation of ballistic missiles

Scud B	missiles deployed
Shahab 2	missiles in development
*	missiles developed but not deployed
Jericho 3	rumour of missiles or development

Guerrilla wars followed the withdrawal of European powers from their empires and the Cold War tendency to fight wars by proxy. At the same time, established states in South America and Europe have faced internal threats from terrorist organizations (map below). Of course, one man's terrorist is another man's freedom fighter, and many such groups have been sustained by foreign money. In South America and Germany robust action against the terrorists did not produce the populist revolt anticipated by the Marxists: it led to their extinction.

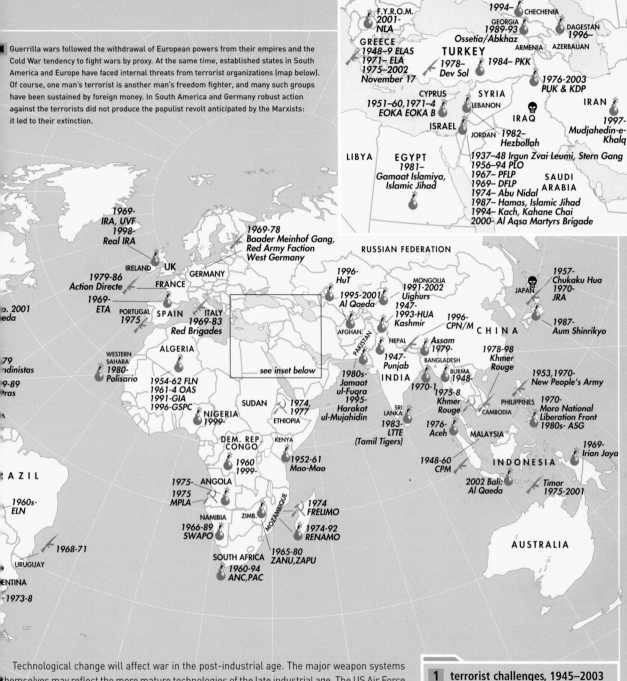

1 terrorist challenges, 1945–2003

- successful Marxist revolutions involving terrorism, with date
- unsuccessful Marxist terrorist challenges, with date and name of group
- nationalist, communal and religious terrorist challenges, with date and name of group
- detected terrorist biological weapons facility

Technological change will affect war in the post-industrial age. The major weapon systems themselves may reflect the more mature technologies of the late industrial age. The US Air Force currently plans to fly its B-52 bombers until they reach 80 years of age.

But even if it is believed that the bombers of the future will look much like those of today, other more dynamic areas will be making fundamental changes in the way wars are fought. Smaller and cheaper micro-circuitry, nanotechnology and biotechnology advances are already finding their way to the battlefield.

The spread of ballistic missiles and weapons of mass destruction – nuclear, biological and chemical – beyond developed nations will likely soon allow even poor, weak countries (such as North Korea) to threaten rich, strong ones and has motivated the United States to start the development of missile defences.

Since the Cold War ended, war has ranged from the highly technological and practically bloodless (for the practitioner) conflict waged in aid of sophisticated statecraft (as in the NATO operations against Kosovo), to religiously motivated terrorism (as in Al-Qaeda's strikes).

Index

JUDITH BRAY

UNLOCKING
LAND LAW

SERIES EDITORS
JACQUELINE MARTIN & CHRIS TURNER

Hodder & Stoughton
A MEMBER OF THE HODDER HEADLINE GROUP

Orders: please contact Bookpoint Ltd, 130 Milton Park, Abingdon, Oxon OX14 4SB. Telephone: (44) 01235 827720.
Fax: (44) 01235 400454. Lines are open from 9.00 – 6.00, Monday to Saturday, with a 24 hour message answering service.
You can also order through our website www.hodderheadline.co.uk.

British Library Cataloguing in Publication Data
A catalogue record for this title is available from the British Library

ISBN-10: 0 340 81564 7

ISBN-13: 978 0 340 81564 9

First published 2004
Impression number 10 9 8 7 6 5 4 3
Year   2008 2007 2006

Hodder Headline's policy is to use papers that are natural, renewable and recyclable products and made from wood grown in
sustainable forests. The logging and manufacturing processes are expected to conform to the environmental regulations of the
country of origin.

Typeset by Dorchester Typesetting Group Ltd.
Printed in Malta for Hodder & Stoughton Educational, a division of Hodder Headline Plc, 338 Euston Road,
London NW1 3BH by Gutenberg Press Ltd.